New Issues in Regional Monetary Coordination

New Issues in Regional Monetary Coordination

Understanding North–South and South–South Arrangements

Edited by

Barbara Fritz

and

Martina Metzger

First published in 2006 by
PALGRAVE MACMILLAN
Houndmills, Basingstoke, Hampshire RG21 6XS and
175 Fifth Avenue, New York, N.Y. 10010
Companies and representatives throughout the world.

PALGRAVE MACMILLAN is the global academic imprint of the Palgrave
Macmillan division of St. Martin's Press, LLC and of Palgrave Macmillan Ltd.
Macmillan® is a registered trademark in the United States, United Kingdom
and other countries. Palgrave is a registered trademark in the European
Union and other countries.

ISBN-13: 978–1–4039–9622–0
ISBN-10: 1–4039–9622–9

This book is printed on paper suitable for recycling and made from fully
managed and sustained forest sources.

A catalogue record for this book is available from the British Library.

Library of Congress Cataloging-in-Publication Data
    New issues in regional monetary coordination: understanding
  North–South and South–South arrangements / edited by
  Barbara Fritz and Martina Metzger.
       p. cm.
    Includes bibliographical references and index.
    ISBN 1–4039–9622–9 (cloth)
        1. Monetary policy. 2. International economic integration.
  I. Fritz, Barbara, 1964– II. Metzger, Martina, 1963–
HG230.3.N48 2005
332.4′566—dc22   2005049332

10 9 8 7 6 5 4 3 2 1
15 14 13 12 11 10 09 08 07 06

Printed and bound in Great Britain by
Antony Rowe Ltd, Chippenham and Eastbourne

Contents

List of Figures and Tables

Figures

Tables

Notes on the Contributors

Peter Bofinger is Professor for Monetary Policy and International Economics at Julius-Maximilians-University Würzburg (from 1992) and a Member of the German Council of Economic Experts (from 2004). He was formerly Vice-President of the same University (2003–4). He has researched monetary theory and policy, European integration, currency theory and policy, transition economics, reform issues of the social security system, and coordination of monetary and fiscal policy. His current research interests are economic policy and reform issues, e.g. the social security system.

e-mail address: bofinger@t-online.de

Fernando J. Cardim de Carvalho is Professor of Economics at Institute of Economics, Federal University of Rio de Janeiro. His research areas and current research interests are macroeconomics, international finance, finance and development.

e-mail address: fjccarvalho@uol.com.br

Heribert Dieter is Senior Research Associate at the German Institute for International and Security Affairs, Berlin, and Associate Fellow at the Centre for the Study of Globalization and Regionalization, University of Warwick. His research areas are international economic relations, globalization and regionalization, financial crises and the reorganization of the international financial system. His current research interests are regional cooperation in Asia.

e-mail address: heribert.dieter@swp-berlin.org

Heiner Flassbeck is Officer-in-Charge, Division on Globalization and Development Strategies, UNCTAD, Geneva. He was State Secretary at the Federal Ministry of Finance, responsible for international affairs, the EU and the IMF; German Institute for Economic Research (DIW); Federal Ministry of Economics, Bonn; German Council of Economic Experts, Wiesbaden. Affiliation/institution: American Economic Association. His research areas and current research interests are macroeconomics and international finance.

e-mail address: heiner.flassbeck@unctad.org

Barbara Fritz is Senior Researcher at the Institute for Ibero-American Studies, Hamburg. Previously she was Assistant Professor at the Free University Berlin. Her research areas and current research interests are monetary issues and exchange rate regimes in developing countries, and economic development in Latin America.

e-mail address: fritz@iik.duei.de

Dirk F. Kohnert is Deputy Director at the Institute of African Affairs, Hamburg. He was Senior Research Fellow at the University of Bielefeld (1981–4), Co-ordinator of the Regional Planning Department, Ministry of Planning, Bissau, Guinea-Bissau (1985–6), and Senior Development Expert GTZ, Cotonou, Benin, 1987–90. His research areas are the socio-cultural dimension of economic development in sub-Saharan Africa; participatory development planning, target-group analysis, poverty-assessment; agricultural extension, and the politics of decentralization and empowerment; project and programme evaluation in developing countries. His current research interests involve the comparative study of cultures of innovation in Africa and Latin America.

e-mail address: Kohnert@iak.duei.de

Jan Kregel is Chief of the Policy Analysis and Development Branch of the United Nations Financing for Development Office. He previously served as a high-level expert in International Finance and Macroeconomics in the UNCTAD. Before joining the UN he was Professor of Economics at the Università degli Studi di Bologna as well as Professor of International Economics at the Johns Hopkins University, Paul Nitze School of Advanced International Studies, where he also served as Associate Director of its Bologna Centre from 1987 to 1990. He is a Life Fellow of the Royal Economic Society (UK), an elected member of the Società Italiana degli Economisti, and a Miembro Distinguido of the Association of Cuban Economists. He has published widely on Keynesian economic theory and development issues.

e-mail address: kregel-ny@un.org

Martina Metzger is Senior Researcher for the Berlin Institute of Financial Market Research (BIF). Before joining BIF, she was Assistant Professor for Macroeconomics at the University of Applied Science in Berlin. She previously served as a research fellow and lecturer at the Department of Economics of the Free University of Berlin; her research areas are monetary theory and policy, exchange rate regimes and international finance; besides monetary coordination projects her recent research interests lie in Basel II, funded social security systems and financial sector's implications of migration.

e-mail address: martina.metzger@bif-berlin.de

Manfred Nitsch is Professor Emeritus of Political Economy at the Latin American Institute, Free University Berlin. His research areas and current research interests are monetary aspects of development, microfinance, Amazonian studies.

e-mail address: manfred.nitsch@t-online.de

Peter Nunnenkamp is Senior Research Fellow at the Kiel Institute for World Economics. His current research interests are implications of globalization for industrial and developing countries; foreign direct investment; foreign aid; financial crises and reforms of the financial architecture.

e-mail address: nunnenkamp@ifw.uni-kiel.de

Ugo Panizza is an economist in the Research Department of the Inter-American Development Bank. Prior to joining the IDB he was an assistant professor in the Department of Economics at the University of Turin (Italy). He also held a visiting position in the Department of Economics at the American University of Beirut and worked as consultant for the World Bank. He holds a Laurea in political science and economics from the University of Turin and a PhD in economics from Johns Hopkins University. His research interests include political economy, international finance (with particular reference to the structure of external debt and the choice of the exchange rate regime in emerging market countries), and public sector labour markets.

e-mail address: UGOP@iadb.org

Beate Reszat is Senior Economist at the Hamburg Institute of International Economics. Her research areas and current research interests are European and international financial markets and monetary policy cooperation. She also serves as a lecturer on European and International Financial Market issues and on Macroeconomics at several universities and academies.

e-mail address: reszat@hwwa.de

Waltraud Schelkle is Lecturer in Political Economy at the European Institute of the London School of Economics (LSE) and Adjunct Professor at the Economics Department at the Free University Berlin. Previously she was Visiting Professor at the Economics Department, Free

University of Berlin, and Research Fellow at Johns Hopkins University (AICGS). Her research areas are monetary integration and welfare state reforms. Her current research interests are fiscal policy co-ordination in EMU and social policy coordination in the EU.

e-mail address: w.schelkle@lse.ac.uk

Jan Suchanek is an economist and journalist. His research areas are currency problems in Africa, neo-colonialism, integration, media and development. His current research interests are cooperation between the European Union and the African Union, community radio and independent media in Africa.

e-mail address: janmaat@so36.net

Preface

The issue of regional monetary coordination has moved to the forefront of the policy and academic agenda, with a large number of developing countries involved in projects aimed at regional monetary coordination. This is due to three factors:

- The successful creation of the euro, and its international projection. Developing economies have paid particularly close attention to the eastern enlargement of the EU. If these countries join the euro zone in the medium term (or even if they choose other arrangements, with the euro as their key currency), the result will be a hitherto unknown model of international monetary coordination between countries with considerable differences in income levels.

- The increasing regionalization of international trade imposes new monetary restrictions on those countries that do not belong to either of the major trading blocs. For these reasons, the formation of regional currency arrangements is increasingly being considered.

- The series of financial crises in emerging markets in recent years has highlighted the difficulties of unilaterally defending a national currency under the present conditions of globalization, free capital movement and the absence of a single globally dominant key currency. The increased exchange-rate volatility between international key currencies due to intensified monetary block-building has underscored the crucial role of extra-regional shocks.

However, research has by-passed the question of the specific conditions and problems of monetary South–South coordination in which, unlike in North–South arrangements, none of the international key currencies, the dollar, the euro or the yen, is involved.

For that reason, we invited outstanding scholars to the Institute for Ibero-American Studies in Hamburg for an international workshop from 7–9 July 2004 to debate the issue of regional monetary coordination from this specific viewpoint.

The contributions of this book, based on the conference papers, seek to provide a fresh analytical perspective on the study of regional monetary cooperation, particularly emphasizing the differences between North–South and South–South arrangements. By bringing together new theoretical approaches and substantial empirical findings from various world regions, our goal is to sketch a framework that will allow for an innovative interpretation and a convincing typology of regional monetary coordination initiatives in Africa, Asia, Eastern Europe and Latin America.

The term 'monetary coordination' as used here covers a broad spectrum of economic policy activities, ranging from *ad hoc* monetary and exchange-rate policy arrangements between neighbouring countries to the creation of a common supranational currency, and including such intermediate steps as the creation of regional liquidity funds, or the establishment of regional monetary systems with adjustable exchange-rate bands and mutual intervention agreements between central banks. The guiding perspective of the contributions of this book is toward the elaboration of macroeconomic constellations that may open up opportunities for stabilization and sustainable development.

In this context, the term 'South' is not entirely a geographical characterization. In accordance with the 'original-sin' argument, the assignment of a country to the typological categories of 'South' or 'North' is determined by its ability to accumulate debt in its own currency ('North'), or predominantly in a foreign currency ('South'). In this sense, many of the Eastern European transformation countries are as much 'southern' as the developing countries of Asia, Africa and Latin America – although a closer look leads to a further differentiation within this group of 'southern' economies and monetary coordination projects.

The articles in Part I of the book deal with qualitative differences between countries of the South and of the North and hence the different potentials of South–South coordination projects as compared with North–South coordination arrangements. They do this by drawing on the original-sin hypothesis, by resorting to historic examples of regional monetary coordination, and by analysing the exchange rate options for developing countries.

Barbara Fritz and Martina Metzger discuss the opportunities and limitations of South–South coordination projects, compared with North–South arrangements. They concentrate on the specific monetary restrictions to which developing countries are subject in stabilizing their exchange rates and initiating a sustainable development process, e.g. currency mismatch, restricted lender-of-last-resort functions, and the costs of original sin. Furthermore, they outline some features of a South–South coordination project which are not identical with conventional OCA criteria, e.g. similar vulnerability with regard to extra-regional factors, a clear hierarchical structure between member countries, and cooperation between macro players both at the domestic and regional levels. They come to the conclusion that South–South coordination projects do indeed have the potential for limiting a mercantilist race to the bottom from the very outset, and can reduce original sin over the medium to long term. However, escaping original sin is not without its costs.

In the second chapter, Ugo Panizza presents a concise summary of the hypothesis and the empirical outcomes of the so-called original-sin hypothesis. The main lesson is that the inability to borrow abroad in domestic currency is the factor that, over the long run, most hampers growth. In the last section of the paper, dealing with monetary cooperation, he concludes that North–South monetary cooperation offers the obvious advantage of automatic redemption for the participating developing country marked by original sin. But even if South–South coordination does not bring with it that advantage, the author argues that at least for monetary unions that include large and well-diversified economies, the increased size of the currency area can raise the interest of international investors in holding this currency in their portfolios.

In her comment to Panizza's paper, Waltraud Schelkle highlights the policy relevance of the original-sin hypothesis for developing countries. She then identifies some 'hidden treasures', such as the importance of foreign direct investment that may strengthen the demand for domestic currency, concluding that one criterion for choosing one's partners for a common currency could be their attractiveness to foreign direct investors, since their demand for the common currency would then spill over to the other members, reducing the degree of foreign debt even in a case of South–South coordination. Schelkle concludes that some of the findings of original-sin research, such as the irrelevance of fiscal performance for the degree of original sin, the efficiency of financial markets, or the minor role given to monetary credibility, represent highly relevant questions for further research.

Historically, the idea of forming a monetary coordination project to reduce the dependence on foreign borrowing by member countries which are short of foreign exchange is not new. After giving an overview of different monetary coordination projects beginning with the former European Payments Union over current projects like ASEAN and the Mercosur, Jan Kregel identifies as major benefits of a monetary coordination project – be it North–North, South–South or North–South – efficiency gains caused by the use of net settlement systems or the pooling of reserves. However, he analyses crucial limitations of such projects, e.g. volatile autonomous capital inflows and the widespread lack of monetary sovereignty of developing countries. He proposes a deepening of regional capital market integration with regard to commercial bank asset portfolios as an alternative to a South–South monetary coordination project.

In his comment, Peter Nunnenkamp states that the phenomenon 'original sin', and the tight external financing constraints under which developing countries suffer, might be caused by both domestic and international institutional deficiencies. Furthermore, he stresses that it is important to differentiate monetary coordination arrangements according to their objectives and the corresponding types, e.g. settlement of payments, agreements for balance of payments support, and monetary unions. He raises the question of what can reasonably be expected from a South–South monetary coordination project if exchange-rate volatility to hard-currency areas is the major problem, and if those hard-currency areas are not involved in the coordination projects.

Heiner Flassbeck focuses on the need for multilateral exchange-rate coordination, be it at the regional or at the global level. A key condition for successful economic performance is the ability to keep the domestic exchange rate at a competitive level. However, especially those developing economies which show higher inflation rates than the international level and have a liberalized capital account are not able to achieve competitive and stable exchange rates. Inflation stabilization requires higher interest rates that attract interest-rate-driven capital inflows, the appreciation of the exchange rate will lead to a loss in international competitiveness and the risk of costly financial crises. Since the exchange rate is by definition a multilateral phenomenon, attempts by many countries to undervalue their currency may end up in a globally harmful race to the bottom that could be prevented by multilateral arrangements. In a world without such multilateral solutions, the only way out, especially for smaller and less competitive developing countries that are not members of a regional monetary union, is to resort to capital import controls.

The articles of the Part II of the book give a detailed overview of selected regional case studies which include, on the one hand, such already-existing monetary arrangements as the CFA zone in Francophone Africa and the common currency zone of southern Africa and, on the other, regions which are striving on an implicit or even explicit basis for monetary integration over the medium term (NAFTA, Mercosur and ASEAN or ASEAN +3), or which will have to define such arrangements in the context of the future enlargement of key currency zones (the eastern European transformation countries).

Based on an analysis of the existing exchange rate regimes adopted by the new EU member countries, Peter Bofinger comes to the conclusion that managed floating is better than expected, while the two corner solutions might be sub-optimal. Furthermore, he discusses the adequacy of ERM II for both the pre-convergence period and the two-year transition period prior to adoption of the euro by the new EU member countries. He identifies several flaws in the current ERM II mechanism, of which the mutual determination of exchange rates, the safeguard clause with regard to intra-marginal interventions with its ECB veto right, and the very limited financial support in case of speculative attacks, are the most damaging. Finally, proposals to overcome the asymmetry of rights and obligations inherent in the current ERM II mechanism are presented.

Before drawing on the case of the Mercosur, Fernando Cardim de Carvalho first discusses the arguments developed in the Optimum Currency Area (OCA) tradition, relates it to issues like price stabilization and exchange rate regimes, and then discusses the special case within OCA of dollarization; finally, he addresses the case of monetary unification of the Mercosur countries. Analysing then the OCA question for Argentina and Brazil, the two biggest economies within Mercosur, Carvalho concludes that the costs of a common currency are too high and offer too little, and argues instead for less far-reaching joint measures, such as the introduction of common protective policies like capital controls, to reduce vulnerability.

Manfred Nitsch comments on the Carvalho paper in the light of the non-neutrality theory of money that posits an international monetary hierarchy. Sketching the monetary options in Mercosur, he concludes that an intermediate solution for the exchange-rate regimes of all participants could help to increase regional convergence of policies and harden the currencies within the region.

Barbara Fritz argues in her paper that although Latin America forms part of the US dollar's 'sphere of influence', its countries and sub-regions are seeking rather divergent monetary strategies. Among them, she first analyses Mexico as a case of implicit monetary coordination within NAFTA. The second case treated in the chapter is Mercosur, with its perspectives for monetary coordination, where Fritz concludes that even if stabilization gains may be small, regional cooperation is worth the effort, because in a highly unstable global financial environment, common regional strategies offer advantages over the national option of defending one's currency.

In the African continent, a series of agreements on monetary coordination exist, two of which stand out. The Common Monetary Area in Southern Africa is regarded as an unusually longstanding monetary coordination project between developing countries. In her paper, Martina Metzger analyses the functioning of the CMA, including issues of institutions, interdependence and convergence. She identifies considerable benefits for the smaller member countries, e.g. low real interest-rate spreads, participation in seigniorage, the existence of a lender of last resort in form of the South African Reserve Bank, and access to foreign borrowing on the South African capital market. Furthermore, the smaller members show a favourable currency mismatch, as they earn forex other than rand while paying for the majority of their imports in rand. Hence, from the point of view of the smaller member countries, the CMA is a North–South coordination project, whereas for South Africa, with its volatile rand exchange rate *vis-à-vis* hard currencies, the CMA is more of a South–South coordination arrangement.

The North–South arrangement of the Franc CFA Zone is another long-standing monetary coordination project in Africa which stabilizes exchange rates between the member countries, as the French treasury guarantees full convertibility with an unlimited supply of liquidity. Although the literature states that the Franc CFA Zone is not optimal according to traditional OCA criteria, Jan Suchanek identifies as major benefits of the monetary coordination arrangement lower inflation rates and higher growth rates for the African member countries of the CFA than for neighbouring countries. The benefit is dearly paid for by a considerable overvaluation of the nominal exchange rates *vis-à-vis* the rest of the world, due to the peg with the French franc – now the euro – which has appreciated enormously against the US dollar during recent years. For the future, he expects limited progress in the ambitious project of a single African currency, as many countries do not fulfill convergence criteria, and due also to unsolved political and military conflicts.

In his comment on the CMA and the Franc CFA Zone, Dirk Kohnert argues that both monetary coordination projects have been shaped by external politics and informal economics. While the CFA Zone is based on the colonial heritage, and is highly dependent on the monetary policy of the Euro zone, the CMA is dominated by the regional giant South Africa, and monetary integration involves the risk of deepened economic and political dependence of the smaller member countries. For the future, he proposes the establishment of specific monetary regimes based on the needs of their member countries, rather than the simple application of economic optimality criteria, which might ultimately be sub-optimal for all members.

Since the Asian crisis in 1997 Asian policy-makers are continuously searching mechanisms to combat volatility of exchange rates and to reduce vulnerability of their countries at the regional level. In his paper Heribert Dieter juxtaposes the traditional understanding of regional economic integration to an alternative model of monetary regionalism, which takes into consideration the link between monetary policies and the financial sectors of the participating countries. Although, the deepening of central bank cooperation and the efforts for the creation of a regional bond market are important and indicate a break with the policies of the past, he also shows the piecemeal progress that is apparent in cooperation in East Asia. One obstacle to further progress constitutes the political context in which this new monetary regionalism is embedded and where the three big players (China, Japan, US) have a blocking power over each other. The author argues that successful regional policy coordination will be as much dependent on Sino-Japanese relations and leadership as on US relations with these two states.

In her comment to Dieter's paper, Beate Reszat asks about the effectiveness of a regional liquidity fund to cope with Asian-style financial crises. Instead, she points to the fact that currency crises could be limited by establishing new rules to the few players, most of them western banks, in the interbank market of the country whose currency is under pressure.

The editors wish to express their sincere thanks to the German Thyssen Foundation for the generous financial support, without which the workshop and this book would not have been possible. Our heartfelt thanks also go to UNCTAD, not only for co-financing, but especially for contributing to the workshop as regards content and discussion. We are very grateful to Laurissa Mühlich for supporting us with the preparation of the workshop, and to Gabriele Neusser and her team for their excellent technical assistance before and during the workshop. We also wish to express our appreciation to Palgrave and especially to Katie Button who was prepared to support us whenever help was needed. And, as always, the authors alone are responsible for the contents of their contributions; the articles do not necessarily express the opinion of the institutions with which they are affiliated.

Barbara Fritz
Martina Metzger

Hamburg/Berlin

Part I

Debtor Economies and Perspectives for Regional Monetary Coordination

1
Monetary Coordination Involving Developing Countries: The Need for a New Conceptual Framework

Barbara Fritz and Martina Metzger

Introductory remarks

As the East Asian crisis has impressively shown, sudden U-turns in capital flows and volatile exchange rates must today be identified as major sources of instability, even in a favourable world economic climate. Countries not engaged in a regional monetary coordination arrangement and therefore unilaterally exposed to these instabilities fall back on a combination of monetary and fiscal policies to avert depreciation, and if – as is regrettably too often the case – the struggle is lost, on competitive devaluations. The balance-sheet effects of devaluations and increased domestic interest rates depress domestic income generation and result in a deterioration of public budgets. Moreover, this policy mix has an extremely deleterious impact on regional integration, as the case of Mercosur compellingly indicates.

Against this background, we would like to elaborate on whether regional monetary arrangements, including a monetary union, might offer a significant potential for handling prevalent economic and financial instability in a more sustainable manner for both a given single member country and for the economies of other developing countries connected with it in a regional integration project. With very few exceptions, the research to date has neglected the question of the specific conditions and potential benefits of monetary South–South coordination in which, unlike in North–South arrangements, none of the international key currencies, the dollar, the euro or the yen, would be involved.[1] Furthermore, most South–South monetary arrangements are 'under construction', and their results still rather uncertain. Nevertheless, we believe it is crucial to intensify the debate on monetary coordination projects, and thus analytically differentiate between arrangements that involve international key currencies and one those that do not – a qualitative difference that most of the existing literature ignores or underestimates.

Therefore, we shall begin with a discussion of the limitations of a South–South coordination (SSC) projects compared with North–South (NSC) coordination arrangements, focusing on the specific monetary restrictions to which developing countries are subjected in stabilizing their exchange rates and initiating a sustainable development process, for example: currency mismatch, a restricted lender-of-last-resort function, and the costs of 'original sin'. Our preliminary conclusion is the argument that although an SSC offers a developing country less potential for stability gains and fewer benefits for the domestic income-generating process than an NSC, the latter is not available as an option for the majority of developing and emerging market economies. Hence, the establishment of an SSC is an option 'competing' not with the establishment of an NSC, but only with the familiar, forlorn option of unilateral management of typical boom-and-bust waves.

This will be followed by a discussion of some features of a South–South coordination project (p. 9). As a point of departure, we use conventional OCA criteria, e.g. trade interdependence and macroeconomic convergence, together with the oft-repeated call to establish independent institutions, especially central banks. We conclude that both the OCA criteria and its institutions are endogenous in the sense that they are the result of a successful monetary coordination project rather than of preconditions, and that cooperation between institutions is more decisive for success than the formal independence of institutions.

Finally, our main findings will be summed up in the Conclusion.

Original sin and regional monetary coordination

'Original sin'[2] is measured by the index of securities issued in domestic currency as a proportion of all the securities issued by a country. The resulting ranking of economies shows that the key currency economies with an original sin of zero are located in the North, and economies with a very high share of foreign to total securities are in the South. Based on broad empirical tests, the authors show that original sin significantly increases economic volatility. Three main reasons for this are:

Currency mismatch. When external debt is denominated in foreign currency, exchange-rate depreciation, by increasing the real value of the foreign debt stock, increases the costs in national currency of servicing that debt. Fears of payment difficulties create a vicious circle, making capital flows highly pro-cyclical and limiting national authorities' capacity to sustain counter-cyclical policies. This makes economies marked by original sin more volatile, and reduces growth rates.

Restricted lender-of-last-resort function and credibility. Foreign currency liabilities restrict the central bank's ability to provide domestic banks with unlimited liquidity, as its capacity of issuing money is restricted to its own currency. The higher the index of original sin, the higher is the financial sector's exposure to liquidity risks that may eventually translate into solvency problems. A high probability of solvency crises not only hinders economic growth by increasing uncertainty, but also creates extremely high contingent liabilities for the public sector in the form of potential bail-outs.

Costs of original sin. The costs of devaluation due to currency mismatch in the short run and the increased uncertainty in the long run cause an output reduction, the amount of which depends on the degree of original sin.

Against the background of this perception of net external debt in foreign currency as the key problem of developing economies with regard to monetary and exchange rate stability, the implications of original sin for regional monetary coordination will be discussed in the following section.

Currency mismatch

Currency mismatch[3] severely limits the possibility of using exchange-rate devaluation as an instrument for cushioning the effects of external shocks. Therefore it is no wonder that much of the debate on the original-sin hypothesis was first centred on the pros and cons of policies of full dollarization.[4] The higher the original sin, the more natural it seems at first glance to opt for abandoning the national currency, adopting instead the currency in which the foreign debt is denominated.[5]

But the differences between unilaterally adopting an international key currency and integrating into a key-currency area in a coordinated manner are decisive. While coordinated integration puts a definitive end to the problem of original sin for the Southern economy and re-establishes a full lender of last resort, unilateral dollarization has quite the opposite effect. When the national lender of last resort ceases to exist, all debt is transformed not into the domestic currency, but rather into the respective foreign currency.

From the perspective of a country marked by original sin, North–South cooperation projects – in contrast to unilateral submission to a hard currency – (NSCs) have the potential for providing all the advantages of reduced interest rates (due to the reduced risks incurred by the country or currency), combined with an expanded lender-of-last-resort function which includes the debtor currency (quite the reverse applies for the ERM II mechanisms; see Chapter 5). In the case of multilateral exchange-rate coordination, all participating central banks formally commit themselves to intervention. However, the most decisive form of intervention is that of the Northern country's central bank seeking to stabilize the intra-regional exchange rate at a level compatible with the foreign-exchange restrictions of the debtor country. A more advanced scenario involving the integration of the developing country into the hard-currency zone could even entail the cancellation of the foreign currency debtor status for the participant economies of the South.

In the medium term however, bilateral entry to the US dollar or euro zone does not seem feasible in practice for developing countries and emerging markets, except for the new eastern European members of the European Union. Therefore, for the majority of economies tainted by original sin, SSCs are the only viable alternative to the choice between either trying to unilaterally stabilize exchange rates, or pursuing no monetary coordination at all.

Restricted lender-of-last-resort function and limited credibility

The key problem of South–South coordination, from the viewpoint of original sin, is that it does not provide a switch from an external debt status to an internal debt position. Whereas the first generation of OCA literature, following Robert Mundell's famous study (Mundell, 1961), puts more emphasis on the symmetries of the participants as a precondition for a common currency, more recent literature has extended its reach to cover monetary aspects, asking whether, and in what form, monetary coordination could lead to successful stability import. While the first generation of OCA approaches regarded monetary coordination between currencies that respond asymmetrically to a key-currency interest-rate shock as anything but an optimal currency area, the second generation of literature, focused on the European monetary integration process, has emphasized the credibility aspect of economic policy within regional monetary coordination,[6] where it is precisely the integration of asymmetric participants that is seen as a key to success.

But this mainstream interpretation is in effect a 'discipline' argument against floating exchange rates. An inflation-prone country, according to this line of thinking, could gain much credibility by placing monetary policy decisions in the hands of a 'conservative' central bank; and in the context of an international exchange-rate arrangement, the political costs of violating the agreement could restrain the government of a Southern economy from depreciating its currency to gain the short-term advantage of an economic boom at the long-term costs of higher inflation.[7] If this were so, one extreme of the corner solution – i.e. a very extreme exchange-rate fix – would put an end to the monetary instability of southern economies.

We argue, however, that in the case of an economy tainted by high original sin, an effective increase in credibility of a southern currency – imported or otherwise – does not depend so much on such a policy switch as on the northern central bank's willingness to intervene in favor of the exchange rate of the southern currency, effectively extending its lender-of-last-resort function (or, in the case of an unsustainable exchange-rate level, enabling gradual devaluation without the destabilizing effects of overshooting).

In this sense, the main credibility gain from monetary cooperation among Southern currencies with a *similar* original-sin index could stem from collective protection against domestic pressures through a regional exchange-rate arrangement. Such an arrangement might help to make policy orientation less inflation-prone, but it would not change substantially the region's exposure to external shocks.

At the same time, the success of an SSC seems to depend on the existence of internal hierarchies, i.e. regional monetary coordination of economies with *unequal* 'original-sin' indices, where the strongest partner shows a capacity to intervene in favour of the weaker ones. Taking this aspect into account adequately could greatly enhance the empirical comparative analysis of cases of regional monetary coordination.

Costs of original sin

Within SSC schemes, regional reserve funds or swap arrangements often are regarded as early and easy steps on the road toward a regional common currency. The idea is that the pooling of national foreign exchange reserves in a regional fund should result in a leverage effect for protection against external shocks, especially speculative attacks.

This indeed is plausible in the case of an external shock hitting the region in an asymmetrical manner, for instance a destabilization of the current account of one of the member states which triggers devaluation expectations, but which does not affect the other members in the same way. But if we assume that the major source of instability derives from the capital account, the symmetric reaction of the regional economies implies that the foreign-exchange reserves pooled in a regional fund are effectively nothing more than the sum of national reserves and intervention capacities. Moreover, given low regional exchange-rate coordination, or none at all, the collective efforts could easily evaporate due to variations in national responses to such an external shock.

One argument that has emerged in the debate on original sin and the possibilities – or impossibility – of fighting it at the national level could moderate the rather sceptical appraisal of regional stabilization funds. A certain degree of protection from the potentially destabilizing financial consequences of original sin can be achieved by accumulating international reserves at the national central bank, even if this implies costs due to the negative interest-rate spread (see Eichengreen, Hausmann and Panizza, 2003, p. 13ff). This is the case for the current strategy of a number of Asian economies, the pooled regional exchange reserves of which would indeed constitute a regional fund with significant weight in the world economy.

Even if such accumulated reserves do not change the original sin index, defined as gross debt in foreign currency compared to total debt, they signal the possibility of moving out from original sin. Foreign currency reserves that quantitatively match a significant part of net foreign debt could be used to sell off part of foreign-currency debt to counter devaluation expectations and the ensuing currency mismatch. Yet the accumulation of foreign exchange stocks large enough to cope with at least a significant part of net external debt represents a viable option only for those economies which, while suffering from original sin, are still able to generate sufficient current-account surpluses to provide net foreign-exchange income. This may be seen as an indicator of a decreasing original sin index, but applies only to a limited number of dynamic Asian countries, not to the majority of southern economies.

Another argument stemming from the original-sin hypothesis is that the only variable that is robustly coordinated with original sin is country size. Hence, as Panizza argues in Chapter 2, it is to be expected at least for monetary unions that encompass large and well-diversified economies that the increase of the currency-zone size may increase its participation in the portfolio of international investors, i.e. decrease the degree of original sin.

At first sight, it is rather obvious that by applying the concept of original sin to the issue of regional monetary coordination involving developing countries, an NSC arrangement – or at least an SSC of Southern economies with significantly different levels of external debt – would offer significant potential for solving the original-sin-derived problems of net debtor economies, i.e. permitting them to limit economic volatility and enhance sustainable economic growth. For monetary unions of large size, a certain decrease of original sin is to be expected, as the increase in currency size could increase the presence of that currency in international portfolios. Therefore, for most Southern economies, it is not only the lack of viable means of achieving access to an NSC arrangement that leads us to insist on the need for discussion of the SSC option. In order to argue how and to what extent SSCs might be a meaningful instrument for countering economic and financial instability, we will examine central features of the SSC model in the following section.

Features of monetary regional coordination

In the following, we will discuss some features of a South–South coordination project. As a point of departure for our arguments we use conventional OCA criteria (Mundell, 1961), e.g. trade interdependence and macroeconomic convergence together with the often-repeated call for the establishment of independent institutions, especially central banks. Against this background, we intend to identify particular criteria which should apply to regional monetary coordination projects among developing countries – and others which, although dictated by conventional wisdom, should not. In so doing, we propose several components of a new, albeit incomplete framework.

Interdependence

Interdependence is often mentioned as one of the preconditions for a successful monetary coordination between two economies. In addition to the mere fact of geographic proximity of two countries, interdependence, especially with regard to trade, still serves as the major selection criterion for the decision as to which country should be selected for deepened monetary integration. It is argued in this context that benefits and costs of coordination are more equally shared among key trading partners than between two economies which are only loosely related. Furthermore, monetary integration is required to maintain and deepen real integration by smoothing out intra-regional exchange-rate instabilities and stabilizing expectations of agents involved in intra-regional activities. Thus, the argumentation draws the line from trade flows and factor movements to capital flows and asset price fluctuations. But if the major source of instability derives from the capital account and not the current account, and if exchange-rate volatility rather than factor mobility enforces financial and economic adjustment,[8] then the potential for reducing this instability by monetary coordination should constitute the decisive criterion for the selection of member countries. This does *not* necessarily imply high trade interdependence at the outset.

As discussed in the last section, a South–South coordination project (SSC) offers neither the advantage of a lender-of-last-resort function nor the switch from an external debt status to an internal debt position. Hence, the question arises as to what (other) benefits can be expected from an SSC (see for example the contributions of Kregel, Nunnenkamp and Kohnert in this book). To gain more clarity on this issue, it is necessary to differentiate between potential benefits at the outset and those arising from a successful process of monetary coordination.

From the outset, an SSC has the potential for limiting the consequences of exchange-rate volatility caused by extra-regional factors and global economic conditions, such as changes in the international interest-rate structure or the euro-US dollar exchange rate. In such cases, an SSC should engage in common managed bloc floating *vis-à-vis* the rest of the world, to pre-empt relative shifts in the intra-regional exchange-rate structure due to shocks from the outside.[9] Thus, we would argue that the SSC should be seen *not* as a buffer absorbing the direct impacts of external shocks on each member economy of the SSC, but rather as a multilateral policy-induced shield pre-empting mercantilist beggar-thy-neighbour-policies between member countries. Therefore, while a monetary coordination project between developing countries is not able to counter the first-round effects of external shocks from the very beginning, it can serve as an instrument for dampening second-round effects, which would otherwise reinforce adjustment costs and induce setbacks in development.

One important precondition for common managed bloc floating is that member countries share a similar vulnerability with regard to extra-regional factors, so that they can expect to be hit in the same way and to a similar extent by external factors. This applies especially to the phenomenon of contagion, which was deliberately induced during the tequila crisis in 1994–5, and the Asian crisis and its aftermath. Again, while contagion as such cannot be avoided by an SSC alone, since the member countries have high levels of foreign indebtedness, the sequencing of events – countries being hit one after the other – can be broken, and thus the severity of adjustment can be dampened. By contrast to non-coordination when contagion triggers a chain reaction of competitive devaluations aimed at gaining mercantile advantages over other competitors under pressure, an SSC can limit the rate of depreciation by keeping the intra-regional exchange rates at the pre-contagion level. Increased monetary coordination between member countries involves, first, the bilateral obligation to marginal and intra-marginal interventions by the respective central banks when current exchange rates deviate from formerly agreed-upon par values; second, financial assistance in the form of the provision of short-term credit denominated in the appreciating member-currency; and, third, an agreement about the privileged use of regional currencies for intra-regional trade and financial flows. Thus, fiscal and monetary authorities of the member countries create the structural preconditions for facilitating intra-regional financial and trade flows by stabilizing key prices for exporters and importers as well as for banks, and hence also their expectations. If private actors of the member countries pick up these opportunities, the SSC will result in a deepening of regional capital markets and an increase of trade interdependence. Hence, in the medium term, even a monetary coordination project involving exclusively developing countries may diminish domestic and, to limited extent, international original sin. Over the long term, a currency union among developing countries, as the most sophisticated form of monetary coordination, could even completely remove bilateral exchange rates, both as an autonomous source of permanent instability and as an additional transmission mechanism for global shocks. Furthermore, by transforming the previously fragmented currency areas to a single currency area for the entire SSC, a currency union could induce further deepening of regional financial markets, with contracts denominated increasingly in regional currency that makes them less prone to crisis, and increases the size of the regional market as such.

Following the original sin hypotheses (see Chapter 2), we expect a decrease in domestic and international original sin as a result of monetary coordination among major developing countries in the medium to long term. For this reason, we would advance the thesis that contrary to traditional contentions, the formation of a regional currency union within an SSC does *not* rob participant economies of a large degree of monetary autonomy, but rather reduces their degree of vulnerability to external shocks and financial crisis.

Convergence

Divergence of nominal parameters within the member countries of an SSC such as inflation rates, budget deficits or debt levels make it more difficult to stabilize intra-regional exchange rates. Therefore, macroeconomic convergence understood as budget discipline and price-level stability is considered favourable for a successful monetary cooperation project. In any case, macroeconomic convergence is said to be an indispensable requirement for the transition to a currency union, for which the convergence criteria laid down in the Treaty of Maastricht can serve as the most referred-to and comprehensive example.

Although we do not deny that macroeconomic convergence facilitates monetary coordination, we would point out that this argument mixes up cause and effect. After widespread financial liberalization in the 1980s and 1990s, developing countries nowadays show a high variability of inflation rates, budget deficits and foreign debt levels *because* they are both unilaterally exposed to sudden portfolio shifts and affected by large-scale capital outflows in sequence, rather than simultaneously. Therefore, considerable divergence in inflation rates, budget deficits and debt levels should not be very surprising. Even if we assume a relatively simultaneous shock (e.g. due to interest rate changes in the US or Euroland), a variability of nominal indicators is not ruled out. Lacking a multilateral coordination mechanism, every country will to a greater or lesser extent unilaterally take such countermeasures as increasing interest rates, devaluation, acceptance of automatic stabilizers or even a partial bail-out. Thus, macroeconomic convergence should be seen not so much as a precondition for enhanced monetary integration, but rather as a result of successful monetary coordination. Or in other words, monetary coordination serves as a vehicle for macroeconomic convergence.

With stable but adjustable exchange rates within an SSC and different inflation rates at the beginning of enforced monetary integration, a market-induced process will automatically set in, at the end of which policy-induced adjustment based on foreign-exchange interventions by the central banks in question, managed devaluations, and interest-rate policies will have to be undertaken in order to correct over and under-valued bilateral exchange rates within the SSC. Alternatively, if coordination fails, the SSC will break up altogether. Thus, an SSC does not relieve countries of the need to adjust and also harmonize at least their inflation levels within the region over the long term (for which, by the way, the EMS member countries required almost twenty years).

The differences between an adjustment under the umbrella of a monetary coordination project and an adjustment without it are the time horizon involved, and the lower adjustment costs.[10] The bilateral obligation to intervene within an SSC serves to create a much lengthier intra-regional period of adjustment for all domestic actors involved in a currency under downward pressure. Experience with nominal pegs, even by developing countries, has shown that delayed par-value changes result both in a decrease in the domestic inflation rate as such and in a reduction in its variability. There is no reason why delayed managed par-value changes within a monetary coordination project should show different results, except that delaying the depreciation and limiting the extent of depreciation is easier with the intervention partners at hand. The reduction of costs stems from the marginal and intra-marginal interventions and support purchases by the central bank of the currency under upward pressure, which otherwise would be borne unilaterally. Thus, we expect that the interest-rate policy of the currency area under downward pressure should be more effective, and therefore on average less restrictive within an SSC than in the case of a unilateral defense of exchange rates.

Nevertheless, the above-mentioned reduction in adjustment costs must not obscure the fact that the main burden of adjustment is still on the side of the country whose exchange rate is confronted with depreciation pressures. Whether the most price-stable central bank of an SSC will be in a position to decrease its interest rates to ease the adjustment of the other member states of the SSC depends on its exchange rate *vis-à-vis* hard currencies. As a point of departure, one could probably assume that it might not. Therefore, even if intervention on the foreign exchange market is symmetrical, the adjustment process as such will be asymmetrical.

Within a regional monetary coordination project, asymmetry also applies to the intra-regional inflation-rate and extra-regional exchange-rate targets toward which adjustment is geared and which will be set by the most stable country. Although inflation differentials between developing countries may be high, they are certainly lower than those between developing countries and industrialized economies. Thus, compared with the extremely low reference values of the inflation rates of hard-currency areas, the benchmarking effect of the most stable country within an SSC could be less harsh.

With regard to harmonization of business cycles, the result is more ambiguous. On the one hand, we identify an integration-induced trend to *roughly* harmonize business cycles as a consequence of the necessary adjustment policies and the deepening of the integration process. Thus, we exclude a market constellation in which all but one member of an SSC are in a severe recession. On the other hand, we do not exclude the possibility that during an upswing, one member country could lag in its activity level and its growth rate, e.g. due to structural problems limited to that country. For these reasons, we assume an assimilation of business cycles in a bust phase whereas intra-regional business cycles might diverge during boom phases, as member countries might be differently able to take advantage of them. With regard to the bust phases, we acknowledge that cycles could be reinforced, thereby increasing variability of intra-regional activity level. But we would consider such harmonization an advantage which would facilitate common bloc-floating and reduce intra-regional instability. By contrast, diverging trends of income generation within the boom phases would require an active policy-induced redistribution within the SSC to compensate for the lack of a market-induced harmonization during the upswing.

Institutions

Institutional change is often considered necessary for the good functioning of a regional monetary coordination arrangement. Thus, the proposed institutional change refers to the establishment of rules and the creation of organizations, which could obviously not be established and created by the domestic or regional market itself. Therefore, institutional change is just another word for state regulation, albeit less suspect. To assess what kind of institutional change or regulation a regional monetary coordination arrangement would require, it is necessary to clarify the objective, the target group and the executing agency. With regard to our subject, regulations should be introduced which would reduce monetary instability and promote the sustainability of an SSC. In the following, we will discuss only regulations which in principle apply to all economic agents active within the SSC, and concentrate on macroeconomic policy, *in concreto* monetary policy, fiscal policy and incomes policy and the respective macro-players' central bank, central government, trade unions and employers' associations.[11]

Monetary policy

It is no exaggeration to state that the issue of the independence of central banks from central governments dominates the debate on institutional change in monetary policy, and that the assertion of its importance has advanced to the level of an oft-repeated truism. Based on the experiences of the 1970s and 1980s, we acknowledge that a fiscal policy which ignores financial and monetary stability can be implemented much more easily with a central bank which is merely a department of the finance ministry. However, from our point of view, this debate is flawed when it comes to discussing criteria for successful monetary coordination.

Yet it is not independence which is decisive for the relationship between monetary policy and fiscal policy, but rather the extent to which monetary and fiscal policy actors cooperate in a consistent manner, which characterizes a successful monetary coordination. If monetary policy is too restrictive, it may not only severely distort domestic budget consolidation, causing domestic revenues to shrink and domestic debt service and social outlays to rise, but it may also turn intra-regional exchange rates upside-down, thus inducing par-value changes. While the first would counteract the goal of stabilization, the latter would tend to undermine the sustainability of the SSC. In the worst case of a non-cooperative central bank, a disastrous combination of an economic slump and wide-spread unemployment, widening budget deficits and an influx of hot money could arise as a result of too-high interest rates. If all domestic macro-actors but the central bank behave in a cooperative manner favourable to the SSC, the central bank will on the one hand benefit from the stabilization efforts of all other actors – as the inflation rate drops – and on the other, from not having to 'pay' for the common stabilization efforts by decreasing its interest rates; on the contrary, it will be passing on the cost of stabilization to other domestic and regional actors, thus increasing their burden. We call this a free ride for the central bank to the disadvantage of the domestic economy and of the monetary integration project as a whole.

Thus, cooperation between macro-players, both at the domestic and the regional level, is essential for successful monetary coordination, while non-cooperative behaviour, especially by a central bank, will call regional monetary integration into question. In the case of a currency union, which describes the most integrated form of monetary coordination, the abolition of the intra-regional foreign exchange market and the transformation of the different domestic central banks to a single central bank constitute the most important institutional changes in this policy area. The establishment of one single central bank will be required to unify monetary policy and to guarantee the coherence of a currency area.

Fiscal policy

What has been said about the necessary cooperative behaviour of central banks naturally applies to central governments as well. If fiscal policy is too expansive, it may not only enforce inflationary pressures, and hence fears of depreciation, but it may also reduce the effectiveness of interest-rate policy through an increase in public indebtedness in domestic or foreign currency. The first results in a setback for inflation assimilation, while the latter reduces the scope of intervention for both the central bank and the central government.

To preclude behaviour by central governments inconsistent with regional monetary coordination, it is often recommended that a formal agreement on explicit quantitative criteria be concluded, to which member states would commit themselves. However, redefining qualitative characteristics as quantitative, checkable criteria is no easy task, as it is necessary to fix, first, which indicators are to be adopted, and second, which target level should be set for the indicators. In our opinion, budget deficits are unsuitable, because in developing countries, both sides of the budget inherently suffer from great uncertainties, and are therefore partly or even predominantly beyond the control of the central governments. Fiscal agents indebted in foreign currency, as is predominately the case of central governments in developing countries, face the risk of steep and sudden increases in capital expenditures, due only to the depreciation of their domestic currencies against key currencies. Furthermore, maturity of domestic public debt is significantly lower in developing countries than in industrialized countries. Thus, central budgets in developing countries, and hence their level of budget deficits, are much more dependent on events and changes on domestic and world financial markets than their counterparts in industrialized countries. Even if all regional macro-actors within an SSC could be brought to a pattern of cooperative behaviour geared toward reducing monetary instability, any external shock which hit exchange rates and resulted in increased interest rates in the region could cause inland revenues to dwindle and, with a certain level of foreign indebtedness and if domestic social security systems are in place, also cause expenditures to rise. With regard to the target level it can be stated that binding budget deficit ceilings generally contain an inherent risk of pro-cyclical enforcement of current market constellations, thereby increasing the variability of inflation and growth rates.

With regard to binding debt level ceilings, a similar argumentation applies. For developing countries it is not reasonable to fix a standardized target level, as the sustainability of public debt depends, first, on the specific currency-mix in which the public debt is denominated and, second, on the various opportunities for raising sufficient revenues in the necessary currency by the repayment deadline. Hence, we would place greater priority on the reduction of foreign-currency debt in favour of debt denominated in domestic currency by the member states of the SSC, even if interest rates on regional currency bonds and credits were higher, and hence even at the expense of lower budget deficits and absolute debt levels. An additional cost of this proposed switch in domestic debt is the lower maturities with which domestic credit lines are vested, in comparison with international credit lines.

As it is not only the public sector which is accumulating foreign debt, central governments in an SSC should keep open the option of implementing region-wide capital-import controls, thereby setting incentives for private agents not to accumulate foreign debt.[12]

In general, one should be cautious in the selection of so-called convergence criteria and the compulsory fixing of target levels, as they are actually based on expectations which result from current market constellations. Targets that initially appear to be quite easily within reach could be difficult or even impossible to meet later on. A formal agreement which does not make allowances for a changing economic situation has the effect of a straight-jacket which deprives fiscal policy of its already low flexibility, and hence leaves governments with no exit options. Thus, instead of enhancing credibility, such an agreement to meet specified quantitative indicators might even considerably damage the credibility of fiscal policy and of regional monetary coordination.

While the formation of a common central bank is widely agreed upon as an indisputable requirement for the formation of a currency union, a similar institutional change for fiscal policy is less seldom proposed, although similar reasons can be put forward for establishing a common macro-actor and unifying fiscal policy. Instead, it is assumed that the decision-making powers in fiscal policy will remain at the national level. Thus, the introduction or even the continuation of already existing fiscal policy rules – for which the most notorious example is the Stability and Growth Pact of Euroland – is suggested to coordinate the nationally biased fiscal policies and to prevent free-ride behaviour after formation of the currency union. However, from our point of view, the lack of a common fiscal policy at the central level constitutes a harmful institutional deficiency for a currency union which cannot be adequately compensated by governments committing themselves to the fulfillment of rules, even if the latter are flexible enough. For that reason, we recommend that the common currency area be provided with institutions which are both adequate and able to function, not only with regard to monetary but also with regard to fiscal policy. This is especially relevant if it is acknowledged that cooperation between monetary and fiscal policy is essential for the success of a regional monetary coordination.

The question occasionally arises why national governments of developing countries do not take the initiative to launch SSCs, if they offer such potential benefits (see Nunnenkamp's comment on pp. 54–8). A monetary coordination project is a continuous process which begins with ad hoc measures by some members moving toward a structured harmonization of specific policy areas and a coordinated policy intervention procedure in a region, culminating in the formation of a currency union. Hence, the evolution of an SSC will entail the loss of national fiscal sovereignty, a loss which will only be compensated by a gain of greater global steering capacity and evolving fine-tuning ability for the whole currency area by means of a unified fiscal policy. With the – from our point of view – essential transmission of fiscal policy from a domestic to a regional level, the then-remaining scope of domestic fiscal policy would be reduced to a level comparable to that of states of a federal union, in terms both of its area of activity and its effectiveness. From the point of view of political economy, this perspective might not be the first choice of existing nationally-oriented decision-makers.

Incomes policy

In contrast to oft-proclaimed flexibility of nominal wages and the labour market (e.g. prominently Eichengreen, 1998), we are convinced that both upward and downward rigidity of nominal wages are essential for the survival of any regional monetary coordination, and especially for that of an SSC. As the labour market inherently does not tend toward nominal wage rigidity, we favour the establishment of central bargaining systems, both at a central domestic and at a regional level within an SSC. We will develop this argument in greater detail in the following, by discussing first a case of upward pressure on nominal wages, and second, a case of downward pressure on nominal wages.

The upward pressure on nominal wages is the result of devaluations due to common bloc floating and intra-regional par-value adjustments during the years of inflation assimilation, which can be assumed to be necessary from time to time. Every devaluation results in a price level push, be it via the transmission belt of current accounts or of capital accounts. If nominal wages are highly flexible, such price level pushes will immediately be transferred into equivalent nominal wage increases, thereby fueling inflation and increasing variability of regional inflation rates. Thus, to prevent a depreciation-inflation-spiral and to dampen growing variability in regional inflation rates from the outset, central banks in the region would have to increase interest rates to such an extent that domestic income-generating processes would be severely depressed to a level at which the destruction of production capacities would thwart the compensation of wage earners for the price-level push. With regard to the goals of monetary regional coordination – reducing monetary instability and improving sustainability – a more adequate alternative would consist of central agreements in which limited real-wage losses would be accepted in return for the regional central banks' pledge to refrain from restraining the income-generating process during the course of devaluations.[13] Such an operative incomes policy relies on (i) a centralized institutionalization of wage-fixing processes in the labour market, with which monetary policy can cooperate in any case; and (ii) a high level of organization, both in the workforce and among employers, so that the outcome of the agreement at the central level will be accepted by the vast majority of local workers and enterprises at least in the formal economy, which also is a lead for activities in the informal economy. If, on the contrary, the labour market is highly fragmented – or flexible – with different wage levels by industry, internal region, sector or trade union/ employers' association, such an incomes policy will hardly be possible.

The downward pressure on nominal wages and therefore the second line of our argumentation for a centralization of incomes policy, especially at a regional level, is based on the success of inflation assimilation within the SSC. If regional inflation rates are gradually brought into line, regional differences, especially with regard to competitiveness in prices, will continually diminish. Instead of competitive devaluations, which would be ruled out by a successful regional monetary coordination, one member country could nevertheless gain mercantile advantages over the others if its domestic wage increases were to lag behind their nominal wage increases. Hence, nationally biased incomes policies within a successful regional monetary coordination always tends to inherit deflationary risks, and may induce a race to the bottom. An instructive, albeit not advisable, example is demonstrated by the non-coordinated wage-bargaining policy existing within the Eurozone. Given the high unemployment and the huge size of the informal economy combined with rudimentary social security systems in developing countries, the deflationary risk in uncoordinated wage policies is considerably higher. Therefore, a central incomes policy at the regional level is required to prevent national free-ride behaviour which, leaving times of devaluation aside, should be based on productivity increases, thereby fully exhausting the inflation-neutral distributional scope.

The lack of a central incomes policy within an SSC marks an institutional deficiency as grave as the lack of a central fiscal policy, which also cannot be compensated for by a formal regional agreement on wage-bargaining lines between different national trade unions (and employers' associations).

Although central wage-bargaining processes do not automatically guarantee nominal wage rigidity, we suggest that an institutionalized incomes policy at the regional level involves the lowest economic costs in comparison to the alternatives. The alternatives would bring with them a slump both in economic activity and of growth due to high interest rates in case of an upward pressure, and in case of deflation, a real appreciation of domestic debt. All this cannot be without negative effects on public budgets. This underscores once again that the design of the three macroeconomic policy areas, monetary, fiscal and incomes policy, involves strong mutual repercussions, and therefore requires close cooperation between the respective actors. Furthermore, the negative effects that inflation assimilation will necessarily impose upon some of the member countries in any case will make redistribution policies between member states via fiscal policy necessary. As the financial scope for far-reaching redistribution in developing countries is relatively low, it is even more relevant that wage bargaining processes not cause additional distributional pressure on public budgets.

Conclusions

Viewing net external debt in foreign currency as the key problem of developing economies, the concept of original sin enables us to differentiate between North–South and South–South regional monetary coordination. Taking into consideration the negative impact of currency mismatch implied by original sin in terms of increased volatility and reduced growth rates, North–South coordination, in the sense of coordinated integration into a key currency region (preferably the currency in which most foreign debt is denominated), seems to be a very attractive option.

By contrast, SSCs, particularly between economies with similar original-sin indices, neither induce changes in net debtor status nor do they broaden the lender-of-last-resort function from the very beginning, except if they integrate a group of medium-range emerging markets, where the increase in currency-zone size resulting from the establishment of a common currency may at once induce an increase of the attractiveness of this currency for international investors' portfolios. Furthermore, depreciation against key currencies cannot be ruled out by an SSC. We argue, however, that with common bloc floating, a mercantilist race to the bottom due to changes in world financial markets or contagion could be prevented. Hence, we assume that in relation to a unilateral defense of the exchange rates at the national level, SSCs have a greater potential for reducing monetary instability and intra-regional exchange-rate volatility. However, in the medium to long term, we also expect a reduction, first, of domestic original sin, gradually followed, second, by a decrease in international original sin as a result of a continuing process of monetary coordination among developing countries. This improvement is due to the creation of structural conditions which facilitate intra-regional trade and financial flows, and induce a deepening of regional capital markets.

The pooling of foreign exchange reserves in a regional fund in order to obtain a leverage effect for protection against external shocks seems to be effective against a type of shock that does not affect the other members in the same way. For symmetrical shocks, however, these reserve funds have to be exceptionally high, thus signaling the possibility of decreasing the original-sin index to achieve additional stabilization effects. Otherwise, and assuming that the major source of instability derives from the capital account, a symmetrical reaction of the regional economies implies that a regional reserve fund effectively is little more than the sum of national reserves and intervention capacities.

One precondition for an SSC is that member countries share similar vulnerability with regard to extra-regional factors, so that they can expect to be hit in the same way and to a similar extent by external factors. However, conventional OCA criteria, e.g. trade interdependence and macroeconomic convergence, are not necessary preconditions, although they facilitate the establishment of an SSC. We rather see inflation assimilation and trade interdependence as endogenous to a lasting process of monetary coordination. With regard to fiscal convergence, greater priority can be placed on the reduction of foreign-currency debt in favour of debt denominated in the domestic currencies of SSC member states, in contrast to fixing standardized so-called convergence criteria, which is not reasonable for SSC members. Escaping original sin is not without costs: particularly, higher interest rates must be paid on regional currency bonds and credits which are generally vested with lower maturity.

Another necessary prerequisite affects the implementation of different policy areas. The extent to which monetary, fiscal and incomes policy are coordinated at the domestic and regional level determines, first, whether the monetary coordination project will continue to exist or, alternatively, break up altogether in a crisis; and, second, at what economic and social costs in terms of growth, unemployment and social misery monetary coordination can be realized.

The conceptual framework we have outlined here is still wide open and entails open questions:

First, much experience remains to be made, as many South–South monetary arrangements today are not much more than sketches and political intentions with a more or less uncertain outcome. Therefore, future research should closely follow the evolution of new South–South monetary arrangements.

Second, a closer look at the degree of monetary integration may bring quite different results in terms of macroeconomic stabilization rewards, as for instance the long history of monetary integration in Europe shows. Therefore, future analysis should pay more intention to that point.

Third, the role of a clear hierarchical structure between SSC members is ambiguous. On the one hand, a clear hierarchical structure seems to be highly favourable to harmonizing intra-regional inflation rates and stabilizing expectation-building by agents engaged in intra-regional activities at the point of the establishment of an SSC. The existence of internal hierarchies commits the strongest partner to intervene in favour of the weaker ones. The process of monetary convergence from the establishment of an SSC to the creation of a full currency union gradually eliminates the intra-regional instability potential, as a result of which the hierarchy should eventually be phased out. On the other hand, if there is a strong hierarchical relationship between potential SSC member countries, a similar vulnerability with regard to external shocks cannot be assumed as a precondition, and the economic basis for a common bloc floating of the SSC *vis-à-vis* the rest of the world will dwindle.

All these questions point to the necessity of intensified research on the perspectives of monetary integration involving developing countries, a question that is highly relevant, both for academic debate and for policy issues.

Notes

1. For an economic definition of the terms 'South' and 'North', see the Preface.
2. Eichengreen, Hausmann and Panizza (2002) and *idem* (2003). For a concise summary of the concept see also Panizza's chapter in this book. The expression 'original sin' stems from the fact that the inability to borrow abroad in domestic currency is not viewed as a consequence of national policy error or weak institutions in the country, but as an outcome of investors'

portfolio decisions concentrated mainly on the five strongest currencies with the highest share in international financial transactions.
3. The effects of increasing uncertainty induced by exchange-rate variations have been discussed intensively in the literature (Aghion *et al.*, 2000, 2004; Allen *et al.*, 2002; Cespedes *et al.*, 2000; IMF, 2003). The debate was motivated by the series of currency crises during the 1990s, especially in Southeast Asia. One of the most outstanding academic results is the so-called third generation of balance-of-payments crises that focus primarily on balance-sheet effects (Chang and Velasco, 2000; Corsetti *et al.*, 1998; Krugman, 1997 and 2003).
4. The expression 'dollarization' is somewhat imprecise, as it is not necessarily only the US dollar which may be chosen as a substitute for the abolished national currency. A number of eastern European countries for example have unilaterally tied their currencies to the euro.
5. This was the message of one of the first articles on the topic (Hausmann, 1999). Later on, the proposal turned towards the creation of a unit of account based on a basket of emerging-market currencies (originally published in Eichengreen and Hausmann, 2002). In addition, it influenced the debate over inflation-indexed or growth-indexed securities in foreign currency to finance developing economies' current-account deficits.
6. See Alesina and Barro (2000); Bayoumi and Eichengreen (1994); De Grauwe (1994); IDB (2002). For a rather sceptical discussion of the argument, see Schelkle (2001).
7. For an important contribution for this argument, see Rogoff (1985).
8. For a review of recent financial crisis and policy responses see Bisignano, Hunter and Kaufman (2000).
9. For a similar argument with regard to Asia see Williamson (2000).
10. For a discussion of adjustment costs in course of a unilateral defense of exchange rates by developing countries see Metzger (1999).
11. For a discussion of macroeconomic cooperation at a regional level in Latin America see IDB (2002), Ocampo (2002), Heymann (2001).
12. For the role of increasing foreign debt for the outbreak of currency crises see Metzger (2001).
13. A similar argumentation applies to a boom-phase when nominal wages might be under upward pressure.

Bibliography

Aghion, P., Bacchetta, P. and Banerjee, A., 'A Simple Model of Monetary Policy and Currency Crises', *European Economic Review*, No. 44 (2000): 728–38.
Aghion, P., Bacchetta, P. and Banerjee, A., 'A Corporate Balance-Sheet Approach to Currency Crises', *Journal of Economic Theory*, No. 119 (2004): 6–30.
Alesina, A. and Barro, R., *Currency Unions*, NBER Working Paper 7927 (2000).
Allen, M., Rosenberg, C. B., Keller, C., Setser, B. and Roubini, N., *A Balance Sheet Approach to Financial Crisis*, IMF Working Paper 02/210 (2002). http://www.imf.org/external/pubs/ft/wp/2002/wp02210.pdf (04/11/2004)

Bisignano, J. R., Hunter, W. C. and Kaufman, G. G. (eds), *Global Financial Crises: Lessons From Recent Events* (Boston, Dordrecht, London: Kluwer Academic Publishers, 2000).

Bayoumi, T. and Eichengreen, B., 'One Money or Many? Analyzing the Prospects for Monetary Unification in Various Parts of the World', *Princeton Studies in International Finance*, No. 76 (1994).

Cespedes, L., Chang, R. and Velasco, A., *Balance Sheets and Exchange Rate Policy*, NBER Working Paper No. 7840 (2000).

Chang, R. and Velasco, A., 'Financial Fragility and the Exchange Rate Regime', *Journal of Economic Theory*, No. 92 (2000): 1–34.

Corsetti, G., Pesenti, P. and Roubini, N., *Paper Tigers? A Model for the Asian Crisis*, NBER Working Paper No. 6788 (1998).

De Grauwe, P., 'The Need for Real Convergence in a Monetary Union', in Johnson, C. and Collignon, S. (eds), *The Monetary Economics of Europe* (London: Pinter, 1994), pp. 269–79.

Eichengreen, B., *Does Mercosur Need a Single Currency?* Center for International and Development Economics Research Paper C98–103 (University of California, 1998).

Eichengreen, B. and Hausmann, R., 'How to Eliminate Original Financial Sin', *Financial Times* (22 November 2002).

Eichengreen, B., Hausmann, R. and Panizza, U., *Original Sin: The Pain, the Mystery, and the Road to Redemption* (2002). http://www.iadb.org/res/publications/pubfiles/pubS-158.pdf

Eichengreen, B., Hausmann. R. and Panizza, U., *Currency Mismatches, Debt Intolerance and Original Sin: Why They Are Not the Same and Why It Matters*, NBER Working Paper No. 10036 (2003).

Hausmann, R., 'Should There Be Five Currencies or One Hundred and Five?' *Foreign Affairs*, Fall (1999): 66–79.

Heymann, D., *Regional Interdependencies and Macroeconomic Crises: Notes on Mercosur* (Buenos Aires: CEPAL, 2001).

IDB [Inter-American Development Bank], *Beyond Borders – The New Regionalism in Latin America: Economic and Social Progress in Latin America* (Washington, DC: IDB, 2002).

IMF [International Monetary Fund], *The Balance Sheet Approach and its Applications at the Fund*, Prepared by the Policy Development and Review Department (2003a). http://www.imf.org/external/np/pdr/bal/2003/eng/063003.htm (04.11.2004)

Krugman, P., *Currency Crises*, Prepared for NBER conference, October (1997). http://web.mit.edu/krugman/www/crises.html (04.11.2004)

Krugman, P., 'Crisis – The Next Generation', in Helpman, Elhanan and Sadka, Efraim (eds), *Economic Policy in the International Economy: Essays in Honor of Assaf Razin* (Cambridge, UK: Cambridge University Press, 2003).

Metzger, M., 'A Never Ending Story: Developing Countries' Choice of an Exchange Rate Anchor', DIW Vierteljahresheft, No. 1 (1999): 86–93.

Metzger, M., 'Of Magic Dragons and Other Strange Beasts: A Reassessment of the Latin American and Asian Crises', *The South African Journal of Economics*, No. 2 (June 2001): 191–217.

Mundell, R. A., 'A Theory of Optimum Currency Areas', *American Economic Review*, No. 51 (1961): 657–65.

Ocampo, J. A., *Introductory Statement at the Inauguration of the International Conference 'Towards Regional Currency Areas'* (Santiago de Chile, March 2002), mimeo.

Rogoff, K., 'The Optimal Degree of Commitment to an Intermediate Monetary Target', *Quarterly Journal of Economics*, No. 100 (Nov. 1985): 1169–89.

Schelkle, W., *Monetäre Integration. Bestandsaufnahme und Weiterentwicklung der neueren Theorie* (Heidelberg: Physika, 2001).

Williamson, J., *Exchange Rate Regimes for Emerging Markets: Reviving the Intermediate Option* (Washington, DC: Institute for International Economics, 2000).

2
'Original Sin' and Monetary Cooperation

Ugo Panizza[1]

Since the seminal paper of Eichengreen and Hausmann (1999), 'original sin', i.e. a country's inability to borrow abroad in own currency, has became a buzzword in both policy and academic circles. The early work on original sin was soon followed by a large series of papers that examined the problem from theoretical, empirical, and historical perspectives (a large number of these papers are collected in Eichengreen and Hausmann, 2005). Work on original sin has also been subject to strong criticism by authors who either did not find the issue a relevant one (Goldstein and Turner, 2004), or criticized some of the findings of the empirical work conducted by Eichengreen and co-authors (Burger and Warnock, 2003), or criticized the proposal for redemption from original sin put forward in the above-mentioned book by Eichengreen and Hausmann (Reinhart *et al.*, 2003).[2]

The purpose of this paper is to briefly describe the main findings of the research agenda on original sin and discuss their implications for the desirability of monetary cooperation both between industrial and developing countries (North–South monetary cooperation) and among developing countries (South–South monetary cooperation).

What do we mean by original sin?

Eichengreen and Hausmann (1999) originally defined original sin as 'a situation in which the domestic currency is not used to borrow abroad or to borrow long-term even domestically'. According to this definition there are two components of original sin: an international component (the domestic currency is not used to borrow abroad) and a domestic one (the domestic currency is not used to borrow long-term even domestically). In later papers, Eichengreen, Hausmann and Panizza

(2003a, 2003b) mostly focused on the international component of original sin.[3] This choice was dictated by two considerations reason. The first is purely practical and is related to the fact that it is extremely difficult to collect data on domestic original sin. The second is related to the fact that while some countries have apparently achieved redemption from domestic original sin, escaping from international original sin seems to be a much more difficult enterprise.

In order to measure international original sin, Eichengreen, Hausmann and Panizza (2003a) collected Bank of International Settlement (BIS) data on outstanding securities issued in international markets. They showed that one striking feature of this market is that nearly 97 per cent of total outstanding international securities (totaling approximately US\$ 5.6 trillion over the 1999–2001 period) are denominated in five major currencies (US dollar, euro, yen, Swiss franc, and pound sterling). Eichengreen, Hausmann and Panizza (2003a) also show that this situation is not due to the fact that residents of the countries that issue these five major currencies issue most of the international bonds. In particular, they show that 85 per cent of outstanding bonds issued by residents of countries that do not issue any of the five major currencies (these bonds total to approximately US\$ 1.3 billion) are denominated in one of these five currencies (Figure 2.1).

Eichengreen, Hausmann and Panizza (2003a) use the same BIS data to build country-level measures of original sin. While in their work they describe three alternative indices, their main focus is on what they call *OSIN3*, which is defined as:

$$OSIN3_i = \max\left(1 - \frac{\text{Securities in currency } i}{\text{Securities issued by country } i}, 0\right)$$

Two things are worth noting about the *OSIN3* index. First of all, the numerator includes all securities issued in currency i and not only securities issued in currency i by residents of country i.[4] The rationale for adopting this strategy is that bonds in currency i issued by non-residents can be used by residents of country i to swap their obligations in foreign currency into obligations in domestic currency. So, *OSIN3* explicitly recognizes that bonds issued in a given currency (no matter what the nationality of the issuer is) create opportunities for swaps.

Second, it is important to recognize that Securities in currency i/ Securities issued by country i, could be bigger than one because the amount of bonds issued in a given currency could be greater than the

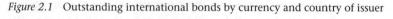

Figure 2.1   Outstanding international bonds by currency and country of issuer

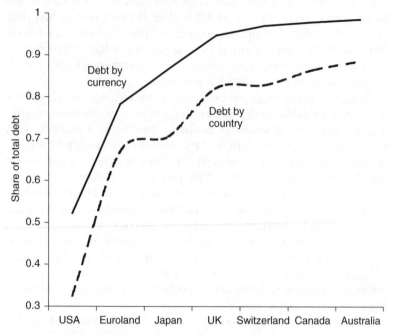

Source: Eichengreen, Hausmann and Panizza (2003a)

amount of bonds issued by residents of the country that issues this given currency (for instance, this is the case for the USA and Switzerland). Therefore, without the bound at zero, *OSIN3* could take on negative values, but countries cannot swap more than the debt they have. Hence, they would derive no additional benefits from having excess opportunities to hedge. This is why the original sin index is bounded at zero.

Figure 2.2 describes average values for the original sin index across groups of countries. The group of countries with the lowest value of the original sin index is what Eichengreen, Hausmann and Panizza (2003a) call 'Financial Centres' (this group of countries is composed of the United States, Japan, Great Britain, and Switzerland), while the second lowest value is for Euroland countries. Interestingly, industrial countries that are not financial centres or that do not belong to Euroland have values of original sin, which are similar to those of the group of developing countries (which is the group of countries with the highest level of original sin).

Figure 2.2 Original sin across groups of countries (*OSIN3*)

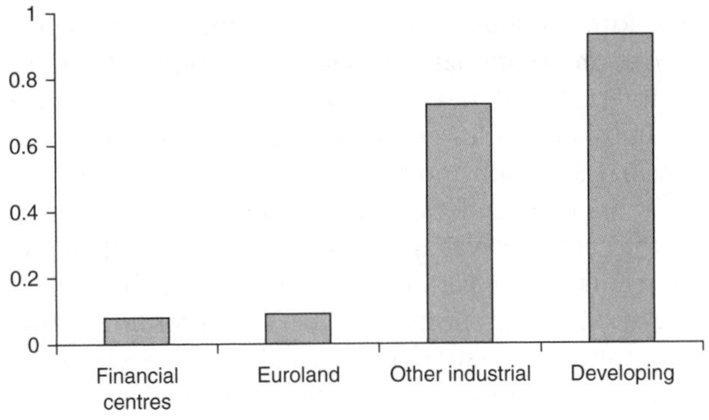

Source: Eichengreen, Hausmann and Panizza (2003a)

Why do we care about original sin?

The previous section demonstrated that original sin is a pervasive phenomenon that affects most countries which are not financial centres or part of Euroland. It is now interesting to ask whether this is just a characteristic of the international financial markets that has no practical consequence or whether it is a phenomenon which has important consequences and hence we should worry about.

Eichengreen, Hausmann and Panizza (2003a) provide strong evidence in support to the latter hypothesis. In particular, they argue that if a country affected by original sin has net foreign debt, then this country will have a currency mismatch in its national balance sheet (the amount of the mismatch will depend on several factors, the size of the tradable sector is one of them). This is important because, in the presence of currency mismatches, swings in the real exchange rate (which are very common in developing countries; Hausmann, Panizza and Rigobon, 2004) will have an aggregate wealth effect and affect a country's ability to service its debt. For these reasons, debt issued by countries that suffer from original sin will be more risky than debt of countries that have similar characteristics but are free from the problem. At the same time, countries that suffer from original sin will tend to limit exchange rate volatility and hence surrender an important policy tool.

Clearly, countries can avoid mismatches by not accumulating foreign debt. This can be achieved by either preventing foreign borrowing (both public and private) or by matching foreign debt with international reserves. However, both of these policies have costs. A country that decides not to accumulate foreign debt will give up all the possible benefits (in the form of additional investment finance and consumption smoothing) of international financial integration. Matching foreign debt with international reserves is also costly because the yield on reserves is almost always lower than the opportunity cost of funds.

Eichengreen, Hausmann and Panizza (2003a) test the above prediction and find that original sin does have important consequences. In particular, when they regress sovereign credit ratings on standard measures of fiscal fundamentals, GDP per capita, and share of foreign debt and original sin, they find a large effect of original sin (according to the baseline estimations, total elimination of original sin is associated with an improvement of ratings by approximately five notches).

Their empirical analysis also shows that original sin is negatively correlated with exchange rate flexibility. In particular, they find that redemption from original sin is associated with a change of one point and a half in the Levy-Yeyati and Sturzenegger (2000) 3-way exchange rate classification. As expected, the empirical exercise of Eichengreen, Hausmann and Panizza (2003a) also finds that countries that suffer from original sin tend to accumulate more foreign reserves than countries which are free from the problem.

Finally, Eichengreen, Hausmann and Panizza (2003a) look at the correlation between original sin and the volatility of growth and capital flows. They argue that there are at least three reasons why original sin should be positively correlated with volatility. First, as was previously discussed, original sin limits a country's ability of conducting a counter-cyclical monetary policy. Second, dollar liabilities limit the ability of central banks to perform their role of lenders of last resort (Chang and Velasco, 2000). Third, the interaction between original sin and real exchange rate volatility increases the uncertainty over the cost of foreign debt service and leads to excessive volatility of domestic interest rates which also increase the uncertainty associated with the cost of domestic currency debt service. This increase in uncertainty leads to an increase of capital flow volatility. As expected, Eichengreen, Hausmann and Panizza (2003a) find that original sin is positively correlated with higher volatility of both GDP growth and capital flows.

What are the causes of original sin?

The previous section argued that original sin does have important consequences; therefore, a logical conclusion is that redemption from original sin would be highly desirable. However, in order to find a cure it is important to understand what the causes of the problem are. Eichengreen, Hausmann and Panizza (2003b) explore six possible explanations (summarized in Table 2.1). Interestingly, they find no correlation between original sin and each of the level of development, institutional quality, monetary credibility and fiscal solvency. In fact, they find that the only variable that is robustly correlated with original sin is country size.

Table 2.1 Theories of original sin and their empirical relevance

Explanation	Link with original sin	Empirical relevance
Economic development and institutional quality	Original sin is merely the miner's canary, signalling the presence of weak institutions and low level of economic development.	GDP per capita and institutional quality can explain differences in original sin across country groups but not within country groups.
Lack of monetary credibility	Borrowers prefer to denominate their obligations in dollars and go bankrupt in the event of large depreciation, rather than borrow in pesos and go bankrupt because of high interest rates. Foreign lenders take account of the fact that the government has less of an incentive to protect their property rights and may choose to inflate away their claims if they denominate them in a unit that they can manipulate and hence they lend only in foreign currency.	Original sin is weakly correlated with past inflation but this weak correlation is due to the presence of few high inflation countries. At best, one can say that having credible monetary policies is a necessary but not sufficient condition for redemption from original sin.
Weak fiscal position	A government that has weak fiscal accounts will have an incentive to debase the currency in order to erode the real value of its obligations. The solution is to index the debt to some real price or to issue short-term debt so as to increase the cost of eroding the debt with inflation.	No statistically significant correlation between fiscal ratios and original sin.
Trade links	Countries that trade heavily with their creditors have an incentive to meet their contractual obligations because failing to do so will provoke commercial retaliation or, at minimum, interrupt the supply of trade credits.	No statistically significant correlation between trade openness and original sin.

Continued

Table 2.1 continued

Explanation	Link with original sin	Empirical relevance
Political economy	If foreigners are the main holders of public and private debts, then there is likely to be a larger domestic political constituency in favour of weakening the value of their claims and foreign creditors will be reluctant to lend in local currency unless protected by a large constituency of local savers.	No statistically significant correlation between size of the domestic financial system and original sin.
International causes	In a world with transaction costs, the optimal portfolio will have a finite number of currencies. These few currencies are the ones that offer better opportunities for diversification, i.e. the currencies of large countries.	There is a strong and robust negative correlation between country size and original sin.

Source: Eichengreen, Hausmann and Panizza (2003b)

Another interesting finding is that when Eichengreen, Hausmann and Panizza (2003b) look at who are the issuers of bonds in exotic currencies (i.e. currencies that do not belong to financial centres or to Euroland), they find that these bonds are mostly issued by non-residents (Figure 2.3) and they argue that this might be due to the fact that markets value bonds that separate currency and credit risk.

These findings led Eichengreen and Hausmann (2003) to formulate a proposal for redemption from original sin based on the idea that the international financial institutions could create markets for local currency emerging market debt by issuing bonds denominated in a basket of different emerging market currencies. Such basket would offer significant diversification benefits and provide emerging market countries with a hedge to be used to swap their foreign currency obligations.

What about monetary cooperation?

So far, I provided a definition of original sin, discussed why it is an important phenomenon and hinted at a proposal for redemption from original sin, but I have not mentioned anything on the relationship between original sin and monetary cooperation. In order to do so, it is necessary to provide a definition of monetary cooperation. According to

Figure 2.3 Share of exotic currency bonds issued by foreigners

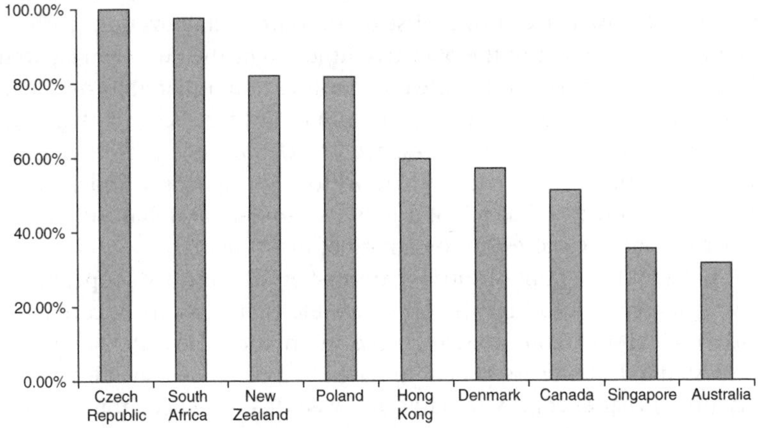

Source: Eichengreen, Hausmann and Panizza (2003b)

a more general definition, monetary cooperation would merely identify a situation in which a set of countries follow similar monetary policies and hence do not allow large swings of their bilateral exchange rates. According to a more strict definition, monetary cooperation would identify a situation in which a set of countries permanently fix their bilateral exchange rates or, in the extreme case, adopt a single currency. In what follows, I will discuss the relationship between original sin and monetary cooperation by adopting this latter strict definition of monetary cooperation.

With this definition at hand, the implications for North–South monetary cooperation are trivial. If a developing country forms a monetary union with an industrial country that is free from original sin, the developing country will automatically achieve redemption. This is why some authors (e.g. Hausmann, 1999) advocated unilateral official dollarization as a solution for original sin. It should be clear that the decision of unilaterally adopting another currency might free a country from original sin but may generate all sorts of other problems (for instance, it could lead to higher volatility and lower growth, see Levy-Yeyati and Sturzenegger, 2003 and Edwards and Magendzo, 2003) and hence should be adopted only after conducting a careful cost-benefits analysis (see, for instance, Panizza, Stein and Talvi, 2001). The situation is different for those countries which have just joined the European Union and that, after a transition period, will adopt the euro. In this case, the accession countries will gain the full benefits that derive from redemption from original sin and will pay limited costs from losing monetary independence for at least two reasons. First of all, output stabilization in these countries will be part of the objective function of the European Central Bank. Clearly, this is not the case for countries that unilaterally decide to adopt a foreign currency (like Ecuador or El Salvador). Second, thanks to free factor mobility and the presence of EU transfers, these countries should be able to better smooth transitory idiosyncratic shocks with respect to countries that adopt a policy of unilateral dollarization and hence do not have access to these kind of instruments.

What about the implications for South–South monetary cooperation? It was argued before that the only variable that is robustly correlated with original sin is country size. Hence, international investors might be interested in holding assets denominated in a currency issued by monetary union that encompasses large and well diversified economies. This suggests that small South–South monetary unions (like the CFA area in Central Africa) are unlikely to achieve redemption from original sin. However, a currency issued by a monetary union among large countries (for instance a currency union among countries belonging to Mercosur or to Asean) might have a chance of becoming part of the international portfolio.

Notes

1. I would like to thank Barbara Fritz and Martina Metzger for inviting me to write this paper, as well as workshop participants and especially my discussant Waltraud Schelkle for helpful comments and suggestions. The paper summarizes part of the research on original sin I conducted jointly with Barry Eichengreen and Ricardo Hausmann. The views expressed in this paper are the author's and do not necessarily reflect those of the Inter-American Development Bank. The usual caveats apply.
2. For an answer to some of these criticisms, see Eichengreen, Hausmann and Panizza (2003c).
3. However, Hausmann and Panizza (2003) also make an attempt to study the causes of domestic original sin.
4. An alternative index that Eichengreen, Hausmann and Panizza (2003a) call OSIN1 focuses on securities issued in currency i by resident of country i.

Bibliography

Burger, J., and Warnock, F., *Diversification, Original Sin, and International Bond Portfolios*, International Finance Discussion Paper no. 755, Board of Governors of the Federal Reserve System (Washington, DC, 2003).

Chang, R., and Velasco, A., 'Financial Fragility and the Exchange Rate Regime', *Journal of Economic Theory*, 92 (2000): 1–34.

Edwards, S. and Magendzo, I. Igal., *Strict Dollarization and Economic Performance: An Empirical Investigation*, NBER Working Papers 9820 (2003).

Eichengreen, B., and Hausmann, R., 'Exchange Rates and Financial Fragility', in *New Challenges for Monetary Policy* (Kansas City: Federal Reserve Bank of Kansas City, 1999), pp. 329–68.

Eichengreen, B., and Hausmann, R., 'The Road to Redemption' (2003), in Eichengreen, B. and Hausmann, R., *Debt Denomination and Financial Instability in Emerging-Market Economies* (Chicago: University of Chicago Press, 2005).

Eichengreen, B., Hausmann, R., and Panizza, U., 'The Pain of Original Sin' (2003a), in Eichengreen, B. and Hausmann, R., *Debt Denomination and Financial Instability in Emerging-Market Economies* (Chicago: University of Chicago Press, 2005).

Eichengreen, B., Hausmann, R., and Panizza, U., 'The Mystery of Original Sin' (2003b), in Eichengreen, B. and Hausmann, R., *Debt Denomination and Financial Instability in Emerging-Market Economies* (Chicago: University of Chicago Press, 2005).

Eichengreen, B., Hausmann, R., and Panizza, U., *Original Sin, Debt Intolerance and Currency Mismatches: Why are not the Same and Why it Matters?* NBER Working Paper 10036 (2003c).

Eichengreen, B., and Hausmann, R., and Panizza, U., *Debt Denomination and Financial Instability in Emerging-Market Economies* (Chicago: University of Chicago Press, 2005).

Goldstein, M. and Turner, P., *Controlling Currency Mismatches in Emerging Market Economies: An Alternative to the Original Sin Hypothesis* (Washington, DC: Institute of International Economics, 2004).

Hausmann, R., 'Should There Be Five Currencies of One Hundred and Five?' *Foreign Policy*, 116 (1999): 65–79.

Hausmann, R. and Panizza, U., 'The Determinants of Original Sin: An Empirical Investigation', *Journal of International Money and Finance*, Vol. 22 (7) (2003): 957–90.

Hausmann, R., Panizza, U. and Rigobon, R., *The Long-Run Volatility Puzzle of the Real Exchange Rate*, NBER Working Paper 10751 (2004).

Levy-Yeyati, E., and Sturzenegger, F., *Classifying Exchange Rate Regimes: Deeds vs Words* (Universidad Torcuato di Tella, 2000), unpublished.

Levy-Yeyati, E., and Sturzenegger, F., 'To Float or to Fix: Evidence on the Impact of Exchange Rate Regimes on Growth', *American Economic Review*, Vol. 93 (4) (2003): 1173–93.

Panizza, U., Stein, E., and Talvi, E., 'Assessing Dollarization: An Application to Central American and Caribbean Countries', in E. Levy-Yeyati and F. Sturzenegger (eds), *Dollarization* (Cambridge, MA: MIT Press, 2001).

Reinhart, C., Rogoff, K., and Savastano, M., 'Debt Intolerance', *Brookings Papers on Economic Activity*, 1 (2003), pp. 1–74.

Comment

Waltraud Schelkle

The paper of Panizza as much as the precedent papers on the 'Determinants' and the 'Pain' of Original Sin (OS)[1] are both a pleasure and a nuisance to comment on. A pleasure because these are excellent empirical papers, exemplary in their exposition of the findings and the scrupulous discussion of the methodological difficulties, for instance as regards the problem of reverse causality. This is then also a nuisance because they leave precious little room for the academic posturing and gaming to a commentator, eager to point out the limitations of the data, the sensitivity to the use of alternative indicators etc. – Ugo Panizza and his co-authors point out all that themselves. Therefore I can only declare defeat and concentrate on the substantive issues.

OS is a most relevant policy issue since it is a barrier for development. It has measurable costs in terms of a risk premium for higher exchange rate volatility. It afflicts the majority of currency areas in the world, more or less severely. OS is also relevant for economic theory since it challenges both conventional 'real' trade theory and old and new theories of monetary integration. Finally, it is stimulating further questions – and what better news is there for researchers than the message that there is yet more research to do.

These three substantive issues that the existence of OS raises will be discussed in the following order: first, the papers' hidden treasures for economic theory will be outlined; then I propose what seem to me important open questions and interesting puzzles; finally, I will draw some policy conclusions.

Hidden treasures

Two challenges for economic theory that the Panizza *et al.* papers contain seem to me particularly noteworthy. First, the phenomenon of OS challenges 'real' trade theory, above all in the context of development. Demonstrating over and over again that comparative advantage in a pure exchange economy raises welfare is not of much use if there is no such thing as a pure exchange economy. Thus, it cannot be assumed that the real exchange rate ensures purchasing power parity within a relevant time horizon.[2] Real trade theory is at best irrelevant because it neglects an important determinant of trade as well as a source of gains from trade, namely whether trading with another country requires payment in hard currency or earns hard currency. At worst, real trade theory is seriously misleading because it ignores the fact that current account imbalances are fairly persistent, which makes for correspondingly stable groups of debtor and creditor countries and has a cumulative effect on development via the interest rate. And yet, avoiding it has also costs in terms of foregone gains from trade or hedging costs as the introduction to the 'Pains' paper rightly points out.

Within the group of debtor countries, there is a surprising differentiation; some suffer from both types of sin, some just from international sin and some from neither. One explanation for this differentiation between serial and simple sinners is the role of FDI. Direct investors exploit price differences between country and currency risk. Again, the new rationale that Panizza *et al.* find for the attractiveness of FDI is another aspect of the flaws of conventional trade theory which considers them only as exporters of scarce capital and perhaps know-how – while it is the import of hard currency as well as the inevitable demand for the domestic currency, thus hardening it, that may be a more redeeming and reliable feature of FDI for the host country. Yet this also means that the clear distinction that is prevalent in the literature between 'good' capital movements, namely presumably long-term FDI, and 'bad' capital movements, that is short-termist portfolio investment, is unwarranted: financial arbitrage and speculative risk assessments are involved in both cases.

Closely related to this is the other challenge for economic theory that the OS phenomenon implies. It is the rationale for monetary integration in terms of an inconsistent quartet of free trade, free capital movements, stable exchange rates and autonomous monetary policy. In light of these findings, the notion of an inconsistent quartet is questionable because the underlying assumption that the authorities of any country have a choice between an autonomous monetary policy and a stable exchange rate is misleading. The majority of countries that are afflicted by OS have no such choice, their monetary policies cannot prioritize domestic goals whatever the choice of the exchange rate regime. Nor can they choose a stable exchange rate in any economically meaningful sense, thus the Panizza *et al.* papers find a higher real exchange rate volatility irrespective of the public stance on floating. Also, the perplexing observation that countries with a floating regime (Chile, India and Poland) have capital controls, while those with fixed rates (Argentina, Hong Kong) have open capital accounts contradicts the inconsistent quartet, which would make us expect stable exchange rates but no free capital movements if authorities want to prevent crisis. To repeat, this can be read as evidence for the phony character of the insinuated choice: in a state of OS, floating is likely to be the default option if interest rate signals ('non-autonomous' monetary policy) fail to stabilize the exchange rate in a reliable and predictable way; the monetary policy is no more or less autonomous than for those with stable exchange rates. The real surprise to me is that capital controls combined with floating rates should have the effect of less domestic OS, and I will come back to that.

Finally, OS is also a challenge for the theory of monetary integration as it has developed as a rationale for economic governance in EMU. A large public debt in particular, fiscal fundamentals more generally do not count for international OS, according to Panizza *et al.* This irrelevance of fiscal performance indicators does not bode well for the notorious 'advantages of tying one's (fiscal) hands' that was the pretext for implementing the Stability and Growth Pact. On the contrary, taken together with the implied finding on the inconsistent quartet, this suggests to me that one should not tie but guide and strengthen governments' hands, because they are desperately needed to make up for the impairments that OS inflicts on monetary policy.

Open questions or research puzzles

Panizza *et al.* do a great job in convincing the reader that OS is indeed an important and widespread phenomenon. While this may not be necessary for the Catholics among us, i.e. those who always suspected that money is *not* just a veil, after reading their papers even the mainstream Lutherans may wonder how some countries can escape OS. To me, this is where more research is needed. How come that some countries live in a state of bliss even though their level of development or a recent history of inflation and lax fiscal management would suggest the opposite? Econometrics can help us only to identify these odd cases which Panizza *et al.* do. It is Poland, the Czech Republic and South Africa that stand out.[3] Qualitative case studies must then find out which factors or combinations thereof can explain their curious redemption. Size in these three cases may not be all that telling because Poland and the Czech

Republic are of significantly different size while assessing the size of the South African economy yields very different results, depending on whether one thinks it is the regional weight or the share in the world economy that counts. Also, the importance of FDI seems to deserve closer scrutiny, for instance why there are such big arbitrage potentials in the case of these countries – but not in others such as, say, Hungary.

Another area of fruitful research is opened up by the question what these findings tell us about the efficiency of financial markets. On the one hand, the evidence of inertia, namely that time-varying factors have very little explanatory power, seems to suggest that financial markets have long memories. On the other hand, evidence of the importance of group assessment indicates that accidental punishment and herding prevails. How can these two sets of findings be reconciled?

Perhaps related to that but still hard to swallow for a monetary catholic/non-neutralist is the finding that there is so little role for monetary credibility. While the irrelevance of fiscal fundamentals can be explained by the fact that the same 3 per cent deficit or 60 per cent debt to GDP ratio may mean very different things for public solvency in different countries. Yet, a history of inflation should indicate to even weakly rational domestic and foreign investors that the country has not managed to protect their property rights. In fact, it could explain that we observe domestic OS but not international OS because domestic investors suffer more from inflation than foreign investors as long as countries manage to keep fairly stable nominal exchange rates despite real appreciation. And yet, Panizza *et al.* do not find any country that suffers (more) from domestic OS but not international. Their explanation is plausible – why should foreign investors trust if even domestic asset holders don't? – and yet I would like to see the explanatory power of monetary credibility tested with other indicators like central bank independence. The impact may be more indirect, analogous to fiscal solvency indicators: *in the presence of OS*, indicators of monetary credibility may have little predictive power because they are seen as risky independently of whether inflation compared to countries with much better credit ratings is really that different. Yet, this does not imply that the inflation history (or central bank independence) was not part of the story that brought OS about in the first place.

Policy conclusions

Two sets of policy conclusions seem to follow from this excellent paper on OS. One set relates to (a) the general policy question of what the monetary authorities of a weak currency area can do on their own after the expulsion from that Garden of Eden, which our economics textbooks describe in glaring and futile detail. The other set relates to (b) how monetary integration could help to ease the punishment, the topic treated in the last section of Panizza's paper.

(a) Defensive action open to monetary authorities of a weak currency area

The evidence that the papers provide on the importance of size but not openness suggests that portfolio decisions determine the occurrence and severity of OS. The real economy or more specifically the current account presumably comes into play only indirectly by feeding the stock of claims that the rest of the world holds against the country. Thus, capital controls must primarily be considered as regards their effect on portfolio decisions. Panizza proposes capital controls to help and alleviate domestic OS, which is the problem that domestic investors do not want to hold longer-term assets, while they do not help or may even aggravate international OS. In other words, the monetary authorities that are afflicted by both have to choose between raising the maturity of domestic debt and persistent or even rising currency mismatch. This amounts to a forceful endorsement of capital controls, given that the authors conclude 'domestic market development is a necessary [if not sufficient] condition for redemption from original sin' (Eichengreen, Hausmann and Panizza, 2003, p. 14). I am less sure than this quote suggests that capital (export) controls are correctly portrayed as a necessary condition for complete redemption since I believe that locking investors in will have to be paid by a higher risk premium. Yet I acknowledge that separating the two forms of OS by capital controls amounts to a trade-off that can be advantageous.

The evidence on the importance of size and FDI but not fiscal fundamentals implies also that the 'advantage of tying one's hands' does not work. On the contrary, the monetary authorities of weak currency areas must obviously be seen to manage the vulnerable status of their economies actively, that is, give reassurances to investors even if that creates Moral Hazard as the related literature on the 'fear of floating' concurs.

(b) How monetary integration could help ease the punishment

These findings would also imply that South–South monetary integration may, at least to some extent, contribute to easing the pains of international OS. A criterion for choosing one's partners could be their attractiveness to foreign direct investors, since their demand for the common currency would then spill over to the other countries, now members, of the monetary union.

Yet, combined with the evidence that belonging to a country group is a significant determinant of OS suggests that redemption can only be sought by asymmetric integration, that is monetary integration with a strong currency area. This does not cover dollarization – currency substitution is not the same as asymmetric monetary integration because the currency supply then becomes even more dependant on the current account balance. A currency union, by contrast, eases exactly that constraint. Evading OS is thus a rationale for most of the new EU members in Central and Eastern Europe to also become members of the monetary union fairly quickly. Yet, it is hard to see what policy lesson this entails for countries outside of the EU orbit. Redemption is only for the lucky few and it is in the nature of redemption that the sinner cannot do much to get the blessing.

Notes

1. At the workshop, Panizza presented two background papers: one on the 'Determinants' of Original Sin (OS), Eichengreen, Hausmann and Panizza (2003); and another one on the 'Pain' of OS; Hausmann and Panizza (2003). The comment was slightly revised after receiving Panizzas's final paper as it is published in the present book.
2. The caveat as regards the 'relevant time horizon' is to take note of the fact that purchasing power parity may hold in the long run – the latest findings suggest, on average, a timespan of 29 years (Taylor and Taylor, 2004, p. 5). Given the frequency of financial crises, this is hardly comforting to policy-makers and central bankers.
3. They also name Hong Kong, Taiwan and Singapore.

Bibliography

Eichengreen, B., Hausmann, R., and Panizza, R., 'The Pain of Original Sin' (2003), in Eichengreen, B. and Hausmann, R., *Debt Denomination and Financial Instability in Emerging-Market Economies* (Chicago: University of Chicago Press, 2005).

Hausmann, R. and Panizza, U., 'The Determinants of Original Sin: An Empirical Investigation', *Journal of International Money and Finance*, Vol. 22 (7) (2003): 957–90.

Taylor, A. M. and Taylor, M. P., *The Purchasing Power Parity Debate*, NBER Working Paper 10607 (Cambridge, MA: National Bureau of Economic Research, 2004).

3
Chances and Limits of South–South Monetary Coordination

Jan Kregel

Introduction: definition of the 'South' and monetary sovereignty

Let us start by noting the definition that has been set for the 'South' in this discussion by the organizers: the inability to sell assets denominated in domestic currency to non-residents. This definition means that even though the title refers only to the South, it cannot be discussed without reference to the 'North', whose domestic currency liabilities will be held by the South as long as there are imbalances in international trade and/or free international capital flows. These countries thus face a foreign currency constraint in financing these imbalances or servicing their external borrowing.

This definition of the South also implies that in the absence of autarchy, the South does not retain what we may call full 'monetary sovereignty'. And in turn this implies that 'South–South' coordination will be subject to limits and constraints set by external activity, while the North will not be subject to these constraints which makes 'North-North' coordination less necessary, although it will be crucial to the success of 'South–South' coordination. In the absence of 'North–North' or 'North–South' coordination, the question becomes the degree of coordination that is possible without consideration and cooperation from the North.

Since the need for monetary coordination will be part of the process of trade and financial integration, it will be part of any discussions of regional trade and financial integration. However, it is important to note that recent international trade negotiations have been dominated by the concept of a new geography of international trade based on the idea that national interests in trade and monetary coordination may not necessarily be dominated by geographical proximity, but by economic similarity or complementarity. This suggests that 'South–South' cooperation is not necessarily the same thing as regional cooperation, although most of the examples that we have of such coordination are on a regional geographic basis.

Examples of regional coordination to reduce dependence on external borrowing

Let us start with what is perhaps the best known example of regional trade and financial coordination: the European Payments Union (EPU). This may now seem far removed from the problems facing a typical developing region, but in the post-war period the reconstructing European countries were all 'South' under our definition (see, for example, Polak, 1943) and much of early development theory was generated by the problems faced by the reconstruction plans in Europe after the First and Second World Wars.

The European Payments Union (EPU)

The EPU was created by Robert Triffin, Special Policy Adviser to the Economic Cooperation Administration, with a capital base provided from the US European Recovery Programme. The EPU followed a series of attempts to provide balance of payments support to the recovering European economies.[1] It was a multilateral netting mechanism that provided for conservation of foreign exchange and the creation of limited intra-system credits so that foreign exchange did not have to be used for intra-EPU payments and intra-EPU trade could be financed from domestic credits. Countries did not have to make initial quota payments in foreign currency, but only settled net monthly changes in their balance with the Union, either with gold or dollars (some of which were ERA funds that created initial debit and credit positions), or their own currency. These balances were calculated in union 'units'. This latter alternative effectively allowed countries to 'borrow' on a limited basis via settlement of net deficits in terms of their own domestic currency.[2] It also allowed for implicit discrimination against US goods in favour of European output because of foreign exchange shortages due to balance of payments deficits, and probably provided the justification for similar conditions for suspension of non-discrimination in Article XII and XV of the GATT. It was in effect a system of European trade preferences.

Fondo Latinoamericano de Reservas (FLAR)

A similar arrangement was created in Latin America in the form of the Fondo Andino de Reservas, formally established in 1976 on the basis of the Cartagena Agreement to assist the integration process in the Andean Community. Unlike the EPU, it was based on member contributions. In 1988 membership was opened to all nations of Latin America and became the Fondo Latinoamericano de Reservas. Its objectives are:

- To support the balance of payments of member countries by granting loans or guaranteeing loans from other lenders.
- To contribute to the harmonization of exchange, monetary and financial policies of member countries, facilitating compliance with commitments acquired in the framework of the Cartagena Agreement and the 1980 Treaty of Montevideo.

The EPU was formed on the basis of US dollar aid but the FLAR was based on members' contributions of a minimum of US$ 250,000 for large countries and US$ 125,000 for small countries (Ecuador and Bolivia). In 2003 the paid-in capital was US$ 1,344,320,582 with Bolivia and Ecuador each 11.3 per cent, and Colombia, Peru and Venezuela each with 22.6 per cent, and Costa Rica with 9.6 per cent.

Besides providing loans for supplementing reserves, meeting balance of payments difficulties and to counter speculation, the FLAR lends to member countries to facilitate programmes to restructure sovereign foreign currency debt. It currently has extended support for balance of payments of US$ 2.140 billion, for liquidity purposes of US$ 2.579 billion, for contingency credits of US$ 375 million, and for debt restructuring of US$ 356 million.

ASEAN Self-help and Support Mechanism and the ASEAN Economic Community

In Asia, the ASEAN countries have taken a different approach, setting up a regional self-help and support mechanism to supplement the existing international facilities by strengthening existing cooperative frameworks among monetary authorities through the 'Chiang Mai Initiative' (CMI) launched by the ASEAN +3 in May 2000. The CMI involves an expanded ASEAN Swap Arrangement and a network of bilateral swap and repurchase agreement facilities among ASEAN countries, China, Japan and the Republic of Korea. The ASEAN Swap Arrangement or ASA was originally established before the regional financial crisis by the

ASEAN central bank and monetary authorities of the five founding members of ASEAN with a view to help countries meet temporary liquidity problems. An expanded ASA now includes all ten ASEAN countries with an expanded facility of US$ 1 billion. Thus far the Swap Network comprises sixteen bilateral swap arrangements (BSAs), including Korea–Philippines, China–Malaysia and Japan–Indonesia, with a total size of US$ 35.5 billion compared with approximately US$ 1 trillion in combined foreign exchange reserves. In view of the need to explore other appropriate mechanisms (in addition to CMI) to further strengthen regional self-help and support in East Asia, a study on 'Regional Self-help and Support Mechanism: Beyond the CMI' was completed in March 2003. The report concluded that conditions were not appropriate for the introduction of a common currency. The 'Roadmap for the Integration of ASEAN in Finance' is the latest regional initiative, which aims to strengthen regional self-help and support mechanisms that will contribute to the realization of the ASEAN Economic Community, launched at the Ninth ASEAN summit in Bali in October 2003. The AEC is the end-goal of economic integration as outlined in the ASEAN Vision 2020 and the Bali Concord II to establish a single market and production base, characterized by the free movement of goods, services, investment, and a freer flow of capital. The AEC will also facilitate the movement of businessmen, skilled labour, and talents within the region. As in the EU, economic integration is expected to lead to the adoption of an ASEAN common currency as the final stage in the realization of the ASEAN Economic Community. Under the Roadmap capital market development, capital account liberalization, financial services liberalization and ASEAN currency cooperation have been identified as areas crucial to the financial and monetary integration necessary for the introduction of a common currency. In the interim, currency cooperation would involve exploration of possible currency arrangements, including an ASEAN currency payment system for trade in local goods in order to reduce the demand for US dollars and help promote stability of regional currencies, such as by settling intra-ASEAN trade using regional currencies. If this were to occur the ASEAN system would have the same short-term goals of conserving foreign exchange reserves via a system of multilateral clearing as the EPU and FLAR. On the other hand, it also has the same long-term goal of a common currency as the EEC. In this respect it is important to note the similarity between ASEAN+3 and the EEC in possessing strong reserve positions built up on the basis of sustained external surpluses.

The European Economic Community Exchange Rate Mechanism and Monetary Union

Although the Werner Report was designed to outline the further steps required for monetary union to complete the European Economic Community, the impetus for the creation of the European Exchange Rate Mechanism in the 1970s also seems to have been driven by a perceived need to pool foreign exchange reserves. However, this need was less the result of a shortage of foreign exchange reserves caused by the external performance of the EEC as an excess supply of US dollars, in part created by US outflows (although the current account was in surplus averaged US\$ 3 billion per year for 1960–71, and only showed deficits for 1971 and 1972, government transfers averaged US\$ 7.5 billion per year, leaving an average official settlements balance of over minus US\$ 4 billion per year), in part by the expansion of the Eurodollar market, which was causing excessive volatility in intra-European exchange rates. It was thus not only the excess supply of dollars, but the volatility of the dollar causing misalignment of rates among European trading partners that had nothing to do with changes in national productivity across countries and thus imposed a form of 'beggar my neighbour' policy on the currencies of the larger members, such as Germany, that was the problem that ERM sought to resolve. Although the original schemes were built on the idea of an 'average' currency that would be a counter to the dollar, the system was eventually built on a 'bi-lateral' grid of exchange rate bands that were largely maintained through intervention via bi-lateral rates of members *vis-à-vis* the dollar and thus did little to reduce the need for member central banks to hold dollar balances. Since the main objective was stability of intra-European rates through stabilization against the dollar this meant that the coordination required was compatibility with German monetary policy. In terms of its role in policy coordination, the ERM thus differed little from the dollar standard or the gold standard.

Mercosur

The final example is that of Mercosur, until now a regional system limited to setting internal and external tariff policies, has recently considered proposals for the creation of a common currency. At present it has no other formal means of monetary cooperation or coordination, although exchange rate volatility between the two major member states has been a continued source of friction since its creation in 1991.

Implications of the various approaches to coordination

Whether or not the system implies a common currency, the major benefits come from the increased efficiency due to the use of net settlements systems or the pooling of reserves through a multilateral clearing system for intra-regional transactions. If there are such efficiency gains, the use of such regional preference systems will allow for the financing of greater overall trade deficits for members in their trade with external countries and thus some increased flexibility by creating a protected zone in which members' domestic currency liabilities are acceptable as substitutes for the currencies of the North. However, these are once over efficiency gains which have only limited use as a policy tool given that there are normally limits to the size of any individual member's issue of his domestic liabilities to the system. It is important to recognize the similarities between the system created at Bretton Woods, which allows member countries the ability to issue domestic liabilities in exchange for foreign liabilities through the Fund up the limits of its quota. A currency union operates in a similar manner, although it differs from the Fund in that it does not require initial quota payments and provides a symmetric adjustment mechanism built on policies and penalties to force surplus countries to contribute to the financing of deficit countries through changes in domestic policies and the potential loss of excess credits to the union. Experience has taught that this is not something that does function well as a basis for 'North–North' coordination, having been one of the major causes of the breakdown of the Bretton Woods System, and has even less possibility of working for 'North–South' coordination. However, it does remain attractive for 'South–South' regional coordination systems for it increases the potential efficiency gains.

Regional coordination in financing imbalances in trade flows and capital flows

All of this has to do with the linkage between coordination of trade flows and financing imbalances. But a large proportion of the difficulties facing 'South–South' coordination stem from autonomous capital inflows. When these flows are in excess of domestic financing needs they exert an impact on domestic monetary and exchange-rate policy and thus on any ability to coordinate policy. Recently a number of developing countries have accumulated extremely large reserves in order to forestall an overvaluation of their currencies, similar to those that had occurred in many countries following stabilization policies in the early 1990s, hurting their countries' export industries' international competitiveness and thereby impairing the future ability to earn the foreign currency necessary to finance imports needed for a balanced growth path. For all developing countries purchases of foreign currency reached a net value of US$ 320.9 billion, last year with the largest purchases by Asian countries, led by China's accumulation of US$ 117.1 billion, India's US$ 31.7 billion, and Malaysia over US$ 10 billion. Russia accumulated US$ 27.2 billion. In Latin America Brazil increased reserves by US$ 11.5 billion and Mexico also had significant accumulation.

These reserves accumulations have a cost that could in part be offset by greater regional cooperation. Buying foreign exchange market increases excess reserves of domestic banks. In order to keep to monetary or interest rate targets central banks must borrow these reserves by issuing stabilization bonds. Since the rates set are above the rate earned from the investment of the reserves in US treasury securities the reserves have what is called negative net carry,[3] i.e. the interest paid to finance the position is greater than the interest earned on the assets; the resulting costs then have to be carried by the developing country's general government budget and consequently by the taxpayer. In the spring of 2004, Korea, which has also been heavily intervening in the foreign exchange market had currency stabilization bonds of more than 30 trillion won (US$ 27 billion) outstanding, with an estimated interest cost of 1.5 trillion won (US$ 1.1 billion) in the current year alone. In Brazil, Chile and South Africa, high costs of the sterilization of the reserve built-up have also been an issue.

The impact of these flows for regional coordination is similar to that caused by excess dollar balances in the EEC in the 1970s since they usually are concentrated in a particular member country's currency, causing an unwanted real or nominal appreciation and loss of competitiveness *vis-à-vis* other members. As noted above, the path taken by the EEC was to pool reserves to stabilize exchange rates within the regional system, but to allow the system to float relative to the dollar. This, of course does not eliminate the appreciation of the entire group relative to the dollar, with differential impact on each individual member, so it really does not solve the problem of the differential impact of capital flows.

One possibility would be the creation of a composite currency, similar to the European Currency Unit, but in difference from that experience it would be actually used as the sole counterpart currency for external inflows. Thus, foreign capital inflows would be converted into the composite currency, with the proceeds held in the central reserve fund and the direct country investment financed through internal swaps of domestic money creation.

Coordination and the problem of monetary sovereignty

The basic difficulty hindering any attempt at coordination is the lack of domestic monetary sovereignty which precludes autonomy in the selection of monetary and fiscal policy variables. As Hy Minsky once observed, anybody can create money by issuing IOUs, the difficult part is getting them to be generally accepted. The definition of 'South' thus comprises those countries that face that difficulty. The easiest way to get your IOUs accepted is to create liabilities that can only be extinguished through possession of your IOU. This is what happens when a government creates a tax liability on its citizens that can only be extinguished through rendering the government's IOU in the form of money issued by the government. As long as you have an open tax liability you will accept the government's IOU since it liberates you from tax prison. To do this you have to sell some good or service to someone who possesses the government's IOU or sell directly to the government to obtain the IOU. It is the fiscal system that thus underlies the monetary sovereignty of the government.

It might appear that this sovereignty depends on keeping the government's IOUs scarce through a fiscal surplus, but a moment's reflection reveals that this is not the case. If households are to meet their tax liabilities, whatever the size, they can only do so if they obtain government IOUs of a similar amount. And this they can do only if in aggregate households sell to the government goods and services or borrow in an amount equal to the tax liability. But this also means that the government's expenditures on goods and services has to be at least equal to the tax liability. If it is less than the liability some households cannot meet their tax liabilities and go into arrears, which represents implicit government lending, or they end up in tax prison. Thus, the sovereignty depends on the government budget never being in surplus.

If any of the government IOUs are held to finance the exchange of goods and services produced by private individuals and sold to private individuals, or are held as precautionary balances, then the government's budget must be in deficit by the amount that households choose to hold in excess of their public tax liabilities. The sovereignty of the government lies in the fact that it can determine the solvency of the system simply by changing its tax or expenditure decisions. But, since sovereignty implies that the fiscal position will always be in deficit, it means that the government also has the ability to set the short-term interest rate.

For example, if the government makes an expenditure that creates IOUs that no one wishes to hold as ready money they will be deposited in a bank. In a system in which banks are subject to reserve require-ments this creates excess reserves for the bank with the central bank. Since the banking system as a whole cannot change the amount of reserves, this means there will be excess reserves available in the system at the prevailing interest rate for interbank borrowing of reserves. As a result, the interest rate will fall to zero, since there is an inexhaustible excess supply of reserves. If the government wishes to maintain a positive interest rate target as part of its monetary policy, the govern-ment must intervene by buying back those IOUs through the issue of other forms of interest paying government debt. But, it retains the abil-ity to set that rate at any level above zero, so it retains sovereignty over the rate of interest. If it chooses to operate in other markets beside the interbank market it can set other interest rates. Note that it is not the 'money market' or the 'capital market' that sets the limit on the govern-ments' ability to borrow – once the expenditures have been made the government can borrow that amount at any rate it chooses.

This helps us understand why the ability to make your own liabilities acceptable is the key to sovereignty and to coordination. Non-residents, who are not subject to government regulation, in particular are not subject to the government's ability to create a tax liability, have no reason to accept the government liability. They thus have reason to sell resources to the government or its residents. They insist on being paid in their own government's liabilities to which they have tax liabilities. Here it is interest to reflect on the fact that the US government makes no exemption for non-resident citizens on its power to impose tax liabili-ties, nor does it exempt resident non-citizens, thus insuring the maxi-mum coverage of its ability to impose tax liabilities and thus the acceptability of its IOUs.

As long as a government can satisfy its needs for goods and services from domestic production and does not purchase the liabilities of other governments it maintains monetary sovereignty in the sense that it can control the level of economic activity through fiscal policy and the rate of interest through its decisions to buy up the excess reserves that result from that policy. This sovereignty can be maintained if it participates in a currency clearing union in which its liabilities are always accepted as par substitutes for the liabilities of other member governments. In such an arrangement it is possible to coordinate monetary policy to maximize domestic employment levels and growth rates for each of the members.

However, if the government requires goods and services that cannot be produced domestically or within the clearing system member's economies its ability to procure them will be limited by its ability to force suppliers to accept its liabilities. In the absence to the ability to impose a tax liability the only way that this can be done is by building an expectation that the liabilities are perfect substitutes for other government liabilities. This expectation comes not from changing fiscal policy, but from the ability to generate foreign reserves, either by current account surpluses, or by foreign borrowing. That is, domestic monetary sovereignty becomes subject to external constraint. This has been recognized as the major impediment to positive development policies since Raul Prebisch's Report to the UNCTAD I Conference in 1964. Indeed, Polak's article on European reconstruction notes the importance of the disposition of foreign inflows in creating foreign currency, generating investments by building up export industries, keeping the propensity to consume and to import low, as the key to sustainability and thus domestic sovereignty. I have used Domar's (1950) analysis of an analogous problem, which notes the importance of the rate of interest on foreign borrowing relative to the rate of increase of capital inflows, with the former lower than the latter, in ensuring sustainability of the external position when development takes place on the basis of foreign borrowing (see Kregel, 2004). Of course regional coordination can do little to improve these conditions aside from the already well-known benefits of trade integration improving the size of the domestic market.

Capital market integration

A number of countries have taken steps to more fully integrate their financial services. ASEAN for example is moving to full financial integration through extending its participation in GATS to all members of the group irrespective of membership in the WTO. There is a well-known literature on the benefits of financial integration for exchange rate stability. Ingram (1962) had already proposed the full integration of commercial bank asset portfolios as a method of solving the problem of exchange rate instability of the US dollar with Europe. For example, if banks hold assets of all members of the regional group, then changes in relative interest rates in response to a deterioration in bilateral balances will cause banks to increase their holdings of assets denominated in the currency of the weaker partner, automatically increasing its ability to finance itself in its own currency. I have used this proposal elsewhere (Kregel, 1990) to argue that this provides an alternative mechanism to fixed exchange rates or a common currency for monetary and financial integration that promotes regional stability. It increases the ability of a 'South' economy to convince members of the region to purchase its domestic currency denominated liabilities and to that extent improves its ability to finance itself with third countries.

Notes

1. A series of bilateral monetary arrangements set up in 1946–7 quickly proved to be insufficient and were replaced by the Agreement on Multilateral Monetary Compensation in 1947 and the Intra-European Payments Agreement in 1948, renewed in 1949. The latter were the first to use Marshall funds to provide what was called 'indirect aid' (Marshall funds were to provide assistance to both recipient countries (direct aid) and to other countries (indirect aid) by providing surplus countries funds that could be used to provide credits to debtor countries. More details may be found in Tew, 1963, Chapters 8 and 9).
2. The amount of such borrowing was determined by the ratio of the net deficit with the union to its 'quota'. If the ratio was 100 per cent the settlement was in gold or dollars, with lower ratios allowing greater settlement in own currency on a formula that allowed full settlement in domestic currency of a deficit equal to 10 per cent of quota. Surplus members received 50 per cent of the net surplus balance in gold or dollars for positions above 20 per cent of quota and zero for positions below 20 per cent. Any shortfall in gold or dollars that might result was covered by a Special Resources Fund provided from ECA funds. See Tew, 1963, pp. 103–5.
3. See UNCTAD, 1999, pp. 109–10 and p. 124, note 15.

Bibliography

Domar, E. D., 'The Effect of Foreign Investments on the Balance of Payments', *American Economic Review*, Vol. 40 (December 1950): 805–26.

Ingram, J. C., 'A Proposal for Financial Integration in the Atlantic Community', *Factors Affecting the US Balance of Payments* (Washington, DC: Joint Committee Print, USGPO, 1962).

Kregel, J., 'The EMS, the Dollar and the World Economy', P. Ferri (ed.), *Prospects for the European Monetary System* (London: Macmillan, 1990).

Kregel, J., *External Financing for Development and International Financial Instability*, paper prepared for the G-24 Technical Group Meeting, Geneva, March 2004 (available on the G-24 web site).

Polak, J. J., 'Balance of Payments Problems of Countries Reconstructing with the Help of Foreign Loans', *Quarterly Journal of Economics*, LVII (February 1943): 208–40.

Tew, B., *International Monetary Cooperation: 1945–63*, 7th edn (London: Hutchison University Library, 1963).

UNCTAD, *Trade and Development Report 1999* (New York: United Nations, 1999).

Comment

Peter Nunnenkamp

The paper is quite surprising in several respects. The first half of the paper provides short summaries of existing mechanisms of South–South monetary cooperation. But the author goes rarely beyond describing what the objectives of these mechanisms are and what instruments are applied. Kregel is fairly reluctant to critically assess and evaluate the reasonability of objectives and the appropriateness of instruments. For example, he simply notes that a common currency has been proposed by some authors for MERCOSUR, without taking a clear position. The same applies to initiatives such as the Roadmap for the Integration of ASEAN in Finance and possible exchange-rate arrangements for this group of countries.

By contrast, the second half of the paper offers some unconventional arguments, instead of dealing with more familiar OCA criteria. Possibly I am so obsessed with the standard line of reasoning that I sometimes find it difficult to grasp Kregel's approach. For instance, the section on 'Coordination and the Problem of Monetary Sovereignty' starts with the assertion that 'the basic difficulty hindering coordination is the lack of domestic monetary sovereignty'. This appears to be in conflict with the traditional line of reasoning, according to which coordination comes at the cost of national sovereignty. However, what follows is a discussion of how governments make the public accept the money they issue, which does not seem to be specific to the South. It remains open to question why many countries face external financing constraints and suffer from 'original sin', whereas some countries, such as Australia, successfully escaped this uncomfortable situation.

The paper is more or less silent on conventional issues, including the symmetry or asymmetry of shocks, trade intensity among participating countries, factor mobility within the group of countries under consideration, structural similarities or divergence. Likewise, the question of whether these OCA criteria are endogenous, an issue which figures prominently in Chapter 1, is hardly addressed in Kregel's paper. I am not sure whether Kregel considers all this to be irrelevant. In any case, it is mildly surprising to me that a paper on South–South monetary cooperation can do without any reference to Mundell, Eichengreen, Hausmann, John Williamson, Frankel and Rose, and other celebrities in the field.

It would be interesting to learn whether the presenters we have heard so far would agree on what they perceive to be the major problem of the South. From Fritz and Metzger I got the message that net external debt in foreign currency is the key problem of the South, as it involves serious mismatches and 'original sin' increases volatility. Kregel seems to agree in the first part of his paper, where he considers South–South cooperation schemes as a means to reduce dependence on external borrowing. In subsequent sections of the paper, however, external financing constraints are said to be the major impediment to economic development of the South. Both aspects of external financing of the South may well have common roots, namely institutional deficiencies at both the international and national level which many development economists consider to be the fundamental reason for persistent underdevelopment. Yet, the notion of external financing constraints seems to imply that 'too little' is the major problem related to foreign capital imports of the South, whereas the notion of 'original sin', by stressing the risk involved for the South, suggests that the problem is 'too much' or 'too volatile' (see Nunnenkamp, 2001).

The next issue that may deserve some more attention concerns the various types of South–South monetary cooperation and the different objectives underlying these types of cooperation. In a recent paper on regional monetary arrangements for developing countries, Chang (2000) draws on Sebastian Edwards in separating three broad types of arrangements: regional agreements for the settlement of payments, agreements for balance of payments support, and monetary unions:

- It would be interesting to learn whether Kregel would agree with Chang (2000) who argues that the popularity of regional payments agreements (such as the one operated by ALADI in Latin America) is likely to decline. This may be because the rapid development of financial technology and the closer integration of international financial markets mean that regional cooperation of this type has less to offer in terms of reduced transaction costs.

- By contrast, regional agreements for balance of payments support are on the rise, mainly because of recent developments in the ASEAN + 3 group. Yet earlier agreements, such as the Latin American Reserve Fund as well as the original ASEAN Swap Arrangement, may indicate the limits of this approach unless the potential 'war chest' is as large as in the case of ASEAN + 3. It is interesting to note that the symmetry of shocks, which is typically considered a 'plus' when a regional group aims at monetary union, may turn out to be a 'minus' when a group subject to contagion aims at self-protection against financial crises. Hence, depending on the characteristics of shocks, a regional group may be well suited for a common currency, but badly suited to ward off financial crises, or vice versa. At the same time, it may be open to question to what extent monetary cooperation can really reduce the cost of the accumulation of reserves observed by Kregel. UNCTAD (2001, p. 111) may be quite right in stating that 'regional arrangements among developing countries may need to involve major reserve-currency countries ... in order to achieve stability and avoid costly crises'.

- As concerns monetary unions between developing countries, the question is whether exchange-rate risk *within* the regional group represents the major problem. According to Levy-Yeyati (2002), the – flawed – logic in part of the literature runs as follows: (i) nominal volatility has negative real effects; (ii) monetary union reduces nominal volatility; hence, (iii) monetary union has positive real effects. However, if it is mainly volatility of the local currency vis-à-vis the US\$ which harms developing countries, the positive real effects of a monetary union among developing countries will probably remain marginal. This reasoning also invites the question of whether the European model is of much use for South–South cooperation. Developing countries regarding the European experience as a model should not forget the EMS crisis of the early 1990s, which, according to UNCTAD (2001), was similar in many respects to emerging-market crises, even though supporting institutions were fairly advanced at that time already. Furthermore, Eichengreen (1998, p. 22ff.) posits that 'no EMS-style arrangement will be viable elsewhere in today's world of high capital mobility'. In any case, the road to monetary union has many traps. Transitional issues include technical challenges such as finding optimal weights for a common currency basket (Dobson, 2002; Schweickert, 2000). More importantly, a common basket peg may well lead to higher intra-regional volatility in real, effective terms when, as in Southeast Asia, the geographical structure of trade and the structure of foreign debt differ considerably within the region.

Against this backdrop, I am curious about what we can reasonably expect from South–South monetary cooperation. Kregel raises a similar question on the first page of his paper about the degree of South–South coordination that is possible without cooperation from the North. As indicated before, the general message of the paper is not completely clear to me. But it does not seem quite as simple as the UN Under-Secretary-General for Economic and Social Affairs, J. A. Ocampo (2003), would like to have it when he noted: 'The small size of existing financial arrangements among developing countries indicates that there is ample room for aggressive South–South cooperation.' Alternatively, the small size of existing arrangements may indicate that there is less to gain than we might wish, because otherwise governments would not have missed the opportunities of South–South cooperation in the first place.

My reading is that much of the relevant literature invites the conclusion that monetary union is neither necessary nor sufficient for developing countries to achieve closer integration in terms of trade, FDI, etc. The experience of the West African Economic and Monetary Union, even though not a pure South–South scheme, illustrates that monetary union is not sufficient. It may not even be necessary if, as Bayoumi and Mauro (2001) as well as Schweickert (2000) observed for the *de facto* US$ orientation of large parts of Southeast Asia, the individual optimization of currency baskets implies fairly stable intra-regional exchange rates. Schweickert (2000) argues that it is difficult to conceive sub-optimal intra-regional exchange rates as long as all countries optimize their exchange-rate relations *vis-à-vis* a few anchor currencies.

The next question is which type of cooperation, and in which policy area regional cooperation is most likely to deliver. In Asia, for example, monetary and exchange-rate cooperation may be inferior (the wrong project, according to Eichengreen, 2002), at the present time at least, to regional projects focusing on the deepening and strengthening of regional financial and capital markets. In that regard, the final section in Kregel's paper may come fairly close to suggestions made by Eichengreen and others on how ASEAN should proceed. Eichengreen (2002) suggests that the Chiang Mai Initiative should be clearly defined as fostering financial stability, not stabilizing exchange rates.

More generally, it is probably for good reasons that UNCTAD (2001, p. 127) notes that 'regional arrangements could fail in the absence of sound domestic institutions and policies'. Dobson (2002) goes one step further. She regards domestic reforms as the most important line of defence; her concern is that the current focus on monetary cooperation, notably in East Asia, may divert attention and resources from reforms of domestic financial institutions, even though financial systems in this region still trail best international practice. Hopefully, she is wrong and her concern will prove unfounded!

Bibliography

Bayoumi, T. and Mauro, P., 'The Suitability of ASEAN for a Regional Currency Arrangement', *The World Economy* 24 (7) (2001): 933–54.

Chang, R., *Regional Monetary Arrangements for Developing Countries* (Rutgers University, 2000), mimeo. http://www.g24.org/chang.pdf

Dobson, W., *East Asian Financial Reform and Integration: Systemic Issues* (Toronto: University of Toronto, Rotman School of Management, 2002), mimeo.

Eichengreen, B., *Does Mercosur Need a Common Currency?* National Bureau of Economic Research, NBER Working Papers 6821 (Cambridge, MA, 1998).

Eichengreen, B., *Whither Monetary and Financial Integration in Asia?* Paper presented at the PECC Finance Forum Conference 'Issues and Prospects for Regional Cooperation for Financial Stability and Development' (Honolulu, 2002) mimeo.

Levy-Yeyati, E., *Comments on: Monetary Integration in the Southern Cone: Mercosur is Not Like the EU?* Österreichische Nationalbank, Working Paper 72 (Vienna, 2002).

Nunnenkamp, P., 'Too Much, Too Little, or Too Volatile? International Capital Flows to Developing Countries in the 1990s', *Journal of International Economic Studies* 5 (1) (2001): 119–47.

Ocampo, J. A., *Statement at the High Level Conference on South–South Cooperation in Marrakesh* (2003) mimeo.

Schweickert, R., 'Chancen und Risiken eines regionalen Währungsverbundes in Südostasien', *List Forum* 26 (3) (2000): 272–86.

UNCTAD, *Trade and Development Report 2001* (New York: United Nations, 2001).

4
Exchange Rate Management in Developing Countries: The Need for a Multilateral Solution[1]

Heiner Flassbeck

The discussion about adequate exchange rate systems for developing countries takes a new turn. Whereas, in the 1990s the official doctrine of the Washington-based finance institutions was the corner solution idea, where developing countries should either absolutely fix their exchange rate against an international anchor currency or float freely, after the Asian crises the international economics community favoured the return to floating. But only a few countries accepted this advice. Most of the countries affected by the storm of the financial crises in Asia and in Latin America decided to use the opportunity of a low valuation of their currencies and the swing from current account deficit to surplus to uni-laterally fix their exchange rate or – at least – to frequently intervene in the currency market to avoid the rapid return of their currencies to pre-crisis levels. The most striking example is China, where the authorities, after the traumatic experience of an overvaluation and a big devaluation in 1994, absolutely fixed the value of the renmimbi against the US dollar.

Beyond this untypical corner solution the unilateral attempts to fix the value of their currencies at rather low levels have created another puzzle for mainstream economic thinking. Due to their current account surpluses and their intervention in the currency markets many develop-ing countries have piled up huge amounts of international reserves and thus have become net exporters of capital. This is difficult to reconcile with the expectation of neoclassical general equilibrium models where poor economies with a low endowment of capital receive the scarce resource from rich countries with an abundant endowment of capital. The fact that the most successful countries in the South have violated that 'law' puzzles many orthodox observers and leads them to argue that holding United States treasuries is a waste of resources as this money could have been used much more efficiently by investing it in fixed capital or by using it to import more investment goods.

For policy-makers in developing countries, the fact that exchange rate movements directly influence the overall competitiveness of a country and have the potential to directly improve the overall trade performance of the majority of their firms and the balance of payments is a promising prospect. On the other hand, the use of the exchange rate as a powerful tool of economic policy is often strictly limited by the influence that the global capital market and the policy of other countries exert on that rate. The exchange rate of any country is, by definition, a multilateral phenomenon, and any rate change has multilateral repercussions.

In the last three decades, developing and emerging-market economies in all the major regions have had to struggle with financial crises or their contagion effects once they have tried to manage the exchange rate unilaterally or even opted for free floating. Nevertheless, in the Bretton Woods era, as well as in the period of floating or managed floating thereafter, some patterns of successful adjustment to the vagaries of the international capital market emerged, which have been increasingly adopted by developing countries' economic and financial policies. Since the Second World War, some experiences of successful catching up – such as by Western Europe, Japan and the NIEs – suggest that, among other factors, long-lasting currency undervaluation can be extremely helpful to fully reap the benefits of open markets. Today, as multilateral arrangements do not exist on a global scale, a strategy to avoid overvaluation by any means has become the preferred tool of many governments and central banks.

This is in stark contrast to the experience of the 1990s in Latin America. During that decade many Latin American countries maintained hard or soft currency pegs with some overvaluation, and used the exchange rate as a nominal anchor to achieve rapid disinflation. This led to an impressive improvement in their monetary stability (Fischer, 2001, p. 9; Mussa *et al.*, 2000) but also to currency appreciations that impaired the competitiveness of exporters in these countries. Today, with inflation rates being relatively low and stable due to favourable domestic conditions, adopting a strategy designed to avoid currency overvaluation has become feasible for a much larger number of developing countries. Indeed, many developing countries (such as China, Brazil and South Africa) have recently sought to avoid a revaluation of their currencies through direct central bank intervention, with the result that they have accumulated substantial amounts of foreign-exchange reserves.

It is clear that for these countries, avoiding currency overvaluation is not only a means to preserve or improve macroeconomic competitiveness, but also an insurance against the risk of future financial crises. The accumulation of current-account deficits, and frequent financial crises, with overshooting currency depreciations, proved very costly in the past. Surges in inflation, huge losses of real income, and rising debt burdens have been a common feature of all recent financial crises.

However, a strategy of avoiding currency overvaluation cannot easily be implemented if the capital account is open. If inflation rates in developing countries exceed those in the developed world, or if there are expectations of an imminent currency appreciation, monetary policy will often face a dilemma in trying to keep the exchange rate stable and yet at a level that preserves the international cost competitiveness of the country's exporters.

The dilemma posed by capital-account openness

Even a slightly diverging inflation trend between two open economies is sufficient for highly volatile short-term international capital flows to force the central bank of the country with high inflation to give up its undervaluation strategy or to face the severe fiscal costs that can be associated with this strategy.[2] Differences in inflation rates are usually reflected in differences in nominal interest rates, with the high-inflation country having higher interest rates than the low-inflation country, even if both countries have similar growth trends and a similar monetary policy stance (e.g. if they try to apply a Taylor rule[3]). The reason for this is that nominal interest rates have to be higher in the high-inflation country if the central bank is to bring the domestic real interest rate in line with the given real growth rate and degree of capacity utilization.

However, short-term capital flows are not driven exclusively by interest rate differentials. Speculators may attack the currencies of countries that follow an undervaluation policy, because they expect a revaluation to occur sooner or later. This means that, contrary to textbook scenarios, in the real world, international investors do not form short-term exchange rate expectations on the basis of the purchasing power parity (PPP) rule.

Since the PPP rule is relevant only over the long term, policy-makers in financially open developing countries need to be aware that international investors in short-term deposits base their decisions on the expected nominal return rather than the expected real return on investments. This is because portfolio investors do not intend to buy goods in the country in which they invest, but simply invest money for a day, a week or three months. If, during that period of time, the inflation divergence between the high-inflation and the low-inflation country does not trigger the generally expected depreciation of the high-inflation country's currency, portfolio investment will be more attracted to the high-inflation than to the low-inflation country. As discussed in *TDRs 1998* and *2001*, most of the financial crises in the post-Bretton Woods era have been characterized by unsustainable nominal interest rate differentials. The differential in nominal interest rates attracts portfolio investment in the currency of the high-inflation country. This, in turn, improves the short-term attractiveness of the high-inflation country's currency, because an appreciation would increase the expected return from such an investment. On the other hand, if governments try, from the outset, to limit the extent of an appreciation of the domestic currency by buying foreign currencies, this will usually add to the confidence of international investors as the high-inflation country's international reserves increase.

Thus, independently of whether high nominal interest rates or the expectation of a revaluation attract short-term capital inflows, the currency of the high-inflation country will tend to appreciate in the short-term.[4] This undermines the fundamental exchange rate in the short term, does not preclude the exchange rate from eventually returning to PPP. In the medium term, the clearly visible deterioration of the international competitive position of the high-inflation country will reverse expectations of international investors: they will lose 'confidence' in the high-inflation country's currency, thus making a correction of the overvaluation unavoidable.

Even in the absence of short-term capital flows, internal and external equilibrium cannot be achieved at the same time by adjusting interest rates, if inflation rates in the two countries diverge, for example, because of different institutional arrangements on the labour market. This is because the central bank cannot fight inflation without attracting capital inflows in the short term, and provoking volatility of capital flows and exchange rates in the medium term. Neither can it lower interest rates without running the risk of failing to reach the inflation target.[5]

Independently of whether a high-inflation country with a fully liberalized capital account chooses to fight inflation by maintaining high interest rates, or to keep the real interest rate at a level at least as high as in the low-inflation country, its currency will attract international investors in short-term assets. The high-inflation country can achieve domestic price stabilization only if it maintains nominal interest rates at a level higher than those of the low-inflation country. But if, in the short run, the inflation differential between the two countries is not matched by a corresponding expectation of depreciation of the high-inflation country's currency, the occurrence of a fundamental disequilibrium will be unavoidable. However, choosing the alternative approach and trying to fix the nominal exchange rate is, in this framework, also very costly. Intervention by the central bank of a developing country implies buying foreign currency against bonds denominated in domestic currency that bear relatively high interest rates, and investing the foreign currency purchased at a lower interest rate in the developed country. Thus a strategy of intervening in currency markets and accumulating foreign currency reserves amounts to a permanent subsidization of foreign investors with domestic taxpayers' money.

Free capital flows between countries with differing rates of inflation usually break the link between interest rate differentials and the risk of currency depreciation, because exchange rates do not follow PPP in the short term. Introducing PPP as a 'theoretical norm' (Schumpeter, 1939) or a political target is the only way out. With exchange rate expectations being 'rational' in terms of PPP, exchange rate expectations should always equal the interest rate differential and the price level differential. But this solution does not apply in reality. Expectations are not formed rationally along the lines of PPP, as un-hedged borrowing offers a short-term profit in most exchange rate regimes only if major imbalances have not occurred.

Patterns of adjustment

The UNCTAD secretariat conducted some calculations in order to examine the evolution of returns on short-term international portfolio investment in a number of developing countries over the period 1995–2003. As a first step, assuming exchange rates to remain stable, the real interest rate that is relevant for the decision of an investor from the United States to make, for example, a three-month investment in a developing country, is the three-month nominal interest rate in the developing country minus the inflation rate in the United States. International investors base their decisions on the inflation rate in their home country, and not on the rate in the country in which they invest, because they intend to re-import the invested money at the end of the investment period rather than to buy goods in the country in which they invest.[6]

The results of these calculations are shown in Figure 4.1 for six countries. The exchange rate regimes that govern the relationship

64

Figure 4.1 Incentives for short-term international portfolio investment in selected countries, 1995–2003 (percentages)

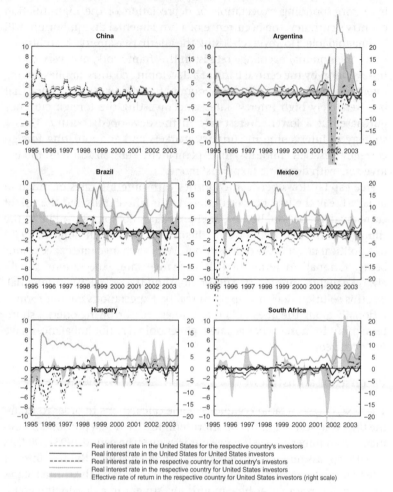

Real interest rate in the United States for the respective country's investors
Real interest rate in the United States for United States investors
Real interest rate in the respective country for that country's investors
Real interest rate in the respective country for United States investors
Effective rate of return in the respective country for United States investors (right scale)

Note: The scenario that underlies the figure is based on a 3-month investment horizon. Real interest rates lower than minus 10 per cent or higher than plus 10 per cent, and effective returns lower than minus 20 per cent or higher than plus 20 per cent are not shown for expositional clarity

Sources: UNCTAD secretariat calculations, based on data from IMF, *International Financial Statistics* and Thomson Financial Datastream

between the dollar and the currencies of these six countries strongly differ. China has maintained a stable currency peg against the dollar for a long time. The figure indicates that from the financial side, this peg is sustainable, as China does not offer real interest rates for international investors that could directly endanger the peg. The incentive to invest in China on a short-term basis, as reflected by the line showing the real interest rate for United States investors, has consistently been either only marginally positive or even negative. By contrast, Mexico and Brazil maintained a very high real interest rate for international investors throughout the second half of the 1990s. Even Argentina maintained positive real interest rate differentials during this period – reflected by the difference between the two solid lines in the figure – despite its hard currency peg with the dollar. Indeed, the real interest rate that underlies decisions of United States investors to invest in the Latin American countries has, in many instances, been much higher than in the United States over a long period. Thus transactions of a huge size must have taken place, assuming that the money and currency markets operated efficiently. The crises in Mexico (in the mid-1990s), Brazil (1999), and Argentina (2001–2) demonstrate that, as a rule, financial crises and the collapse of the exchange rate are preceded by phases of enormous effective returns and extremely high interest rates for foreign investors. Only in 2002 did Mexico manage to bring inflation and its short-term interest rate down, and to avoid attracting foreign investors with offers of high financial yields. Brazil, on the other hand, still offers investors very attractive conditions.

In addition to the interest rates calculated at a fixed exchange rate, a second step in the calculations takes account of the actual change in the bilateral exchange rate in order to calculate the effective rate of return for United States investors in the developing country. This rate (shown by the shaded area in Figure 4.1) reflects the *ex post* observed change in the exchange rate, but provides no information on the rate that the investors expected. Indeed, the calculations are based on *ex post* known interest and exchange rates, which may differ from the rates the investors expected. As such, the results of the calculations do not allow any assessment of the actual size of capital flows that may have been induced by the configuration of these rates at any point in time. At some points there may have been huge flows, while at others there may have been no flows at all. While these limitations need to be kept in mind when interpreting the results, the calculations reveal the dilemma of developing countries that liberalize their capital account without being able to keep their inflation rate at the level of the developed economies.

Hungary and South Africa are examples of countries with rather flexible exchange rate regimes and high de facto exchange rate volatility. Since 2002, both countries have tried to reduce domestic inflation by maintaining relatively high interest rates. This has resulted in a decline in competitiveness due to real currency appreciation. Figure 4.1 shows that the real interest rate incentive for foreign investors is significant and induces short-term capital inflows, causing an adverse impact on the real exchange rate. During 2003, for example, a three-month investment in South Africa could yield as much as 10 to 20 per cent, which may add up to an annual rate far beyond 50 per cent.

Argentina and Brazil followed similar approaches in the second half of the 1990s but with varying rigour. Argentina fixed its exchange rate very strictly to the dollar, offering a positive and, over many years, fairly stable real rate of return to foreign investors; this rate increased sharply in the run-up to the crisis of its currency board system and led to the collapse of that system. Brazil adopted a crawling peg, visible in the stable difference between the real interest rate for United States investors and the effective rate of return. This system per se was less restrictive than the Argentinean one on the external side, but had to be complemented by higher domestic interest rates to avoid a return of inflation. Under conditions of free capital flows, the Brazilian soft peg offered very high real rates of return until the beginning of the crisis in 1999. However, even after the crisis, the Brazilian central bank did not fundamentally change its policy of maintaining a high level of interest rates relative to that in the United States. The resulting recent rise in capital inflows has put sharp pressure on the Brazilian real to appreciate.

Looking at the experience of a larger group of economies, Figure 4.2 reveals sharp differences in patterns of adjustment. In this figure, the real interest rate for a United States investor is correlated with the effective rate of return for that investor. The economies are grouped according to the attractiveness of their currencies for international portfolio investors. If the nominal exchange rate is perfectly stable, there is no scattering of the points and the correlation is very high, as is the case for China. The position of the curve (right of the zero point or on the zero point) indicates whether, in terms of the interest rate differential, the country has been attractive (Argentina, Brazil) or not (China) for international investors. In group 1 (column 1 of the figure), the countries aim at a rather low nominal interest rate, with or without fixing the exchange rates. In Malaysia, Singapore and Chile, the exchange rate is not as stable as in China, but these three countries' central banks avoid giving incentives to foreign investors to speculate on an overvaluation.

Figure 4.2 Alternative exchange rate regimes and incentives for short-term portfolio investment in selected economies, 1995–2003

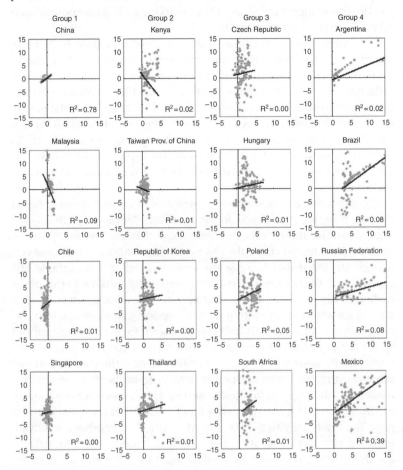

Note: For the calculation of the real interest rate and the effective rate of return, see text
Vertical scale: Effective rate of return in the respective economy for United States investors
Horizontal scale: Real interest rate in the respective economy for United States investors

Sources: UNCTAD secretariat calculations, based on data from IMF, *International Financial Statistics* and Thomson Financial Datastream

In group 2, the interest rate incentives are fairly small and the effective returns (including exchange rate changes) scatter quite remarkably along the vertical axis. This means that these economies – as demonstrated by the Republic of Korea, Taiwan Province of China and Thailand – avoid one-sided flows by maintaining high exchange rate volatility and low interest rates.

Countries in group 3, consisting mainly of transition economies, have adopted a floating exchange rate regime but with some interest rate incentives for international investors, as the inflation rate in these countries was relatively high during the 1990s.

The fourth group of countries follows a different approach. By keeping the exchange rate fairly stable and offering incentives for financial investors, their central banks try to use the exchange rate to stabilize inflation. This implies prolonged periods of rather risk-free arbitrage for international investors. These hard or soft pegs are sustainable only if the high interest rate does not depress the rate of domestic investment, or if an appreciation of the real exchange rate can be avoided. In most cases, however, these conditions do not apply. Sooner or later, the currency peg, soft or hard, has to be discontinued and replaced by a new system.

The examples of intermediate systems of managed floating (as in Poland, Hungary, the Czech Republic, South Africa, or in Brazil and Argentina after their currency crises) show that the variability of the exchange rate may increase the risk for the international investor at certain points, but it may increase the reward as well. If, for example, the country with the floating currency has been going through a crisis phase with real depreciation, the exchange rate expectation tends to turn around for a time, as the international investors expect revaluation and not a new devaluation. This has been the recent experience of Brazil and South Africa. To avoid a quick and strong real currency revaluation, which would destroy the gains in competitiveness the country has just achieved, the monetary authorities intervene by buying foreign currency and piling up international reserves. This is costly for the country involved, as its interest rates are higher than the rates it can earn by recycling the money to the country of origin or to another safe haven. In these circumstances, it is difficult, if not impossible, to strike a balance between the domestic needs to fight inflation and the negative repercussions of incentives for foreign investors in portfolio capital on domestic growth and employment.

Multilateral solutions are the answer

The message of the preceding analysis is a simple one. If the nominal short-term interest rate in a financially open emerging-market economy exceeds that in a developed country by more than the growth differential, the nominal exchange rate of the former should depreciate at a (annual) rate that equals the difference in (annual) interest rates. If this is not the case, the situation is not sustainable, as either the high interest rate or the overvalued exchange rate hampers sustainable economic development in the emerging market economy.

Hence the political choice to combine floating of the currency with restrictive domestic monetary policy to bring down inflation will destabilize the external account. Speculation on uncovered interest rate parities will yield high returns to arbitraging international portfolio investors, as nominal and real interest rates in the developing economies are higher than in the leading industrialized economies. The currencies of the high-inflation countries will tend to appreciate, thereby, temporarily, even increasing the incentive for foreign investors to buy domestic assets and the incentive of domestic borrowers to borrow abroad.

Overall, the dilemma for developing-country policy-makers of a situation in which international investors earn high rates of return in their countries, despite falling real income, domestic profits and employment, cannot be resolved under conditions of free capital flows. Developing-country policy-makers are usually unable to reduce interest rates to stop the speculative capital inflow, because doing so would endanger the credibility of their monetary policy domestically. The political will to achieve economic stability is reflected in the decision to keep nominal interest rates high. How long an external economic imbalance following an exchange rate peg or an appreciation can be sustained is an open question. With growing visible external imbalances the developing country's exchange rate policy will begin to lose credibility in markets. Once investors are convinced that the anchoring country will not be able to manage slowing down the growth of its external debt smoothly, confidence will deteriorate. This will lead to renewed crisis, a reduction of reserves and eventually a depreciation of the country's exchange rate.

In any case, exchange rate changes are necessary to compensate for the opening scissor blades of the price and cost developments between a high-inflation and a low-inflation country. As long as developing countries are not able to perfectly converge in nominal terms with the developed countries, devaluations are unavoidable in order to preserve the competitiveness of the high-inflation countries. However, exchange rate changes, and in particular, real exchange rate changes, that determine the competitiveness of the whole economy, cannot be left to the market. Given the arbitrage opportunities between high- and low-inflation countries, a rule of competitive neutrality of the exchange rate, like the PPP rule, has to be enforced by governments and/or central banks. Ideally, such a rule should be the result of multilateral agreements, as exchange rate changes always have multilateral repercussions. But if the international community is not able to agree on rules to avoid competitive devaluations and huge destabilizing shocks, countries will continue to manage the floating of their currencies unilaterally.

Managed floating, however, faces an adding-up problem on the global scale. Not all countries can simultaneously manage the movements of their exchange rate and achieve their targeted rates. The exchange rate, by definition, is a multilateral phenomenon, and attempts by many countries to keep their currencies at an undervalued rate may end up in a race to the bottom – or in competitive devaluations – that would be as harmful for the world economy as in the 1930s. Moreover, given the size of international short-term capital flows and the inherent volatility of these flows, only those developing countries that are big and competitive enough to withstand strong and sustained attempts of the international financial markets to move the exchange rate in a certain direction, will be able to manage the floating successfully. A small and open developing economy will hardly be able to continue fighting a strong tendency to appreciate over many years or even decades.

Multilateral or even global arrangements are clearly the best solutions to this problem. The idea of a cooperative global monetary system would be to assure, on a multilateral basis, the same rules of the game for all parties involved, more or less in the same way as multilateral trade rules apply to every party equally. That is why the main idea behind the founding of the International Monetary Fund in the 1940s was to avoid competitive devaluations. In a well-designed global monetary system, the need and the advantages of the currency depreciation of one country have to be balanced against the disadvantages to the others. As changes in the exchange rate, deviating from purchasing power parity, affect international trade in exactly the same way as changes in tariffs and export duties do, such changes should be governed by multilateral regulations. Such a multilateral regime would, among other things, require countries to specify their reasons for real devaluations and the dimension of necessary changes. If such rules were strictly applied, the real exchange rate of all the parties involved would remain more or less constant, as strong arguments for creating competitive advantages at the national level would rarely be acceptable.

In a world without a multilateral solution to the currency problem, the only way out for high-inflation or high-growth countries that are not members of a regional monetary union is to resort to controls of short-term capital flows or to follow a strategy of undervaluation and unilateral fixing. If developing countries are able to avoid destabilizing inflows and outflows, either by taxing those flows or by limiting their impact through direct intervention in the market, the hardest choices and misallocations due to erratic exchange rate changes can be avoided; but the resort to controls or permanent intervention should not replace the search for an appropriate exchange rate system at the regional or global level.

Notes

1. This paper is based on UNCTAD, *Trade and Development Report: Policy Coherence, Development Strategies and Integration into the World Economy*, Chapter IV (2004).
2. Diverging inflation trends in open economies are much more important for the viability of an exchange rate strategy than the usually discussed 'asymmetric shock', first introduced by Mundell in his paper on optimum currency areas (Mundell, 1961). With diverging inflation trends grounded in different labour market regimes, the arguments used to defend hard pegs or dollarization (e.g. Calvo, 1999) no longer apply, as long-lasting remedies to preserve competitiveness are sought and not just one-off measures.
3. The monetary policy rule presented by Taylor (1993) postulates that the central bank should base the setting of the short-term interest rate on the current situation with regard to inflation and the business cycle.
4. A striking example of this is Hungary's recent switch from a crawling peg to a flexible exchange rate following a strategy of inflation targeting. Immediately after the move, although the country had an inflation rate of around 10 per cent (compared with 2 per cent in its main trading partner Germany), its currency appreciated sharply, as Hungary offered much higher nominal interest rates than Germany.
5. Laursen and Metzler (1950, pp. 277–8) summarize the experience of the 1930s in a similar way: 'Exchange rates at that time underwent frequent and substantial fluctuations ... the fluctuations that occurred nevertheless created serious doubts concerning the effectiveness of a flexible-exchange system in equalizing a country's international payments and receipts.' They conclude that 'a regime of flexible exchange rates would not be successful unless capital movements were subject to some kind of control'.
6. The same reasoning applies for a developing-country enterprise seeking a low-interest, short-term credit. In other words, the enterprise will have an incentive to obtain the credit in the United States if the nominal interest rate in the United States is lower than in its home country.

Bibliography

Calvo, G. A., *On Dollarization* (University of Maryland, VA, 1999). http://www/bsos.umd.edu/econ/ciecpn5.pdf

Fischer, S., *Exchange Rate Regimes: Is the Bipolar View Correct?* (2001), speech delivered at the meeting of the American Economic Association, New Orleans, 6 January 2001. http://www.imf.org/external/np/speeches/2001/010601a.htm

Laursen, S. and Metzler, L. A., 'Flexible Exchange Rates and the Theory of Employment', Metzler, L. A. (ed.), *Collected Papers* (originally published 1950; Cambridge MA: Harvard University Press, 1978).

Mundell, R. A., 'A Theory of Optimum Currency Areas', *American Economic Review*, 51 (September 1961): 657–65.

Mussa, M., Masson, P., Swoboda, A., Jadresic, E., Mauro, P. and Berg, Y., *Exchange Rate Regimes in an Increasingly Integrated World Economy*, Occasional Paper 193 (Washington, DC: International Monetary Fund, 2000).

Schumpeter, J. A., *Business Cycles: A Theoretical, Historical, and Statistical Analysis of the Capitalist Process* (New York and London: McGraw Hill, 1939).

Taylor, J. B., 'Discretion Versus Policy Rules in Practice', *Carnegie-Rochester Conference Series on Public Policy*, 39 (1993), pp. 195–214.

UNCTAD, *Trade and Development Report* (New York and Geneva: United Nations, various years).

Part II

Cases of Regional Monetary Coordination

5
Exchange Rate Policies and Institutional Arrangements in the Transition Process to European Monetary Union

Peter Bofinger

Introduction

After their accession to the European Union, the countries of Central and Eastern Europe will be confronted with the difficult task of designing an exchange-rate strategy for their transition to the European Monetary Union (EMU). This requires above all a timetable for the major institutional steps, membership in ERM II and finally, entry into the EMU. In addition, countries will have to decide on the exchange rate policy they will follow in the pre-ERM II period and, given the wide ±15 per cent margin, to some extent also during their period of ERM II membership.

For both questions – the timetable and the overall design of exchange-rate policy after EU membership – it seems useful to start with an analysis of the experience of the candidate countries over the past few years. Such an assessment has the important advantage that three completely different approaches have been adopted, so that a very broad comparison is possible.

The experience since 1999

Figure 5.1 shows that since the start of EMU in 1999, the exchange rates of countries in central and eastern Europe have developed in quite different ways.

- The group of countries that decided for *fixed exchange rates* (Bulgaria, Estonia and Latvia) has maintained a completely constant exchange rate *vis-à-vis* the euro, or the SDR in the case of Latvia.

Figure 5.1 Exchange rates of candidate countries *vis-à-vis* the euro (January 1999 = 100)

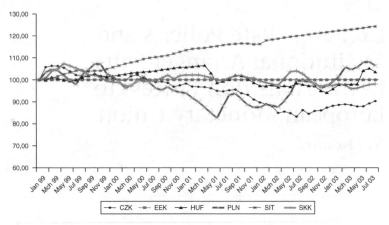

Source: Bundesbank Research Data Bank

- The group of countries with *flexible exchange rates*, which includes the Czech Republic, Poland and Hungary (since May 2001), has experienced rather strong fluctuations in their bilateral euro exchange rates. The Czech koruna appreciated *vis-à-vis* the euro until the summer of 2002. Since then, massive interventions (Figure 5.2) have led to a partial correction, so that the koruna is now only 10 per cent above its value of January 1999. Thus, the Czech National Bank can now also be regarded as a managed floater. The Polish zloty appreciated until May 2001; since then it has depreciated, so that its euro rate is today about 8 per cent weaker than in January 1999. Polish foreign exchange reserves show that this country is the most consequent free floater in the region. The Hungarian forint appreciated strongly after the crawling peg was abandoned, but since autumn 2002 this process has completely reverted again, with the support of foreign exchange market interventions.
- The group of countries with pronounced *managed floating* includes Slovenia and Romania. Since 1999, both currencies have followed a very stable depreciation path *vis-à-vis* the euro. However, as Figure 5.3 shows, the fluctuations of the Slovenian tolar from month to month were much more controlled than those of the Romanian leu. Slovakia can be also regarded as a managed floater. In contrast to Slovenia and Romania, it has allowed its currency to fluctuate around a constant level *vis-à-vis* the euro.

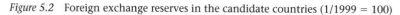

Figure 5.2 Foreign exchange reserves in the candidate countries (1/1999 = 100)

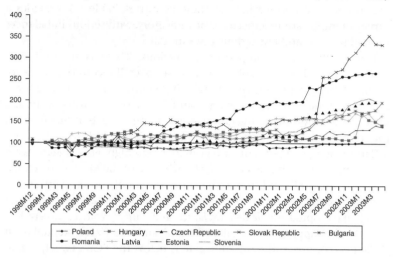

Source: international financial statistics

Figure 5.3 Monthly fluctuations of the euro exchange rate of the tolar and the leu

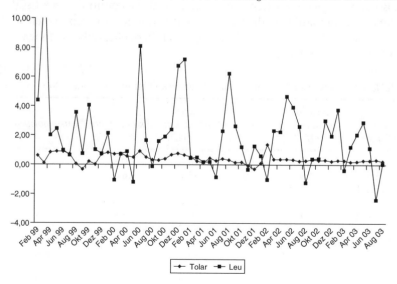

Source: Bundesbank Research Data Bank

Given these quite different approaches, it seems useful to compare the macroeconomic performance of these countries. Table 5.1 provides a survey of important macroeconomic indicators, with serious imbalances printed in bold, and less serious cases in italic.

The result of this comparison is obvious. There is no candidate country which has been able to achieve an overall record of macroeconomic stability. Unemployment and a high current-account deficits are a serious problem in almost every country. The only country without a major disequilibrium of overall macroeconomic targets is Slovenia. In the country group with *fixed exchange rates*, inflation is close to the ECB's inflation target of 2 per cent, and growth is very high. Fiscal balances are also compatible with the 3 per cent benchmark of the Maastricht Treaty. However, especially in Estonia, the current account shows a very strong deficit, and unemployment is very high in Bulgaria. The countries which have opted for *flexible exchange rates* suffer from relatively low growth; this applies above all to Poland and the Czech Republic. In these two countries, the inflation rate is below the ECB's target, which can already be regarded as a weak form of deflation. Hungary, which adopted flexible exchange rates much later, shows better growth performance and a more healthy inflation rate. In spite of weak growth performance, the Czech Republic has a strong current-account deficit; this also applies to some extend to Poland. All three countries have fiscal deficits incompatible with the 3 per cent threshold. Unemployment is very high in Poland, and high in the Czech Republic; only in Hungary is it at an acceptable level.

Table 5.1   Macroeconomic indicators of European Union candidates (2003)

Country	Real GDP (annual change 2001–03)	Inflation rate	Current account in % of GDP	Fiscal balance in % of GDP	Unemployment rate (2002)
Bulgaria	4.6	2.4	**−4.6**	0.8	**17.9**
Czech Republic	**2.3**	0.6	**−5.7**	**−6.8**	7.3
Estonia	5.3	1.5	**−12.6**	0.4	**9.1**
Hungary	3.4	**4.5**	**−5.7**	**−5.6**	5.6
Latvia	6.5	2.7	**−7.3**	**−3.1**	**12.8**
Poland	**1.8**	0.9	*−3.3*	**−5.3**	**19.9**
Romania	5.1	**15.4**	**−4.8**	*−2.7*	**6.9**
Slovakia	3.9	**8.4**	**−6.3**	**−3.5**	**18.6**
Slovenia	2.8	*5.6*	0.9	*−1.5*	*6.0*

Sources: IMF, *World Economic Outlook*, September 2003; DB Research Data Bank; Eurostat

In the group of *managed floaters*, the growth performance is satisfactory, but inflation is a major problem in Romania and Slovakia, while Slovenia has been able to reduce its inflation rate somewhat. In Slovakia, the current account is in a deep deficit. All three managed floaters have been able to meet the 3 per cent criterion. As in most candidate countries, unemployment is a problem, above all in Slovakia.

Implications for the official dogma

After the Asian crises, official and academic circles came to the conclusion that intermediate exchange-rate systems are prone to currency crises. According to the so-called 'unholy trinity', the only viable options in a world with free capital movements are either absolutely fixed or freely floating exchange rates. The experience of the EU candidate countries does *not* fully confirm this view.

The experience with fixed exchange rates

The candidate countries that have adopted absolutely fixed rates have been relatively successful in terms of growth and inflation. However, both the high current-account deficits and the high unemployment rates of these countries indicate that growth has been import-driven. Their experience is in line with the view that a fixed exchange-rate strategy is useful for relatively small and open countries. This can be shown with a very simple model for monetary macroeconomics in closed and open economies.[1]

The output gap (y^d) is determined by the real interest rate (r) and the change of the real exchange rate (Δq):

$$y^d = a - br + c\Delta q + \varepsilon_1 \tag{1}$$

In the short run, the inflation rate (π) is determined only by domestic inflation expectations, which, for the sake of simplicity, are assumed to be identical with the central bank's inflation target (π_0), and by the output gap:

$$\pi = \pi_0 + dy + \varepsilon_2 \tag{2}$$

In a world of fixed rates and free capital movement, the uncovered interest parity (UIP) condition is:

$$i = i^* + \alpha \tag{3}$$

Thus the domestic real interest rate becomes

$$r = i^* - \pi + \alpha \tag{4}$$

One can see that this implicit real interest-rate rule is identical with a Taylor rule that violates the Taylor principle, since the real interest rate declines if the inflation rate increases:

$$r = (i^* + \alpha) + (-1)\pi + 0y \tag{5}$$

However, this destabilizing effect can be avoided if the country is so small that changes in the real exchange rate have a stronger effect on aggregate demand than changes in the real interest rate, i.e. if $c > b$ in equation (1).

The change of the real exchange rate is given by

$$\Delta q = r - r^* - \alpha \tag{6}$$

Inserting equations (6) and (4) in (1) yields an aggregate demand dependant on the inflation rate:

$$y^d(\pi) = a - b(r^* + \alpha) - (b - c)\pi^* + (b - c)\pi + \varepsilon_1 \tag{7}$$

Thus, the destabilizing effect of inflation on aggregate demand via the implicit Taylor rule can be compensated if $c > b$. In this case, in a π/y-space, aggregate demand declines if the inflation rate increases, which is the same result as with a stabilizing Taylor rule in a closed economy.

The required high degree of openness can be observed most clearly in Estonia, where exports are 50 per cent of GDP, and imports make up almost two thirds of GDP. In Latvia and Bulgaria, the openness is somewhat less pronounced with exports of about 30 per cent of GDP, and imports of 50 per cent (Latvia) and 43 per cent (Bulgaria).

The disappointing, but not surprising experience with flexible rates

In retrospect, the performance of flexible rates has not been convincing. Poland, the Czech Republic and later Hungary have suffered from a strong nominal appreciation of their currencies, which can hardly be explained by underlying macroeconomic fundamentals. This outcome is not astonishing, but rather confirms the well-known evidence for

Table 5.2 Inflation differential *vis-à-vis* the euro area

Country	1999	2000	2001	2002	2003
Bulgaria	1.5	8.3	5.2	3.5	2.6
Czech Republic	1.0	1.8	2.5	−0.5	−1.4
Estonia	2.2	1.9	3.5	1.3	−0.3
Hungary	8.9	7.7	6.9	3.0	2.7
Latvia	1.3	0.5	0.2	−0.4	1.0
Poland	6.2	8.0	3.2	−0.4	−1.2
Romania	44.7	43.6	32.2	20.2	13.1
Slovak Republic	9.6	9.9	5.0	1.0	6.5
Slovenia	5.1	6.8	6.1	5.2	3.9

Source: IMF, *World Economic Outlook*, September 2003

flexible exchange rates in all other areas and periods, summarized e.g. by Isard (1995) as follows:

> In short, neither the behavioral relationships suggested by theory, nor the information obtained through auto-regression, provided a model that could forecast significantly better than a random walk. And furthermore, while the random walk model performed at least as well as other models, it predicted very poorly.

Thus, especially in the case of Poland and Hungary, it was a very risky strategy to abandon a functioning crawling peg for freely floating exchange rates. While the Samuelson–Balassa effect is often mentioned as a justification for strong real appreciation, is certainly not sufficient to explain a nominal appreciation in Poland or the Czech Republic, which reached almost 20 per cent while the inflation differential *vis-à-vis* the euro area was still relatively high (Table 5.2). In the case of the Czech Republic, the productivity differential *vis-à-vis* the euro area is not more than 2 percentage points per annum. The high current account deficit of the Czech Republic is also a clear sign for an overvalued currency.

In the framework of our simple model, the situation in these countries can be described as follows. In contrast to fixed rates, the central bank can now base its policy on a standard loss function:

$$L = (\pi - \pi_0)^2 + \lambda y^2 \tag{8}$$

If one assumes that the exchange rate is not determined by fundamental factors, the real exchange rate can be described as a very simple random walk:

$$\Delta q = \eta \tag{9}$$

where η is a random white noise variable. Inserting (9) in (1) together with the loss function permits derivation of the optimum real interest rate for the central bank:

$$r^{\text{opt}} = \frac{a}{b} + \frac{1}{b}\varepsilon_1 + \frac{d}{b(d^2 + \lambda)}\varepsilon_2 + \frac{c}{b}\eta \tag{10}$$

Thus, the optimal policy requires that the central bank react to demand and supply shocks *and* also to the changes in the real exchange rate, which can be regarded as an additional shock. In contrast to this approach, Poland, the Czech Republic and Hungary pursued an interest-rate policy which disregarded the exchange-rate movements and thus created a deflationary bias. As a result, especially in Poland, monetary policy became excessively tight by the end of 2001 (Figure 5.4).[2]

In sum, the Polish experience since 1999 and the actual macroeconomic situation do not support the rather positive assessment made by Borowski *et al.* (2003, p. 3): 'From the perspective of the last 3 years it can

Figure 5.4   Monetary conditions index in Poland

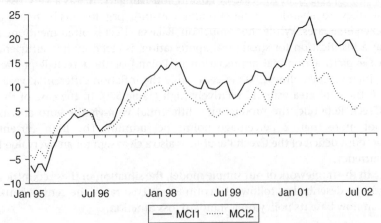

Source: international financial statistics

be said unambiguously that the floating exchange rate was good for the Polish economy. Not only did it solve the problem of long run inconsistency of monetary policy, but also immunized the economy against external shocks that could have otherwise caused a currency crises.'

Intermediate solutions better than expected

The most important contradiction to the 'two-corner solution' ideology is the rather successful performance of Slovenia. For several years, this country has followed a very stable path in terms of its exchange rate *vis-à-vis* the euro. By contrast with the mainstream view,[3] this policy was not prone to capital inflows, although it had liberalized its financial markets by the end of the 1990s. Interestingly, proponents of the mainstream simply disregard the experience of Slovenia. For instance Wyplosz (2003, p. 4) states: 'Central banks can intervene to lean against the wind, but the accumulated experience is that such interventions invite speculative attacks more often than they discourage them.'

Consequently, his paper completely neglects the Slovenian experience. The success of managed floating in Slovenia was not a coincidence, but rather the result of a comprehensive strategy for the simultaneous management of the interest and exchange rates. The elements of such a strategy are explained in detail by Bofinger and Wollmershäuser (2001). It requires that the interest and exchange rates be targeted in such a way as to simultaneously achieve both:

- an internal equilibrium which minimizes the loss function, and
- an external equilibrium which is defined as an exchange-rate path in line with the uncovered interest parity.

The latter safeguards a country from strong portfolio inflows, which are in most cases driven by excess returns, i.e. a domestic interest rate that exceeds the foreign rate and at the same time a constant exchange rate. Such an exchange-rate path has the important advantage that the central bank can sterilize capital inflows without cost. If the domestic interest rate exceeds the foreign rate, sterilization is associated with interest-rate costs, since the foreign assets that are acquired provide a lower return than the domestic assets that have to be issued to absorb the excess liquidity. At the same time, depreciation of the domestic currency increases the value of the central bank's foreign assets, which compensates for interest-rate costs. Thus, Wyplosz (2003, p. 5) is also wrong if he states: 'There is no known solution to the capital inflow problem.' The solution is an exchange-rate path determined by UIP. Figure 5.5 shows the interest rate

Figure 5.5   Changes in tolar/euro rate and tolar/euro interest-rate differential

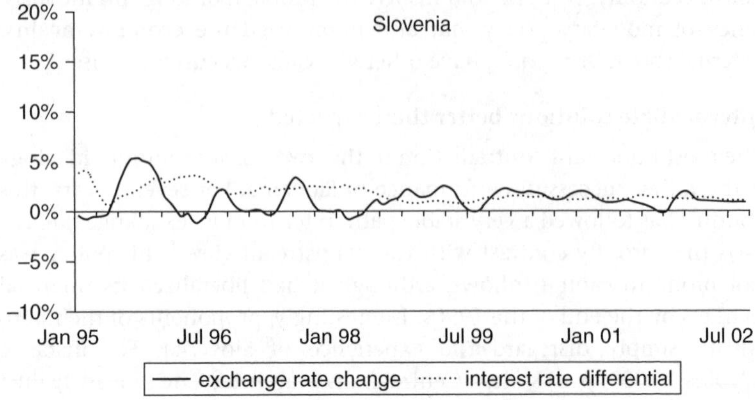

Sources: Bundesbank Research Data Bank and international financial statistics

differential between Slovenia and the euro area and the change in the tolar/euro rate. The experience of Slovenia also refutes the view that countries are unable to target their currency with sterilized intervention. Its central bank targets the exchange rate with interventions on the foreign-exchange market, and the interest rate with interventions on the domestic money market. As the Slovenian banking system is in a net-debtor position *vis-à-vis* the central bank, the money market rate is targeted by issuing short-term money market paper.

The current debate on exchange-rate policy in China and Japan additionally proves that countries are able to target their exchange rate, especially if it is under appreciation pressure.

What strategy for EMU entry?

After their accession to the EMU, the new member countries have to decide on

- the final date for EMU entry, and,
- if the time until transition exceeds two years, on their exchange-rate regime in the pre-convergence-test period.

As far as the first topic is concerned, all new entrants are well advised to delay the start of the convergence test period. Our survey of the macroeconomic situation represented in Table 5.2 shows serious imbalances in all countries; above all, current-account deficits are very high. Thus, it would be premature to adopt in the near future an exchange rate parity that would have to be applied for final EMU entry. The risk of overvalued parity is especially high in the case of the Czech Republic, where the real exchange rate appreciated by 25 per cent from 1999 to 2003. Of course, this analytical uncertainty is also an argument against the solution of early unilateral euroization.

In case they undergo a waiting period before the convergence test, countries have to decide on an exchange-rate strategy and on possible membership in ERM II. In its resolution 'on the establishment of an exchange-rate mechanism in the third stage of economic and monetary union', the European Council stated:[4] 'Participation in the exchange-rate mechanism will be voluntary for the Member States outside the euro area. Nevertheless, Member States with a derogation can be expected to join the mechanism. A Member State which does not participate from the outset in the exchange-rate mechanism may participate at a later date.'

We will discuss the pre-convergence-test period first, and then analyse the specific problems of the last two years of the transition process to the EMU.

Exchange-rate strategies for new members in the PCTP

EU membership requires that the new member countries observe Article 124 of the Treaty: 'Until the beginning of the third stage, each Member State shall treat its exchange-rate policy as a matter of common interest. In so doing, Member States shall take account of the experience acquired in cooperation within the framework of the European Monetary System (EMS) and in developing the ECU, and shall respect existing powers in this field.'

Given the very general character of this article, each new member country is still confronted with the three alternatives of fixed rates, free and managed floating. The experience of the last five years clearly speaks against market-determined exchange rates during this waiting period. Strong fluctuations of a freely-floating exchange rate not only create unnecessary macroeconomic frictions, they also make it difficult to determine whether a given exchange-rate level can be seen as a sustainable equilibrium for later EMU entry. In this respect, the experience of ERM I is very useful. As Figure 5.6 shows, several EMU members had maintained a very stable rate *vis-à-vis* the D-mark – and thus also among each other – for many years before they finally determined their EMU entry rate.

Figure 5.6   The Deutsch mark exchange rates in the ERM I

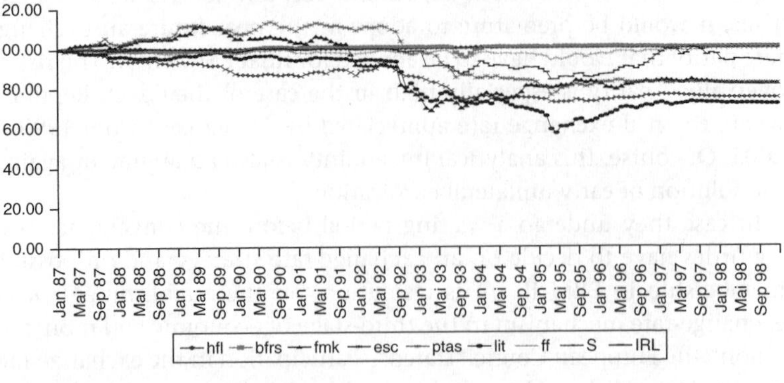

Source: Bundesbank Research Data Bank

Thus, Poland, Hungary and the Czech Republic would have to redefine their exchange rate strategy in order to avoid serious macroeconomic risks on their path to EMU entry. Since euroization must be excluded, the only viable option is the strategy of managed floating. Figure 5.2 shows that the Czech Republic and – to some extent – Hungary have already adopted a more active exchange-rate management during the past year. As already mentioned, a successful management of the exchange rate requires that the exchange-rate path follow the interest rate differential *vis-à-vis* the anchor currency. The prevailing interest-rate differential of Poland and Hungary *vis-à-vis* the euro would allow gradual depreciation of these currencies until ERM II entry. This could provide a substantial correction for existing macroeconomic imbalances. The situation of the Czech Republic is more difficult, since its interest-rate differential to the euro is close to zero. Thus, it would not be possible to target a gradual depreciation without causing major currency outflows. Given the serious imbalances in the Czech macroeconomic situation, the only solution would be a managed floating that starts with an outright devaluation of 10 per cent and then targets a constant euro exchange rate.

Of course, the strategy of managed floating is not a panacea. Its most important flaw is the asymmetry of the constraint of foreign exchange reserves. While a country can cope with appreciation pressure on its currency (as long as the exchange-rate path follows UIP), its ability to defend an exchange-rate path against depreciation pressure is very limited. A second major flaw of managed floating is its unilateral perspective, which provides a leeway for a beggar-thy-neighbour policy. Both flaws could become relevant after EU membership:

- a candidate country could come under the pressure of foreign-exchange markets which would force it to devalue strongly, although such an adjustment were not warranted by its macroeconomic situation,
- a candidate country could try to manipulate its exchange rate downwards in order to achieve a more competitive exchange rate in the EMU.

Both outcomes would not be in the interest of present EMU members, since they would lead to a deterioration of their competitiveness. While Article 124 addresses these problems in principle, it provides no concrete advice for coping with them. This is all the more the case as long as new member countries stay outside ERM II. In this case, exchange-rate policies would be conducted in a conceptual vacuum, especially since academic and political circles still have great difficulties understanding the mechanics of managed floating.

In this context, it is important to note that managed floating is not incompatible with the very popular strategy of *inflation targeting*. As shown by Bofinger and Wollmershäuser (2001), the exchange and the interest rate are targeted together in order to achieve an internal equilibrium. This equilibrium can be defined by a loss function based on an inflation target which attributes a specific weight to the inflation gap.

ERM II in the pre-convergence-test period

The conceptual problems in the pre-convergence test period would not change very much with ERM II membership. This institutional framework is very much shaped by the structures of its predecessor, ERM I, which was designed as a scheme with narrow margins and frequent parity adjustments. In addition, ERM I was characterized by a co-existence of several large players (the Bundesbank, Banque de France, Bank of England, Banca d'Italia). Thus, the ERM II framework suffers from serious inconsistencies which become obvious if we discuss its institutional features in detail. The most important institutional features of ERM II are:

- the definition of central rates and fluctuation bands,
- the rules for marginal and intra-marginal interventions,
- the provision of short-term financing facilities for interventions,
- an exit option, especially for the ECB.

Central rates and fluctuations bands

According to the resolution of the Council, an ERM II member country must define a *central rate vis-à-vis* the euro for its currency. This leads to an asymmetric hub-and-spoke structure of the system, since the ECB is not required to do the same for the euro *vis-à-vis* the currencies of ERM II members. This is the main difference from ERM I, which was based on a *'parity grid'*, i.e. a matrix of mutual parities, which led to a formal symmetry of the system.[5]

In line with the regulations for the ERM I since August 1993, the *fluctuation band* of ERM II is ±15 per cent. In ERM I until July 1993, the 'normal' fluctuation margin was ±2.25 per cent; a wide band of ±6 per cent was also possible, but it was only used by Italy.

As far as parity definitions and adjustments are concerned, the resolution calls for a coordinated procedure:

> Decisions on central rates and the standard fluctuation band shall be taken by mutual agreement of the ministers of the euro-area Member States, the ECB and the ministers and central bank governors of the non-euro area Member States participating in the new mechanism, following a common procedure involving the European Commission, and after consultation of the Economic and Financial Committee. The ministers and governors of the central banks of the Member States not participating in the exchange-rate mechanism will take part but will not have the right to vote in the procedure.

These regulations are very well suited for a strategy of managed floating. First, the *broad fluctuation margins* provide sufficient breathing space for exchange-rate paths determined by interest-rate differentials. Even if one assumes that a currency exhibits an interest-differential of 10 percentage points in relation to the euro, it could be kept within the band at a constant central rate for three years: It would start in the first year at the ceiling of the band and gradually move towards the floor by the end of the third year. Additional flexibility is provided by the possibility of discretionary realignments. A second positive feature of ERM II is the requirement that parity adjustments be made by *mutual agreement*. This removes one of the main risks of unilateral managed floating, the fact that an individual country is always tempted to use this strategy for a beggar-thy-neighbour policy. Of course, the advantage of coordinated exchange-rate management increases with the number of countries in central and eastern Europe participating in ERM II. It is important to note that such an arrangement is not mainly in the interest of the new EU members, but above all in the interest of present EMU countries. It gives them a possibility to prevent exchange-rate dumping by CEE countries, which could impair their competitiveness.

Rules for interventions

In line with our assessment of foreign exchange markets the resolution explicitly addresses the problems of purely market-determined exchange rates: 'The mechanism will also help to protect them [ERM II members – PB] and the Member States adopting the euro from unwarranted pressures in the foreign-exchange markets. In such cases, it may assist Member States outside the euro area participating in it, when their currencies come under pressure, to combine appropriate policy responses, including interest-rate measures, with coordinated intervention.'

In addition, the agreement between the ECB and possible ERM II members distinguishes between *marginal* interventions, i.e., those required to prevent a breach of the margins, and *intra-marginal* interventions, i.e. those within the margins. The agreement stipulates that:

- 'Intervention at the margins shall in principle be automatic and unlimited. However, the ECB and an ERM II central bank can suspend these interventions if they conflict with the objective of price stability.'
- 'The ECB and participating non-euro area NCBs [national central banks – PB] may agree to coordinated intra-marginal intervention.'

It is obvious that the agreement is still very much shaped by the arrangements of the original ERM I with its narrow ±2.25 margins. In this system, shocks have very rapidly forced a currency to the limits of the band, so that marginal intervention was required. Nevertheless, intra-marginal interventions also played an important role in the original ERM, but they were never given equal treatment with marginal interventions.[6] If a new member country decides to pursue a policy of managed floating within ERM II, the subordinate role of intra-marginal interventions will constitute a major disadvantage. It is obvious that such interventions are necessary for targeting a currency within the ±15 per cent band. They are certainly more important than marginal interventions which only come into play if intra-marginal interventions have been insufficient to stop a speculative attack. Thus, under managed floating:

- intra-marginal interventions are required to keep the exchange rate on a target path, while
- marginal interventions are only needed in emergency cases, where intra-marginal interventions have failed, so that control over the exchange rate has been lost.

Financing of interventions ('Very short-term financing facility')

Compared with a unilateral managed floating, ERM II membership would provide the CEE countries access to the seemingly generous 'very short-term financing facility' (VSTF). However, the ECB agreement's preference for marginal interventions is also mirrored in the regulations for the financing of interventions:

- In the case of *marginal* interventions, VSTF is 'in principle automatically available and unlimited in amount';
- For *intra-marginal* interventions, VSTF can also be used, but it requires agreement by the ECB, and the cumulative amount made available for such interventions is limited to a ceiling laid down for each ERM II member country. In addition, it is expected that the debtor central bank make 'appropriate use' of its own reserves.

As the asymmetry of the reserve constraint is one of the main difficulties of a strategy of managed floating, the provision of additional funds is certainly very helpful. However, in the case of intra-marginal interventions the *ceilings* laid down by the agreement are very tight. Denmark, which is currently the only ERM II member, could obtain maximum support of €520 million. If one relates the ceilings to a country's GDP, Poland would qualify for about €450 million. Compared with Poland's foreign exchange reserves, which total about $25 billion, the additional leeway provided by VSTF is almost negligible.

In both cases the *maturity* of the credits is indeed very short-term. The unlimited facilities for marginal interventions have to be repaid after three months. They can automatically be renewed once, but this is also limited by the narrow ceilings of the agreement. Thus, in the case of an outright speculative attack, the overall financing mechanism is not very effective. This became obvious in the ERM crises of 1992–93 when France had to give up the ±2.25 margin in August 1993 after a strongly increased debtor balance, although its macroeconomic fundamentals were no worse than those of Germany.

The exit option

In the view of the Bundesbank, one of the main flaws of ERM I was the lack of a clearly defined exit option for the central bank with a strong currency.[7] This concern was taken up by the authors of the Council resolution: 'However, the ECB and the central banks of the other participants could suspend intervention if this were to conflict with their primary objective. In their decision they would take due account of all relevant factors, and in particular of the need to maintain price stability and the credible functioning of the exchange-rate mechanism.' While such a regulation could have been helpful for the Bundesbank in ERM I, where it was confronted with up to nine central banks, some of which were of almost similar size, in the case of the ECB and its relations with CEE countries, such a safeguard clause seems no longer appropriate. It is difficult to image that even strong *interventions* for Poland, as the largest CEE economy, but with a GDP and a monetary base of only $3\frac{1}{2}$ per cent of the present euro area, could directly threaten the ECB's attempts to maintain price stability.

In the relationship between a hegemonic ECB and its satellites in the CEE, the main risk is that some ERM II country could pursue a non-stability-oriented fiscal and monetary policy which would cause a strong depreciation of its currency, and which in the longer run could impair the price stability of the whole currency area. As in this case, interventions in and of themselves would not be the right therapy; it would be helpful if the ECB could suspend interventions from the very outset. A simple framework for a modified exit option could be based on the '*broad guidelines*' laid down in Article 99 of the Treaty which were not available when the original ERM was established. In the context of an ERM II exit option, the following two paragraphs would be especially important:

- Paragraph 3: 'In order to ensure closer coordination of economic policies and sustained convergence of the economic performances of the Member States, the Council shall ... regularly carry out an overall assessment.'
- Paragraph 4: 'Where it is established ... that the economic policies of a Member State are not consistent with the broad guidelines ... or that they risk jeopardizing the proper functioning of economic and monetary union, the Council may ... make the necessary recommendations to the Member State concerned.'

Thus, an exit option could be designed in such a way that a country would automatically lose access to VSTF if the Council decided according to Paragraph 4 that its policies were no longer compatible with the broad guidelines.

Overall assessment

In its present institutional set-up, ERM II has very little to offer candidate countries during the pre-convergence test period. In principle, it mainly limits a country's national discretion in its exchange policy, since:

- Exchange rates have to be decided mutually.
- Intra-marginal interventions require the consent of the ECB.

At the same time, ERM II offers very limited financial support for countries suffering from speculative attack, especially if they are trying to avoid a drop in their exchange rate to the margin of their parity. With this asymmetry of rights and obligations for ERM II members, it is not surprising that e.g. the Czech National Bank (2003, p. 1) has come to a rather negative assessment: 'the Czech National Bank views participation in ERM II merely as a gateway to joining the eurozone, and does not recommend staying in the mechanism for any longer than the minimum required period of two years'.

Such a decision, while understandable from a national perspective, has negative implications for the exchange-rate policy in an enlarged European Union. By staying outside ERM II, countries reserve the ability to determine their euro exchange rate unilaterally, which could interfere with the unhampered functioning of the common market. On the other hand, if the Union wants to have a say in a country's exchange rate policy, it is also under the obligation to support it in periods of speculative attack.

A reformed ERM II

Therefore, it seems useful to reconsider the entire ERM II framework. In our view, it would be possible to modify the Council resolution as well as the ECB agreement in such a way as to make it attractive for new members to join ERM II as soon as possible. This requires above all that a much stronger role be assigned to *intra-marginal interventions*. First, it would be necessary to stipulate in Article 4 of the agreement that an ERM II member country have general permission to undertake intra-marginal interventions at its own discretion. This would reflect the fact that under a managed floating regime, the exchange-rate and interest-rate policies are integral elements of an autonomous national monetary policy. Thus,

Table 5.3 Ceilings in an extended VSTF

Country	GDP (€ billion)	Ceiling (€ billion)
Bulgaria	13.0	0.8
Czech Republic	55.0	3.2
Estonia	5.5	0.3
Hungary	49.5	2.9
Latvia	7.7	0.5
Lithuania	12.2	0.7
Poland	171.0	10.0
Romania	40.0	2.3
Slovakia	20.9	1.2
Slovenia	19.5	1.1
		23.1

Source for GDP data: Deutsche Bundesbank (2001)

if an ECB agreement is required whenever intra-marginal interventions are carried out, this could interfere with an effective national monetary policy, and it could blur monetary-policy responsibilities.

Second, in order to support a smooth exchange-rate policy of accession countries, the *VSTF ceilings* would have to be increased considerably. The example of Denmark shows that the amounts have been kept constant in nominal terms since 1979 which explains their very small size compared to present levels of foreign exchange reserves. For Table 5.3, it is assumed that ceilings would be about twenty times the size of the present agreement, so that Poland would be entitled to a finance volume of €10 billion. The ceilings for the other countries were calculated according to their nominal GDPs. For all accession countries in central and eastern Europe, this would lead to an aggregate ceiling of about €23 billion.

A comparison of the aggregate ceiling with the amount of refinance credits provided by the ECB, which total about €200 billion, demonstrates that even such a generously extended VSTF would not constitute a problem for the ECB's monetary policy management.

Such a modification of VSTF would not only be in the interest of the accession countries, it could also be helpful for the present EMU members. By making ERM II much more attractive, accession countries would be more willing to join it than under present conditions. As already mentioned, this gives the old members a say in the exchange-rate policies of the entrants, which would in turn help prevent possible exchange-rate dumping.

Additionally, access to a much more generous VSTF could be made dependent on the observance of the 'broad policy guidelines'. This would create a strong incentive for national policy-makers to adhere to these guidelines, which would foster macroeconomic stability in the entire European Union.

ERM II in the convergence test period

Under the Maastricht Treaty, exchange-rate stability is regarded as a necessary qualification for EMU entry. Accordingly, Article 121 requires 'the observance of the normal fluctuation margins provided for by the exchange-rate mechanism of the European Monetary System, for at least two years, without devaluing against the currency of any other Member State.'

The economic rationale of this criterion is very weak. Why should a country that is able to meet the inflation and fiscal-policy criteria be excluded from EMU entry, simply because it has been attacked on the foreign-exchange markets? As already mentioned, it is today rather non-controversial that market-determined exchange rates do not systematically reflect macroeconomic fundamentals, so that it makes little sense to use foreign-exchange dealers as judges of a country's EMU qualification.

An additional problem of the exchange-rate criterion is the confusion about 'normal' fluctuation margins. When the Treaty was drafted, the word 'normal' was used to make clear that the narrow ±2.25 per cent margins are required, and not the wider ±6.0 margins. Since the widening of ERM I, margins of ±15 per cent have become 'normal'. Given the very weak economic rationale for the exchange-rate criterion, a generous interpretation of this criterion is certainly warranted.

But even if this criterion were to be given greater leeway, the newcomers would again be confronted with the institutional flaws of ERM 2. Thus, they could suffer from insufficient financial support in situations of speculative attack, and they would have to agree with the ECB on intra-marginal interventions. With the institutional modifications suggested above (pp. 87–94), membership in ERM 2 could be made much easier without jeopardizing price stability in the euro area.

ERM II membership in the pre-accession stage

Given these advantages of a modified ERM II, the question arises whether it would be adequate to open it, too, to countries in central and eastern Europe which are still in the accession stage. Under legal aspects, such an opening would be not too difficult, since in the tradition of the original EMS and ERM, the whole ERM II has to be designed outside the EU Treaty. As already mentioned, it simply rests on a resolution by the Council and on an agreement between the ECB and the national central banks. Both legal documents could be easily amended and modified to permit ERM II membership for accession countries.

Again, a more generous treatment of the accession countries would be in the mutual interest of both old members and newcomers. For both sides, stable and mutually agreed-upon exchange-rate paths are a better solution than unilaterally determined exchange rates prone to major shocks.

Summary

Experience since 1999 has shown clearly that freely flexible exchange rates have been a sub-optimal framework. It also demonstrates that the intermediate solution of managed floating can be handled in such a way that the capital-inflow problem is avoided. Thus, by pursuing managed floating instead of freely flexible rates, a country can obtain an additional degree of freedom which will help avoid the macroeconomic disequilibria from which Poland, Hungary and the Czech Republic are currently suffering. Due to these imbalances, all candidate countries should avoid a strategy of introducing the euro as soon as possible. The experience of the ERM I shows that most EMU members followed a long trial-and-error process with rather stable rates before determining final conversion rates.

For such a long transition period, the strategy of managed floating provides a simple and effective framework that is also compatible with the strategy of inflation targeting. Two main risks are associated with this strategy. For new members, the asymmetry of the reserve constraint limits their control over the exchange rate in situations with strong speculative attacks. For old members, there is a danger that the unilateral targeting of the exchange rate could be used for exchange-rate dumping. Thus, both sides should have an interest that such managed floating be operated within a common framework.

Unfortunately, the ERM II in its present form is not very useful for this purpose. It suffers from an institutional structure that was designed for a situation with narrow bands and relatively similar players. As a result, it provides very limited resources for interventions *de facto*, and is almost useless for the most likely case of interventions carried out before the ±15 per cent band is reached. Thus, ERM II restricts the room for maneuver of the candidate countries without offering them anything real in exchange. Thus, it is not surprising that the Czech National Bank wants to keep its time in this uncomfortable waiting room as short as possible.

Given the mutual interest of old and new members in a common framework for exchange-rate policies during the transition process to the EMU, it would be advisable to reform ERM II in such a way that its main flaws are avoided: Its ceilings could be extended substantially without jeopardizing the ECB's monetary policy, the limitations on intra-marginal interventions could be abolished, and access to the credit facilities could be made contingent upon meeting the broad policy guidelines. Such a more generously designed ERM II would also reduce the attractiveness of euroization, which is the only other alternative to freely floating rates.

In the convergence-test period, ERM II membership without tensions is regarded as a necessary qualification for the EMU. As the economic rationale for this criterion is very weak, it would again be useful to have a modified ERM II which would make it easier for the candidate countries to keep their currencies on track until their final transition to the EMU.

Finally, a modified ERM II could also be considered as a framework for the exchange-rate polices of those accession countries which will enter the EU later. Again, there is a mutual interest in avoiding excessive currency fluctuations.

Notes

1. The complete model is in Bofinger *et al.* (2002).
2. MCI1 is based on deviations of the real exchange rate from the average of 1995, MCI2 is based on the annual change of the real exchange rate.
3. See, for example, Begg *et al.* (2003, p. 25): 'A – if not the – major challenge for accession economies attempting to navigate the transition to membership in the euro area is the capital inflows problem. Large capital inflows would seem inevitable when capital markets are open, exchange rate flexibility is limited, and interest rates are still coming down to EU levels.'
4. Resolution of 16 June 1997 (97/C 236/03).
5. *De facto*, ERM I was an asymmetric system, since the reserve constraint forced countries with weak currencies to adjust their policies to that of the Bundesbank, which was always the central bank with strongest currency.
6. Limited possibilities for such interventions were made possible by the Basle-Nyborg agreement of 1987.
7. Otmar Emminger, the Bundesbank's president during the period from 1977–9, in November 1978 wrote a letter to the German government in which he declared that the Bundesbank would make use of an opting-out provision in case of interventions which threatened monetary stability in Germany; see Emminger (1986).

Bibliography

Begg, D. *et al.*, *Sustainable Regimes of Capital Movements in Accession Countries*, CEPR Policy Paper No. 10 (2003).

Bofinger, P. *et al.*, 'The BMW Model: Simple Macroeconomics for Closed and Open Economies: A Requiem for the IS/LM-AS/AD and the Mundell-Fleming Model', *Würzburg Economic Papers* No. 35 (2002).

Bofinger, P. and Wollmershäuser, T., 'Managed Floating: Understanding the New International Monetary Order', CEPR Discussion Paper No. 3064 (November 2001).

Borowski, J. *et al.*, 'Exchange Rate Regimes and Poland's Participation in ERM II', *Bank and Credit* No. 01/2003 (2003).

Czech National Bank, 'ERM II and Exchange-Rate Convergence Criterion', Information Material for the Czech Government (2003). http://www.cnb.cz/en/pdf/ERM_II_vlada_15_07_03_en.pdf

DB Research Country Infobase, http://dbresearch.de.

Deutsche Bundesbank, *Monthly Bulletin* (October 2001).

Emminger, O., *D-Mark, Dollar, Währungskrisen: Erinnerungen eines ehemaligen Bundesbankpräsidenten* (Stuttgart, 1986).

European Council, *Resolution 97/C 236/03* (1997).

Isard, P., *Exchange Rate Economics* (Cambridge, 1995).

IMF, *World Economic Outlook* (September 2003).

Wyplosz, C., *Briefing Notes to the Committee for Economic and Monetary Affairs of the European Parliament* (2003). http://www.europarl.eu.int/comparl/econ/pdf/emu/speeches/20000620/wyplosz/default_en.pdf

6
Perspectives for a Monetary Union between Argentina and Brazil

Fernando J. Cardim de Carvalho

Introduction

Besides some vague references contained in some official documents, the possibility of having the Common Market of the South (Mercosur) extended to include a monetary union between the four country members, and particularly between Argentina and Brazil, was first raised by Carlos Menem, then president of Argentina, during his last year in office. After a few years of relatively rapid growth, Argentina was going through the first stages of the deep recession from which it only began to recover in 2003. Several imbalances plagued the Argentine economy by the end of the 1990s, but the abandonment by Brazil of its semi-fixed exchange rate regime in January 1999, and the quick and steep devaluation of the real that followed it, dealt a lethal blow on the uno-a-uno exchange rate regime that Argentina had sustained since 1991.

Menem's proposal was by and large received as a theatrical move, a step in his bid for re-election. It was made without any previous consultation with the Brazilian government, Argentina's main partner at Mercosur. In fact, there were indications that Mr Menem hadn't even consulted with his own staff. The overvaluation of the peso, fixed at the rate of one peso to the dollar for almost a decade, was undeniable, but Argentine economists, especially those connected with the country's government, insisted that the regime would still be able to survive if Brazil could be convinced to adopt a similar currency board regime, instead of floating its currency, as it did. Proposing a monetary union was mostly an attempt to shift the responsibility (and blame) for the overvaluation of the peso to the Brazilian monetary authorities.

Understandably, the proposal was received as a non-starter by the Brazilian government. Since it had not been presented as an official proposal from the Argentine government, Brazil was able to dismiss it as mostly a personal speculation by Mr Menem about a possibly desirable future outcome of the process of integration in the region. Nevertheless, a few conservative economists in Brazil seized upon the idea, because it was seen as an opportunity to introduce into the political agenda a debate on the adoption of Maastricht-like reforms that would restrain the use of fiscal and monetary policies by local authorities. In fact, a common currency in and of itself was not nearly as important to them as, for instance, the possibility of imposing limits on fiscal deficits, or of creating an independent central bank for the region.

For the moderate left, Mercosur has been important for two reasons. On the one hand, it had helped to consolidate the move toward redemocratization after the military regimes in the region had folded up. Regional political solidarity in the Mercosur area has prevented at least one military coup, in Paraguay. On the other hand, Mercosur opened the alternative for the block, and more particularly for Brazil and Argentina, to maintain some measure of autonomy in the face of the larger powers of world capitalism, the US, and, more recently, the European Union. In fact, the autonomy strategy itself is inspired by the trajectory of the EU, as a third force between the United States and the Soviet Union. In this view, the most important aspect of Mercosur is the political rapprochement between Argentina and Brazil, and if monetary unification can help solidify it, the thinking goes, it should be supported. Thus, although launched in the debate for entirely artificial reasons, the currency union proposal ended up opening a serious discussion on both the desirability of monetary unification in the Mercosur area, and the conditions for its success. However, some enormous difficulties stand in the way of such an initiative. Even if one is persuaded that its shortcomings are no greater than its advantages, it is impossible to ignore that important barriers remain even for much smaller additional steps toward greater integration. Here, we would like to explore the main arguments for and against monetary unification between Argentina and Brazil. In the next section we examine the standard arguments in favour of monetary unions, developed in the Optimum Currency Area (OCA) tradition. Then we compare monetary unions, as an extreme form of fixed exchange-rate regimes, to the option of floating exchange rates. Next we look at the criteria (laundry-list style) for the identification of OCAs in the case of Argentina and Brazil.

Optimum currency areas

The theory of optimum currency areas

In modern economic theory, the case for monetary unions is made via the model of the *optimum currency area* (OCA). As is usually the case, arguments and visions of common currencies, even of a world currency, can be found in the works of many of the founders of economic theory. However, the inspiration for the debates of the last decades comes from R. Mundell, and particularly his 1961 paper in the *American Economic Review*.

In this seminal paper, Mundell argues that there is no reason for optimum currency areas to coincide with national territories. Even a small country, and certainly bigger ones, may be heterogeneous enough to make macro-stabilization-oriented monetary policies inefficient. Ideally, an OCA would be an area within which factors of production would be fully mobile. Since capital is usually highly fungible, especially in modern times, it is with respect to the mobility of labour that significant restrictions would be found. A given monetary policy could be efficient either if the area is homogeneous enough so that the effects of a shock (and of the corresponding countervailing policy) would be symmetrical among agents, or that, even if constituted by heterogeneous sub-areas, the mobility of labour were high enough within the area as a whole so that labour could move from the sub-areas where its reward is diminished toward those where it is increased. Thus, the mobility of factors (and of labour in particular) was the most important criterion for establishing the boundaries of an OCA.

In fact, the first generation of OCA models also emphasized the degree of commercial integration as another important criterion for defining an OCA (cf. McKinnon, 1963). The higher the degree of integration between two economies, the less efficient adjustment mechanisms based on relative price changes (like those triggered by floating exchange rates) would be. Therefore, a set of countries that traded among themselves in a more intense fashion would be another candidate to be an OCA.

International labour mobility is, as is well known, in fact very limited. In larger countries, even national mobility of labour may be somewhat restricted. On the other hand, many, if not most, countries are very heterogeneous. It seemed that OCA theory was an argument in favour of sub-national currencies instead of monetary unions, as it came in time to be.[1] Mundell himself realized the paradox of an argument that starts as a criticism of floating exchange rates and ends up suggesting that there should be an even larger number of independent currencies than already exist.[2] Mundell rejected this conclusion, however, arguing that currencies are in fact *means of communication*, vehicles for assessing exchange values and liquidating obligations. The more fragmented a monetary system is, the less efficiently the currency performs those functions. In other words, there are economies of scale in the use of currency, so that the costs of establishing a common currency per 'unit' of transaction decrease with the size of the area.[3] In sum, the opportunity to design precisely focused monetary policies is an incentive to define smaller OCAs; by contrast, the economies of scale of a common currency push in the opposite direction. *Ceteris paribus*, at any given moment, the existing number of currencies appear as the solution to a satisfaction-maximization problem defined along these lines.[4]

The gains to be derived from a common currency described above are believed to be empirically illustrated by the discrepancies between the volumes of intra-national and international trade. Studies of the volume of trade among Canadian provinces along the border with the United States are frequently mentioned in the literature. They show that trade between the provinces is tens of times greater than trade with neighbouring states in the United States. It seems reasonable to assume that the only difference between Canadian provinces and American states is the different currencies each group uses. Empirical studies realized so far, however, have not supported the hypothesis that international trade would be highly sensitive to exchange-rate factors.

Even as this dilemma remained fundamentally unsolved, Mundell himself seemed to change his views about the appropriate conditions for defining an OCA.[5] In fact, as pointed out by McKinnon (2000), one could see Mundell's presentation of OCA in the early 1970s as practically the exact opposite of his initial formulation. While in 1961, to use more modern terminology, Mundell emphasized the *symmetry of shocks* as a condition defining OCAs, because if two regions suffered the same shock (and with similar intensity) they would choose similar monetary policies, by 1970, his view as summarized by McKinnon seemed to have become precisely the opposite: 'If a common money can be managed so that its general purchasing power remains stable, then the larger the currency area – even one encompassing diverse regions or nations subject to "asymmetric shocks" – the better' (McKinnon, 2000).

The views are not, in fact, as contrasting as they may seem. In both versions, Mundell emphasizes mobility as a condition for defining an OCA. A larger area may be able to absorb more shocks, so monetary policies would be less needed to induce adjustment. If that area is diversified, adverse local shocks may just induce factor migration to the unaffected areas, so that monetary policy could be dispensed with. The difference between the two approaches seems to be that in the initial paper, Mundell focused on how monetary policy could be used to stabilize the economy, while in the later papers he focused on whether monetary policy would be necessary at all to achieve stabilization.[6] Thus, the larger the currency area, the higher the probability that (local) adverse shocks could be absorbed by the normal operation of the economy without the need for intervention by the authorities.

Two important shortcomings of the conventional literature on OCA are the slight attention paid to either financial constraints on and incentives for monetary unification, or to political variables. As to financial variables, there is a striking contrast between the academic discussion of the OCA concept and the actual political debate around concrete proposals, such as those that led to the creation of the euro, where financial matters are of paramount concern. A few exceptions in the academic literature should be noted. Stockman (2000) discussed the convenience for Mexico of a monetary union with the United States precisely from this point of view. The focus here is on the fact that having a common currency implies having a *common central bank*. A central bank, however, is usually responsible for more than monetary policy.[7] It usually also deals with financial regulation, and acts as a lender of last resort for the banking system.[8] Thus, the financial impact of a monetary union is an essential element in the decision over whether or not to join it.[9]

The political aspect of the matter is, of course, more complex. There are several layers of arguments to be considered here. First, there is the problem that currencies are usually associated with national sovereignty. Adopting a single currency has been one of the most important symbols identifying new nation-states over the last few centuries. These feelings may seem irrational to some economists, but how economists feel about the matter is irrelevant.[10] An easier point to grasp, perhaps, is the fact that a number of monetary unions were established as a step in processes of *political* unification. Monetary unification was part of the German unification process in the late 1800s, for instance, as it was again after the fall of the Berlin Wall in the late 1980s and early 1990s.

Mundell was not oblivious to the political factor. He stressed it in 1961, when examining the perspectives for monetary union in Europe: 'In Western Europe the creation of the Common Market is regarded by many as an important step toward eventual political union, and the subject of a common currency for the six countries has been much discussed' (Mundell, 1961, p. 661).[11] The relevant trade-offs in this case would not be between the economic gains of having independent monetary policies *vs* the gains of higher predictability in trade activities, but between the loss of the domestic power of choice over monetary policies *vs* the gains of forming stronger political units (as was certainly the view of France's General de Gaulle, for instance).[12]

A political union, finally, raises another important aspect of monetary unions: the compensation for weaker participants. When a common currency is just one element of a federal entity, weaker members are for example compensated for their loss of monetary (and exchange-rate) independence through transfers. Many researchers have noted this. Frankel (1999), for instance, states: 'Consider ... a rather special form of integration: the existence of a federal fiscal system to transfer funds to regions that suffer adverse shocks. The existence of such a system ... makes monetary independence less necessary.' McKinnon also stresses the connection between monetary and political union, when discussing Mundell's proposals for a common currency in Mercosur in 2000: 'Of course, without political unity and financial stability, the introduction of such a stand-alone regional currency is only a remote possibility' (McKinnon, 2000). The political will to promote unification can supersede economic barriers to initiatives like the creation of a common currency, if the political dividends one expects to obtain from political union are significant enough. As we will discuss below (pp. 111–12), this may actually be the strongest argument for a common currency between Argentina and Brazil in a not-so-distant future.

OCA and price stabilization

It is reasonably clear that OCA theories were not formulated with developing economies in mind. Although most of the literature does not specify the mechanisms through which monetary unions could be established, OCA proponents clearly have institutions in mind which are created by some kind of mutual agreement, as was the case with Euroland. Countries that chose to join a union should, all of them, benefit from the arrangement.

When discussing the case of developing countries, most people think of different arrangements, at least when Latin American or transition economies are considered. Here, the rationale for monetary unification is not the search for mutual gain, but the attempt by inflation-prone countries to gain credibility for their price-stabilization strategies by tying their hands as regards monetary policy. In other words, it is not the constitution of common currency areas *per se* that is discussed, but the eradication of monetary-policy independence in countries that are not considered fit to run their own macroeconomic policies.

Stockman's discussion of the possibility of monetary union between Mexico and the United States raises the issue that much, if not most, of the literature on monetary unification related to developing countries is in reality about *dollarization* instead of OCAs. Dollarization, by contrast to the creation of an OCA, is the unilateral acceptance of the US dollar as the national currency by another country. It is not really monetary unification, since the rules of the game as to issuance of money, seigniorage gains, lender-of-last-resort facilities, etc., do not change with dollarization, since the United States does not in fact accept any responsibility for the decisions of other countries.[13]

According to some economists, currency unions such as dollarization or the creation of currency boards would compensate for the loss of independence in monetary policy (and, of course, in exchange-rate policy) with such a degree of credibility in the solidity of the country's commitment to price stability that interest rates would be drastically reduced (because of the decrease in country risk), allowing the country to grow beyond what would otherwise have been possible.[14]

Fixed versus floating exchange rates

OCA models and other systems of fixed exchange rates (including some intermediate exchange rate regimes) are built on strong *parti pris* exhibited by proponents against floating exchange rates. In 1997 for instance, Mundell, reflecting on the evolution of his views on the matter, wrote of the post-Bretton Woods period of floating exchange rates: 'Not surprisingly, two decades of flexible exchange rates have been too much of a bad thing' (Mundell, 1997).

Already in his 1961 paper, long before the collapse of the Bretton Woods system, Mundell warned that a floating exchange-rate regime was not a feasible alternative to fixed exchange rates. The perception that floating exchange rates were not sustainable was stronger among Europeans, as Wyplosz wrote: 'The alternative option of letting exchange rates float was never acceptable to Europeans' (Wyplosz, 1997, p. 4). He added that exchange rate fluctuations proved to be too intense and too durable after 1973 (from 20 per cent to 50 per cent for two to three years). This pattern of fluctuations is 'just not compatible with fully open markets and the complete removal of border posts' (ibid., p. 8).

It is generally argued that different exchange rate regimes may better suit very large and very small economies.[15] Small economies have no choice but to seek integration in international trade, since they cannot provide for the needs of their populations.[16] On the other hand, the largest economies may exhibit a very high degree of self-sufficiency.

Small integrated economies would most obviously benefit from fixed exchange rates, given the predictability this would impart to revenues and expenses related to international trade. Larger economies, on the other hand, with more diversified productive structures, could benefit more from floating exchange rates.

Frankel (1999) argues that a more relevant argument to explain the choice of exchange-rate regimes may be the origin of the shocks to which the particular economy may be subject. Floating exchange rates would be better for countries more vulnerable to external shocks, since they would allow a quicker, and possibly less painful, adjustment. Fixed or pegged exchange rates better suit countries subject to more frequent internal shocks. Of course, a monetary union may be a more complex arrangement, where exchange rates are fixed between the currencies of the countries that join it, while they are allowed to float against other currencies. In fact, most currently existing cases of monetary union are precisely of that type. Keeping in mind that monetary unions are just an extreme form of fixed exchange rates, one is taken back to the central dichotomy addressed by OCA theory: the contrast between symmetric and asymmetric shocks, and the two rationales for currency unification.

Is there a case for monetary unification between Argentina and Brazil?

As we saw above (p. 103), the most frequently proposed modality of monetary unification for inflation-prone developing countries is dollarization.[17] In this section, we quickly dispose of this proposal, and proceed to examine the case for monetary unification between Argentina and Brazil along lines more akin to the original OCA model.

Dollarization

It is clear that most proponents of the reduction of the number of national currencies today are in fact referring to some particular groups of countries, notably Latin American and transition countries. They generally assume the inability of certain countries – particularly developing countries – to sustain price stability on their own. Under these conditions, the debate actually shifts from the virtues and shortcomings of monetary union *per se* to the related, but not quite identical, question of whether such countries should adopt the currency of a developed country so as to anchor the value of their own currencies, and to which form such an anchoring process should assume.

Thus, the debate actually centres on two different questions: first, whether all national economies, particularly those of developing economies, are endowed with institutions strong enough to guarantee price stability on their own; and second, under which conditions a currency union, which is merely one way of anchoring one currency to another, could be efficient.

For our purposes here, we can dispose of this question quickly. The literature on dollarization concerns price-stabilization strategies for economies suffering from high inflation. In such economies, confidence in the domestic currency may have eroded to such an extent that no domestically created independent form of money will be able recover the unit-of-account function necessary to support a system of money contracts. If that is the case, fighting inflation can be more effective if the country's government – assumed to be the main culprit – signals to private agents that it is giving up its powers of monetary creation and management, and opting instead for a strong foreign currency as the measure of value.

Of course, in principle, this could be achieved simply by fixing the exchange rate between the domestic currency and a foreign anchor currency. There is, however, the problem of credibility: the public may not believe the domestic currency will be managed in such a way as to support the fixed exchange rate, because the possibility of increasing the supply of domestic money may be too tempting for the local government. Two schemes may send a stronger, and more credible, signal: currency substitution, by which the country directly adopts the foreign currency as its own legal tender, eliminating the domestic currency; or currency union, with binding rules connecting both currencies in an irrevocable bond.

Some economies have adopted the first modality, mostly by *dollarizing* their economies, that is, by adopting the US dollar as their own legal tender. Other economies have sought to establish a strong bond between currencies without getting to the extreme point of actually giving up a domestic currency, as was the case with the Cavallo Plan in Argentina, an example of a currency board arrangement.[18] The results of these strategies are well known in the empirical literature: they are efficacious in controlling inflation, but impose severe real costs on the economy. The resulting overvaluation of the domestic currency causes deficits in the balance of payments to emerge, forcing either a contraction of the economy or an increase in foreign debt. Also, dependence of the local currency on the foreign anchor as its base of confidence is not easy to overcome. Exit strategies are hard to design in theory, and even harder to apply in practice.

In any case, this debate has now largely been closed in the Mercosur area. Except for hold-outs of the 1990s, such as former president Menem, who seemed until recently still to plan some kind of political comeback, Argentines do not seem to be willing to engage in such an experiment again. In Brazil, dollarization was never seen as a serious option.[19]

Thus, in a sense, the debate on monetary unification in the Mercosur area harks back to the 'classical' framework proposed by Mundell when advancing his theory of optimal currency areas. The point of the debate over the creation of a single currency for Argentina and Brazil is certainly not one about anchoring the Argentinean peso to the Brazilian real, or the reverse, but rather about investigating whether those two countries could define an optimum currency area.

Are Argentina and Brazil an optimal currency area?

As discussed above, in the most common formulation of OCA theory, three criteria are advanced to define optimum currency areas: the symmetry of shocks, the degree of trade integration, and factor mobility.

If shocks hit two economies differently or with different intensity, policies that could be optimal for one of them might not be optimal for the other. The more two economies share shock and reaction patterns, the likelier it is that a common monetary policy, such as would result from monetary unification, will suit both of them. Moreover, if two economies are hit by shocks in a similar way, it is unlikely that changes in exchange rates would be efficient in fixing the imbalances that could emerge between them. Thus a high symmetry of shocks is a condition favourable to monetary integration.

The degree of integration between the economies is also intuitively favourable to unification. The more integrated two economies are, the more one will benefit from whatever is beneficial to the other. Thus, for instance, if an economy is going through a recession that makes an expansive policy an adequate choice, it is likely that the other economy will also be suffering a recession, and that both would benefit from a common expansive policy.

Finally, factor mobility is little more than just another name for economic integration. Even though movements of capital and, even more, of people are usually problematic from many points of view, integration ultimately aims at creating a single economic space. Therefore, the freer the movements of capital and people in a given area,

Table 6.1 Argentina: destination of exports and origins of imports (US$ million)

Area	1994		1995		1996		1997		1998		1999		2000		2001		2002	
	Exports	Imports	Exports	Imports	Exports	Imports	Exports	Imports	Exports	Imports	Exports	Imports	Exports	Imports	Exports	Imports	Exports	Imports
European Union	3,890	6,139	4,465	6,008	4,562	6,901	3,989	8,301	4,585	8,691	4,712	7,119	4,598	5,757	4,579	4,598	5,146	2,028
Nafta	2,083	4,819	2,026	4,819	2,327	5,565	2,393	7,133	2,550	7,098	3,173	5,777	3,739	5,629	3,616	4,420	3,829	2,027
Mercosur	4,803	4,783	6,769	4,593	7,818	5,800	8,995	7,506	9,260	7,967	7,071	6,298	8,393	7,197	7,459	5,907	5,723	2,896
Total	15,839	21,590	20,963	20,121	23,810	23,731	25,222	30,323	25,856	31,437	23,332	25,508	26,251	25,148	26,610	20,321	25,709	8,989

Source: www.mercosur.org.uy

Table 6.2 Brazil: destination of exports and origins of imports (US$ million)

Area	1994		1995		1996		1997		1998		1999		2000		2001		2002	
	Exports	Imports	Exports	Imports	Exports	Imports	Exports	Imports	Exports	Imports	Exports	Imports	Exports	Imports	Exports	Imports	Exports	Imports
European Union	12,202	8,972	12,912	13,798	12,836	14,242	14,513	15,874	14,748	16,826	13,736	14,984	14,784	14,065	14,865	14,822	15,113	13,069
Nafta	10,501	7,944	9,755	12,474	10,494	14,187	10,820	16,490	11,418	15,862	12,430	13,462	15,643	14,873	16,801	14,659	18,659	11,758
Mercosur	5,921	4,583	6,154	6,839	7,305	8,302	9,047	9,517	8,878	9425	6,778	6,720	7,733	7,795	6,364	7,010	3,311	5,615
Total	43,545	33,079	46,506	49,972	47,747	53,346	52,994	59,838	51,140	57,550	48,011	49,222	55,086	55,835	58,220	55,581	60,362	47,231

Source: www.mercosur.org.uy

the better the allocation of resources that can be achieved, and the more a common macroeconomic policy (and, in fact, other policies as well) may benefit the economies involved.

The symmetry of shocks between Brazil and Argentina depends on which shocks one is considering. An important class of shocks in recent years has been related to autonomous flows of capital to and from emerging countries. These flows, however, may be rooted in different causes, which affect each country in different ways. Inflows of foreign capital, particularly portfolio investment, may generally represent a somewhat symmetrical shock, with similar timing and effects in both cases. Both Brazil and Argentina, for instance, received excessive inflows of capital during the early to mid-1990s, with similar results, such as, e.g., the overvaluation of their currencies. When the excess liquidity in international financial markets dried up, both countries shared similar difficulties. However, shocks represented by capital outflows may be more idiosyncratic. The experience of Brazil and Argentina is no different from what has been witnessed in other emerging market economies. Capital account liberalization has not only made the circulation of foreign capital easier, it has also facilitated capital flight by residents, a phenomenon which is usually a response to domestic stimuli. Thus, capital flight in Brazil in January 1999 caused no exchange crisis in Argentina, and the Argentine crisis of December 2001 had little effect on Brazil. Again, the turbulence of mid-2002 in Brazil seems to have been caused by strictly idiosyncratic factors.

Capital flows have been the main source of external shocks to these economies in recent years. In the 1990s, Argentina opened its capital account much more completely than did Brazil. After the 2001 crisis, the situation was reversed. Be that as it may, the degree of shock symmetry is relatively low between the two countries, even though it could be increased by some convergence of institutional structures. The low degree of commonality between macroeconomic shocks is shown in Figure 6.1. There is no visible common pattern in GDP variations in Brazil and Argentina during the 1990s, even after 1994, when both countries were able to stabilize prices.[20]

Economic integration between Brazil and Argentina is also problematical. There is little 'natural' complementarity between the two economies. Both countries are large, relatively rich in raw materials and primary production, and capable of supporting a reasonably diversified manufacturing sector. The strong development of oil production in Brazil after the shocks of the 1970s eliminated one potential area of complementarity. Attempts to develop varieties of wheat suitable for higher temperatures

Figure 6.1   GDP annual growth rates: Argentina and Brazil

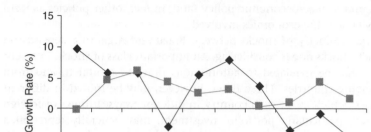

Source: www.eclac.org

may eliminate another. As to manufactured goods, the competition between Argentine producers and those of southern Brazil has been the source of permanent tension.[21] The volume of trade between Mercosur countries has certainly become non-negligible to both Brazil and Argentina, and more particularly to the latter (see Tables 6.1 and 6.2). Nevertheless, it remains a very conflict-prone relationship, with many sectors constantly questioning the trade arrangements made between the Mercosur countries, and safeguards being frequently adopted or demanded.

Finally, factor mobility, especially of labour, is still very limited, although this may be less a problem than in other areas, such as NAFTA or even the EU. Labour regulations are still very different, so that movements other than emigration are still a problem. In fact, economic integration between Brazil and Argentina was originally, and has largely remained, a political goal. It has always been relatively clear to many that the chances of actually integrating both economies would depend on a process of re-division of labour that would be long and possibly painful. It was generally perceived, on the other hand, that the rivalry between the two countries was fed by military regimes intent on finding enemies that could serve the political mobilization purposes that usually support dictatorships. Democratization, on the other hand, brought with it the opposite view: that civilian regimes should support each other, especially in the crucial years when democratic institutions have not yet been consolidated.

Political convergence, if not necessarily unification, was also seen as a means for strengthening the international presence of both countries. Argentina had for a long time attempted a strategy of political approach to the United States, to the point of taking part on some of the latter's military initiatives, albeit in a rather symbolic manner. The statement by Menem's foreign minister that the Argentine government sought 'carnal relations' with the US was widely known in South America. However, both before and after the Menem era, it was clear to both governments that closer ties between them was a condition for strengthening their position in the Americas, even if it remained weak in the larger context.

For these reasons, Mercosur has since its inception never been merely about common markets and economic institutions, any more than this was the case of the European Community created by France and Germany. Studies of monetary unification experiences have repeatedly pointed out that, in fact, many, if not most, of the conditions listed for the formation of OCAs may be endogenous. Trade integration, factor mobility and shock symmetry may all increase *after* a currency area is established, as the European Union experience seems to strongly suggest. In fact, the only really crucial condition may be the one that the literature treats in the least detail: the desire to reach political unity.

In this context, one can see that monetary unification actually has a low priority, in part because current conditions, either in terms of the state of both economies or in terms of policy instruments and structures do not seem propitious for such a step, and also because it would not necessarily contribute substantially to advancing the *political* cause of unification in the near and medium-term future, given that many other questions, particularly those related to industrial localization, remain to be resolved.

A common currency could, certainly, contribute somewhat to the stabilization of trade flows between the two countries. Both countries now adopt floating exchange rates. But exchange rates, especially in Brazil, are very volatile, primarily because of financial transactions with the US dollar that were largely liberalized in the 1990s. In the absence of capital controls, the Brazilian economy is very vulnerable to balance-of-payments shocks, which manifest themselves primarily through nervous changes in the exchange rate. The same vulnerability, on the other hand, has a strong influence on the determination of domestic interest rates. Argentina, in contrast, adopted extensive capital controls on both inflows and outflows after the December 2001 crisis. Interest rates are much lower and exchange rates are more stable than in Brazil.

In addition, Argentina is still undergoing a period of uncertainty regarding the behaviour of such important aggregates as public debt, while Brazil is persisting in its attempts to follow IMF macroeconomic policy guidelines. The weight of inherited imbalances, on both sides, makes it very difficult to envisage which institutions could be created to ensure the success of a currency union, even if the other problems discussed above could somehow be resolved or minimized.

One point is, however, very clear: it would definitely be in *neither* country's interest to reproduce Maastricht-like pre-conditions for monetary unification, as proposed by some economists.[22] The opposition to such conditions is not due to the idea that they are not enforceable in developing countries. Rather, the Maastricht Treaty, and the Stability and Growth Pact which accompanied it, seem to be no more than a glorified revival of the Treasury View, that one would suppose to have been buried by Keynes, albeit with the addition of new classical appreciation for independent central banks. This is not the place to critically examine the meaning of central-bank independence, and the rather obsolete ideas on fiscal balance present in the Pact.[23] Suffice it to note that the virtual repeal of the Pact stipulations by France and Germany indicates how misdirected those stipulations are.

Conclusions

Fixed exchange rates reduce price uncertainty and stimulate trade. It was for no other reason that a fixed, but adjustable, exchange-rate system was created at Bretton Woods in 1944. Trade is still relatively unimportant in both Brazil and Argentina. Mutual exports are a significant share of each country's total exports, but foreign trade is still a low proportion of their GDP. Despite the tensions between Argentine and Brazilian producers, trade could certainly expand and benefit the region.

It is certainly much less clear, however, that trying to create a common currency, or even setting the creation of a common currency as a long-term goal, would significantly boost integration. A stronger effort at macroeconomic policy coordination would be helpful to strengthening both economies. Even more important would be the adoption of common protective devices, such as capital controls, given that external vulnerability to adverse capital flows was and still is, directly or indirectly, the source of most of their problems. In this context, a common currency would seem to demand too much and offer too little.

Notes

1. This conclusion seems more or less inevitable in the case of Mundell (1961). McKinnon's (1963) case, however, based on trade integration, rather than labour mobility, is more ambiguous.
2. As Mundell (1961) correctly pointed out, fixed exchange rates are in and of themselves a form of unifying currencies.
3. See, for instance, Alesina, Barro and Tenreyro (2002), pp. 4–5: 'these small countries may lack the size needed to provide effectively some public goods that are subject to large economies of scale or to substantial externalities. Money may be one of those goods: a small country may be too small for an independent currency to be efficient.'
4. Löchel (1998) proposes a model in which a threshold is determined starting at which a common currency becomes preferable to a national currency based on considerations such as the ones stated here. The natural conclusion of the model, however, is that once the threshold is reached, monetary integration should be complete, an implication that runs against the available evidence.
5. As McKinnon (2000) pointed out, this change of position explains the apparent paradox of having Mundell as a strong supporter of the euro, even though Euroland could hardly qualify as an OCA if his criteria were taken seriously.
6. According to McKinnon, Mundell was a 'Keynesian' in 1961, willing to intervene in the economy, but became '[neo-]classical' later.
7. The restricted nature of the European Central Bank notwithstanding.
8. As Stiglitz and Greenwald (2003) show, even if the central bank is restricted to decisions about monetary policy, it will influence those two functions, because, to a certain extent, the three areas (monetary policy, financial regulation and provision of liquidity to banks) are interchangeable. So one may say that, the ECB produces financial regulation without realizing it.
9. In Western Europe, the creation of capital markets of similar size to that of the United States was a strong argument in favour of the euro. So far, the results have been disappointing, given the inability of Euroland countries to harmonize their regulation and tax systems.
10. See, for example, Alesina, Barro and Tenreyro (2002), who suggest that national pride should be redirected toward winning in the Olympics! Such irony shows the intellectual poverty of economists addressing such problems.
11. See also Hawkins (2002).
12. It may not be a coincidence that resistance against the euro comes from countries like England, which also strongly resists the federalist tendencies of continental European countries.
13. Argentina tried to obtain some consideration of its needs by the Federal Reserve when it proposed to move from its currency board to full dollarization in the late 1990s, but was rebuffed by the US authorities.
14. Some authors suggest that nothing of substance is really lost in terms of monetary independence, at least in developing countries with open capital accounts, since they are already prevented from adopting counter-cyclical monetary policies. Interest rates have to be raised when recession conditions in these countries spark episodes of capital flight, or when policy credibility is

low for any other reason. As to the possibility that gains in exchange-rate and price stabilization may be overestimated, see Levine and Markovic (2001).

15. Frankel (1999) argues that this principle is valid not only in terms of the choice between fixed and floating exchange rate regimes, but also in terms of intermediate regimes. Going against the modern trend in favour of either irrevocably fixed or purely floating exchange rates, Frankel defends the view that intermediate regimes may offer better choices for different countries, depending on the specifics of each country.

16. See, for instance, Rose (2001).

17. One should keep in mind that dollarization is a bit of a misnomer since it is frequently used to refer to the adherence to any strong currency, be it the US dollar, the euro or the yen.

18. Eichengreen (1998) describes the Cavallo Plan as 'Byzantine'.

19. It is interesting, for instance, that Alesina, Barro and Tenreyro (2002), who seem to be interested in the question of unification precisely as a stabilization device, conclude that Brazil would probably gain by anchoring its currency mostly to the euro, while Argentina might not have anything to gain from any anchoring. Levine and Markovic (2001) are also critics of dollarization as a commitment device.

20. As Hawkins (2002) warns, one must be careful when using GDP series to identify macroeconomic shocks, since they exhibit the joint result of the shock *and* of the policies implemented to deal with it.

21. One should keep in mind that both Brazil and Argentina are *developing* countries, where, almost by definition, economic structures are still transitory. This makes the disputes around the localization of industries in the region all the more dramatic, certainly more so than in Western Europe, for instance.

22. One example of such a proposal is Giambiagi (1999). It should be noted, however, that Mundell (1997) states that '[t]he Maastricht approach is not the only route to monetary union'. Wyplosz (1997) explains the treaty as a compromise between the demand by Germany that a new currency reproduce essential traits of German monetary regulation, and the demand of the remaining participants for a voice in the monetary policy process.

23. A criticism of the proposal of central bank independence from a Keynesian point of view is offered by Carvalho (1995/6). Criticisms of the Maastricht's conditions and the Stability and Growth Pact, as examples for Mercosur are given by Arestis *et al.* (2003).

Bibliography

Alesina, A., Barro, R. and Tenreyro, S., *Optimal Currency Areas*, NBER Working Paper Series, WP 9072 (2002).

Arestis, P., Ferrari Filho, F., de Paula, L. F. and Sawyer, M., 'The Euro and the EMU: Lessons for Mercosur', in Arestis, P. and de Paula, L. F. (eds), *Monetary Union in Mercosur: Lessons from EMU* (Aldershot: Edward Elgar, 2003).

Carvalho, F.C., 'The Independence of Central Banks: A Critical Assessment of the Arguments', *Journal of Post Keynesian Economics*, 18 (2), Winter (1995/6).

Eichengreen, B., *Does Mercosur Need a Single Currency?* NBER Working Paper Series, WP 6821 (1998).

Frankel, J., *No Single Currency Regime Is Right for All Countries or at All Times*, NBER Working Paper Series, WP 7338 (1999).

F. Giambiagi, 'Mercosur: Why Does Monetary Union Make Sense in the Long-run?' *Ensaios BNDES*, 12, December (1999).

Hawkins, J., *Financial Aspects of Regional Currency Areas*, 2002. http://sceco. univ-aix.fr/cefi/colloques/hawkins.pdf

Levine, R. and Markovic, M., 'How Much Bang for the Buck? Mexico and Dollarization', *Journal of Money, Credit and Banking*, 33 (2), May (2001).

Löchel, H., *The European Monetary Union and the Theory of Optimum Currency Areas* (1998). http://www.bankakademie.de/Homepage/HFB_edu/Navigator/Faculty/ Show/simple/Prof_Loechel_E

McKinnon, R., 'Optimum Currency Areas', *American Economic Review*, 53 (4), September (1963).

McKinnon, R. *Mundell, the Euro, and Optimum Currency Areas*, 2000. http://www-econ.stanford.edu/faculty/workp/swp00009.pdf

Mundell, R., 'A Theory of Optimum Currency Areas', *American Economic Review*, 51 (4), September (1961).

Mundell, R., *Optimum Currency Areas* (1997). http://www.columbia.edu/~ram15/ eOCATAviv4.html

Rose, A., *Common Currency Areas in Practice* (2001). http://www.sfu.ca/~kkasa/ rose.pdf

Stiglitz, J. and Greenwald, B., *Towards a New Paradigm in Monetary Economics* (Cambridge: Cambridge University Press, 2003).

Stockman, A., 'Optimal Central Bank Areas, Financial Intermediation, and Mexican Dollarization', *Journal of Money, Credit and Banking*, 33 (2), May (2000).

Wyplosz, C., 'EMU: Why and How It Might Happen', *Journal of Economics Perspectives*, 11 (4), Fall (1997).

Comment

Manfred Nitsch

Is Mercosur ripe for monetary integration?

Since its foundation, Mercosur has been rather successful as far as infrastructure, trade, foreign investment and political democratization are concerned. However, various monetary regimes and policies have been sources of crises and serious tensions.

The discrepancy between Cavallo's *Convertibility Plan* of 1991 and Cardoso's *Plano Real* in 1994 as well as Brazil's devaluation of the real in 1999 and the crisis that hit Argentina in 2001 have led to an intensive search for options and solutions in the monetary field (see Berg and Borensztein, 2000; Calvo and Reinhart, 1999; Eichengreen, 1998; Giambiagi, 2000; Sangmeister, 2000 and 2001). Uruguay and Paraguay have tried to stabilize their real exchange rates within a certain band with the US dollar, avoiding both the rigidity of Argentina and the costs of managing their float with a bias toward overvaluation, like Brazil before 1999 (see IMF, 2001). But both countries were also hit hard by the Argentine developments so that a certain openness for new solutions can be detected throughout Mercosur. With the imminent solution of Argentina's acute moratorium crisis, fresh debates on options in the monetary realm are to be envisaged, to which Fernando Cardim de Carvalho (FCC) is making an important contribution. The following comment is an attempt to carry his rather convincing arguments a bit further.

FCC places the question as to whether Argentina and Brazil should form a monetary union in a historical context, referring to the recent experience of those two countries as well as to the euro in Europe and to full dollarization in countries like Ecuador and El Salvador. He leaves out the smaller Mercosur member states and the associated countries, as well as the vision of comprehensive South American integration of such leaders as Lula and Kirchner, which might be understandable and justifiable from a purely economic viewpoint. However, FCC himself emphasizes the fact that integration always has an overarching political dimension, which should not be ignored by analysts. The European experience shows the eminent importance of the smaller states and their special interests when it comes to regional cooperation and integration, particularly in the monetary field.

From a European viewpoint, not only the latent rivalry with the USA with regard to market access in Latin America and to monetary hegemony in the global financial markets is of interest, but also the question as to whether the European Union and the euro process could provide a model for South American integration. As is to be expected, the euro had sparked a vivid debate on monetary affairs in the economics profession, some highlights of which should be of interest in commenting FCC. Since the policy conclusions vary considerably, it is not *l'art pour l'art* academic disputes which are at stake, but rather entrenched interests and sometimes fundamentally differing views of society as a whole.

A fresh look at the theories of money and monetary integration

In the neoclassical tradition, money can be seen as a veil over the real economy, providing a means of exchange on spot markets and a store of value. Disturbances and crises are the results of policy rather than of market failures, since market economies fundamentally tend toward stable, full-employment equilibrium. When confidence in politics and local currencies is lacking, anchoring strategies such as currency board arrangements and even full dollarization look like the logical outcomes of today's globalization trend. Perhaps some kind of compensation for the loss of seigniorage should be envisaged as part of the abandonment of national 'funny money' as an obsolete item of local folklore. Mainstream economics tends toward that point of view.

The other view on money, which is the one I prefer, sees money as a means of deferred payment in the tradition of Keynes, who strove for a 'monetary theory of production' (Keynes, 1933). In an uncertain world, the denomination of debt – and that is what a currency is about – becomes crucial for production, employment and growth, since modern enterprises are modeled as capital-market driven and dominated entities. Banks and other financial intermediaries are seen as precarious and fragile edifices built on trust and always subject to the threat of bank runs. Confidence rests on a reliable central bank with responsibilities for the control of inflation as well as the functioning of the banking system, and serving as a lender of last resort in a permanent fleet-in-being type manner, not only as an exceptional *deus ex machina* in the case of individual illiquid banks.

Debt is not the only item denominated in this or that currency; wages, taxes and public expenditure are, too. In a world of free unions and collective bargaining, nominal wages are negotiated between employers and trade unions, and it is here, on the labour market, that inflation rates are determined. Similarly, the political sovereign, the electorate, elects parliaments which determine the budgets of the executive branch of government, and thus decide the fiscal aspect of the inflationary or deflationary processes. Money is hence more than a means of payment in spot markets and a store of value in the balance sheets of savers and investors; it is the denominator of claims and debts, taxes and budgets, salaries and cost-accounting in an uncertain future and a dynamic environment. The coherence of a capitalist, democratically ruled society depends on the interplay between incomes, fiscal and monetary policies. To abdicate monetary autonomy signifies making labour relations less meaningful, or even putting free labour relations and political democracy at risk. The modern nation-state is built on the 'Westphalian model', meaning the system established after the Thirty Years' War in Europe (1618–48), in the Peace of Westphalia, which established the sovereign territorial state and the fundamentals of modern international law, and endowed each nation with a currency of its own.

This view of monetary affairs can be carried a step further, modeling not only a monetary theory of production and allocation but – with the recognition of Schumpeter's theory of economic development (1912) – one of accumulation and growth. Schumpeter's entrepreneur does not save and invest his own resources, but rather is endowed *ex nihilo* by his banker with a loan, which enables him to establish an innovative firm buying assets from the '*Wirt*', a cue word of Schumpeter's which is not easily translatable, meaning an economic agent who uses his own resources in a traditional way. In addition, the entrepreneur uses the bank loan to hire labour. The banker in turn has to rely on a central bank as a lender of last resort when indulging in this type of risky business, because deposit-taking does not precede the creation of credit but follows it. And if the *Wirt* and the employee prefer cash to bank deposits, the banker runs into trouble, because he can create credit, but not money. The first author to pinpoint this interplay between commercial banks and the central bank was Bagehot with his seminal *Lombard Street*

(1873), in which he described the imperative of the lender of last resort as: that of lending freely at a penalty rate, against good collateral. Writing her doctoral dissertation in the tradition of the Berlin School of Monetary Keynesianism (see Collignon, 2002; Fritz, 2001; Nicolas, 1995; Nitsch, 1998, 1999 and 2002; Riese, 1997 and 2004; Riese and Spahn, 1989; Roy, 2000; Roy and Betz, 2000; Schelkle, 2001), Porcelluzzi (2004) recently drew on historical case studies to emphasize the importance of the permanence of an open discount window to ensure an adequate money supply in normal times, not only in case of crises. In an open economy, the Central Bank has to defend its currency against competition in the portfolios of all economic agents. Higher nominal as well as real interest rates are therefore normal for claims denominated in weaker currencies, reflecting the risk of devaluation. That is something like a country risk rather than an indicator for overvaluation which could be eliminated by an appropriately calibrated devaluation. Interpreting the exchange rate as an asset price, the emphasis on confidence and uncertainty leads to the conclusion that there might not be any floor or base to which the exchange rate would have to fall in order to clear the market, because the public may just not be prepared to hold any peso- or rupee-denominated assets in its portfolios. Hyperinflation has often established this scenario as the dominant memory, so that any inflationary move can lead to a panic rush toward full dollarization, as in Ecuador. The resulting global pattern is a hierarchy with some key currencies on top, which promise to revaluate, other convertible currencies with flexible exchange rates but with no structural revaluation or devaluation bias, and then the whole spectrum of weak and very weak currencies, which have to offer ever higher nominal and real returns. Pyramid climbing and descending is possible, and that is the daily game being played by monetary authorities and investors. Every currency is permanently on the move upward or downward, and holding claims or running into debt in this or that currency is not only a question for the rich and powerful, but also for families of migrant workers and small businesses all over the world. That is why 'original sin' is somewhat of a misnomer, when used for countries or currencies in which you cannot run into debt, because no creditor accepts them – since as in theology, 'sin' indicates a categorical, not a gradual difference, whereas there is always more or less US dollar or *boliviano* debt, as long as the dollar (or euro) is not adopted as the only legal tender.

This approach runs counter to the prevailing purchasing power parity view, which assumes the existence of a market equilibrium, because the exchange rate is seen as a goods market phenomenon which ignores portfolio reshuffling. Without reliance on purchasing power parity, however, the defence of one's own currency becomes even more precarious and subject to trust and herd behaviour. That is why the Keynesian view, as propagated here, identifies non-inflationary fiscal and income policies as key elements of any 'progressive' (not only 'conservative' as FCC suggests) economic policy in a capitalist constitutional setting, since (1) the lowering of the nominal as well as the real interest rate is essential for favouring investment; (2) fiscal discipline and not running into international debt but striving for a surplus in the trade and current account favours national autonomy and employment; and (3) the defence of the country's own currency with the option of re- or devaluations according to the outcome of wage negotiations and democratic budgeting, contributes to the meaningfulness of democracy and freedom of labour.

Another interesting point with regard to the theoretical approach is FCC's reliance on the Optimal Currency Area (OCA) discussion. In Europe, the OCA issue was hotly debated as the basis for the introduction of the euro, and in this context, the basic contract between the stronger and the weaker states, regions and sectors within the areas of integration was identified and re-discussed: the strong can use their economies of scale and scope and become even more competitive, but they will let themselves being taxed, and the transfer funds, be they called 'coherence' or 'regional' or 'agricultural', will be channelled to the weak, as a kind of compensation. That had been the grand design as long as trade and transfers were at the forefront of the policy instruments (see Tomann, 1997). With monetary integration, a new *quid pro quo* appeared for the weaker states: their interest rates were lowered with the introduction of the euro so that no further increase in transfer funds had to be promised in the Maastricht Treaty. On the other side, stronger currency countries such as Germany would not have to fear real interest rate hikes as long as the partners stick to labour and fiscal discipline as stipulated in that Treaty. One of the academic architects of the euro warned pretty early that a 3 per cent deficit would be too rigid (Collignon, 1997), but even if those magic figures are modified and made more flexible in the near future, the basic contract should remain intact.

Last but not least, the OCA concept has rightly been criticized for being too static and allocation-oriented, whereas money is endogenous and monetary affairs are to be interpreted also in terms of accumulation processes and prospects. With regard to Mercosur, infrastructure comes to mind, recalling the role of railway construction in German unification during the nineteenth century, but the Schumpeterian monetary theory of development sketched above fits into this picture as well, with a prominent role for the central bank, be it in the form of a joint institution, or of separate national banks.

On the basis of these theoretical considerations, the options for monetary policies in the Mercosur can be outlined.

Monetary options in Mercosur

The various possibilities and options for monetary policies can be ordered in the matrix shown in Figure C6.1, in which flexible, fixed and intermediate solutions with regard to the rest of the world and within the Mercosur are depicted.

Ever since the Peace of Westphalia in 1648, every sovereign state or nation has had the right to issue its own currency. In principle, flexible exchange rates are the rule, even though weaker currencies have always been pegged to stronger ones, and sometimes, as in the Bretton Woods era after World War II, a hegemonic system has prevailed. Of course, those rules did not apply to colonies, so that after decolonization, an own currency became as much a symbol of the independence of each new nation as a flag or an army.

This monetary geography (see Cohen, 1998) is changing, particularly with the euro, but also around the dollar, since not only Panama and Liberia, but also, recently, Ecuador and El Salvador have adopted the US dollar as legal tender in their countries. Thus, the corner solutions are full flexibility on the one hand side and full dollarization on the other.

In Europe, the path toward the European Central Bank and the euro can be described as flexible or sometimes intermediate with regard to the outside world, and now fixed within the euro zone, but intermediate within the European Monetary System, which is not congruent either with the euro zone or with the European Union. The Maastricht process can be seen as intermediary in the sense that internally, the parities were converging, with flexible exchange rates toward the outside. For some time, the 'snake in the tunnel' symbolized an intermediate regime both toward the rest of the world and internally, with different bands and corridors. However, such a strategy is probably not feasible in practical terms in Mercosur; as a reference model, a subtropical snake in the tunnel could make sense. Learning from Europe could also mean that a clearing system could provide a first step, as it did in post-war Western Europe.

Among the fixed parity solutions, Cavallo's convertibility plan of 1991 provides an example for fixing the currency toward the outside while floating more or less freely within Mercosur. And toward the end of the Argentine convertibility period in 2001, the suggestion arose as to whether Brazil should also peg its currency to the US dollar, as FCC reports; 'quasi-dollarization' would have been the result. The *Plano Real* of 1994 and the devaluation of the real in 1999 are measures falling into the 'intermediate' field with regard to the outside world, and the 'flexible' category within Mercosur.

The scheme in the matrix is a logical one; power, interests and also the probabilities of outcome are left out. When turning to scenarios and options, the crucial question is whether weak currencies have anything to gain from joining strong currency areas, as Ecuador has done, whether they should stay alone and sovereign, or cooperate and eventually form a currency union with their equally weak neighbours.

Because of the interdependencies between incomes and fiscal and monetary policies, dollarization seems to be a very risky option, since labour relations as well as democratic pressure tend to lead to higher inflation rates than in the USA, which means that there is a tendency to have all the symptoms of overvaluation and lack of competitiveness within a few years, without the safety valve of devaluation, let alone the option to undervalue the currency and to grow via export surpluses. Deflation policies have proved to be rather depressing, and debt accumulation is not sustainable, so that emigration has become a way, if not the major way, to deal with the economic problems of El Salvador and Ecuador.

The alternative corner solution is national pyramid-climbing through export drives and undervaluation of the currency. That would also mean trying to harden one's currency inside the country, fighting dollarization of deposits and long-term contracts, or at least setting incentives against it. With regard to outside debt in one's own currency, i.e. redemption from 'original sin', South Korea has shown that export credits are a way to introduce the won into the international sphere, and international investments by potent domestic firms are a method used by China to become less of a weak-currency 'sinner'. However, strategies such as these usually redound against the weak neighbours, rather than affecting the strong partners in the world markets, so that, in view of the experience with the real devaluation of 1999 and the Argentine crisis of 2001 and afterwards, and taking into consideration the potential benefits of infrastructure-deepening among the Mercosur countries, this path of unilateralism with beggar-thy-neighbour side effects can neither be expected nor recommended.

What is left supports FCC's conclusions, namely that a common currency demands too much in terms of national autonomy and offers too little in terms of additional lender-of-last-resort potential or

Figure C6.1   Monetary regimes in areas of cooperation and integration

		Own currency/ies			US$
Within		Flexible	Intermediary	Fix	
Towards rest of the world					
Own currency/ies	Flexible	Westphalian regime	Maastricht process	Euro	
	Intermediary	Plano Real	'Snake in tunnel'	–	
	Fix	Cavallo '91	–	Quasi-dollarization	
US$		Full dollarization			

confidence on the side of investors and savers. However, more flexible ways and means of cooperation, such as a certain convergence of policies and common endeavours to boost integration and to harden the currencies, are to be expected and welcomed, so that intermediate solutions on both sides, with a 'snake' in mind, seem appropriate. The summit of Florianópolis in December 2000 has already produced declarations in the direction of a *'pequeño* Maastricht', i.e. stabilization objectives like Europe's Maastricht Treaty. Further steps in favour of accumulation, hardening of currencies, export drives and mobility of labour are still to come.

Bibliography

Bagehot, W., *Lombard Street: A Description of the Money Market* (originally published 1873; London: John Wiley, 1999).

Berg, A. and Borensztein, E., *Full Dollarization: The Pros and Cons*, IMF Economic Issues No. 24 (Washington, DC, 2000).

Calvo, G. A. and Reinhart, C. M., 'Capital Flow Reversals, the Exchange Rate Debit and Dollarization', *Finance & Development*, September (1999): 13–15.

Cohen, B. J., *The Geography of Money* (New York: Cornell, 1998).

Collignon, S., 'Fatale Drei-Komma-Null. Über Konvergenzkriterien und den Zeitplan der Währungsunion', *Wirtschaftswoche*, No. 15, 3 April (1997): 28.

Collignon, S., *Monetary Stability in Europe* (London/New York: Routledge, 2002).

Eichengreeen, B., *Does Mercosur Need a Single Currency?* National Bureau of Economic Research, Working Paper 6821 (Cambridge, MA, 1998).

Fritz, B., *Entwicklung durch wechselkursbasierte Stabilisierung? Der Fall Brasilien* (Berlin, 2001).

Giambiagi, F., 'Mercosul: a unificação monetária faz sentido?', *Política externa* (São Paulo), Vol. 8, No. 3 (2000): 26–53.

IMF, *Uruguay, Washington 2001* (IMF Country Report No. 01/46).

Keynes, J. M., 'A Monetary Theory of Production', Aftalion *et al.*, *Der Stand und die nächste Zukunft der Konjunkturforschung*, Festschrift für Arthur Spiethoff (München: Duncker & Humblot, 1933), pp. 123–5.

Nicolas, A., *Geldverfassung und Entwicklung und Lateinamerika*, Studien zur monetären Ökonomie, Vol. 16 (Marburg: Metropolis, 1995).

Nitsch, M., 'Entwicklungstheorie unter Unsicherheit: Das Investitionsrisiko als Motor und Störquelle von Entwicklung', *Entwicklung & Zusammenarbeit*, August (1998): 200–2; reprinted in: Thiel, Reinold E. (ed.), *Neue Ansätze zur Entwicklungstheorie* (Bonn: Deutsche Stiftung für internationale Entwicklung, 1999) (DSE Themendienst Nr. 10), pp. 312–20; Spanish translation: 'La teoría del desarrollo bajo condiciones de inseguridad. El riesgo en las inversiones como motor y fuente de distorsión para el desarrollo', in Thiel, Reinold E. (ed.), *Teoría del desarrollo. Nuevos enfoques y problemas* (Caracas: Nueva Sociedad, 2001), 101–7.

Nitsch, M., 'Vom Nutzen des monetär-keynesianischen Ansatzes für Entwicklungstheorie und -politik', in Schubert, Renate (ed.), *Neue Wachstums- und Außenhandelstheorie. Implikationen für die Entwicklungstheorie und -politik*, Schriften des Vereins für Socialpolitik NF Vol. 269 (Berlin: Duncker & Humblot, 1999), pp. 183–214.

Nitsch, M., 'Optionen für die monetäre Kooperation im Mercosur', in Calcagnotto, Gilberto and Nolte, Detlef (eds), *Südamerika zwischen US-amerikanischer Hegemonie und brasilianischem Führungsanspruch. Konkurrenz und Kongruenz der Integrationsprozesse in den Amerikas*, Schriftenreihe des Instituts für Iberoamerika-Kunde, Vol. 56 (Frankfurt/M.: Vervuert, 2002), pp. 61–72.

Porcelluzzi, A. A., *Bagehot and the Open Money Supply Approach*, unpubl. doctoral dissertation, FB Wirtschaftswissenschaft, Freie Universität Berlin (Berlin, 2004).

Riese, H., 'Stabilität und Entwicklung – Anmerkungen zur Integration der Dritten Welt in die Weltwirtschaft', in Braig, Marianne, Ferdinand, Ursula and Zapata, Martha (eds): *Begegnungen und Einmischungen. Festschrift für Renate Rott zum 60. Geburtstag* (Stuttgart: Heinz, 1997), pp. 81–107.

Riese, H., *Money, Development and Economic Transformation, Selected Essays by Hajo Riese*, edited by Jens Hoelscher and Horst Tomann (Basingstoke and New York: Palgrave, 2004).

Riese, H. and Spahn, H.-P. (eds), *Internationale Geldwirtschaft*, Studien zur monetären Ökonomie, Vol. 2 (Regensburg: Transfer, 1989).

Roy, T., *Ursachen und Wirkungen der Dollarisierung von Entwicklungsländern. Ein Erklärungsansatz unter besonderer Berücksichtigung Boliviens*, Studien zur monetären Ökonomie Bd. 26 (Marburg: Metropolis, 2000).

Roy, T. and Betz, K., *Währungskooperation im Mercosur*, Diskussionsbeiträge des FB Wirtschaftswissenschaft der FU Berlin No. 2000/15, Volkswirtschaftliche Reihe (Berlin, 2000).

Sangmeister, H., 'US-Dollars für alle in Lateinamerika?', *Brennpunkt Lateinamerika. Politik, Wirtschaft, Gesellschaft*, No. 7, 14 April 2000.

Sangmeister, H., *Zehn Jahre MERCOSUR. Eine Zwischenbilanz*, Ibero-Analysen, Vol. 9 (Berlin, 2001).

Schelkle, W., *Monetäre Integration. Bestandsaufnahme und Weiterentwicklung der neueren Theorie*, Wirtschaftswissenschaftliche Beiträge No. 181 (Heidelberg: Physica, 2001).

Schumpeter, J., *Theorie der wirtschaftlichen Entwicklung* (1912/1934/1987), English translation: *The Theory of Economic Development* (Cambridge: Harvard University Press, 1949).

Tomann, H., *Stabilitätspolitik. Theorie, Strategie und europäische Perspektive* (Berlin: Springer, 1997).

7
So Far from God and So Close to the US Dollar: Contrasting Approaches of Monetary Coordination in Latin America

Barbara Fritz

Introduction

The current international monetary system is commonly characterized as divided into three great currency blocs, with one key currency (the US dollar, the euro and the yen) playing the crucial role in each region. If these currency blocs are defined as regions with lower exchange-rate variability within each of the groups than across groups,[1] this doubtlessly applies most particularly to Euroland, where the creation of the euro simply did away with intra-regional exchange rates. The western hemisphere, however, clearly does not meet this criterion. Exchange-rate variability between countries of North and South America is very high, dramatically highlighted by frequent exchange-rate crises of the Latin American economies.[2]

Therefore, in terms of currency blocs, the western hemisphere can best be seen as an informal dollar bloc (Jameson, 2001, p. 6). There is no doubt that the US dollar is the absolutely dominant key currency in Latin America. In the Latin American economies, *de facto* dollarization as the result of a market-driven process of currency substitution, measured as the proportion of foreign currency deposits in the domestic financial system to total deposits, is high, albeit with significant intra-regional differences.[3] The degree of dollarization is also evidenced by another indicator. The United States Treasury (2000) puts the value of all Federal Reserve notes in circulation abroad – the bulk of which presumably is to be found in Latin America – at between 50 and 70 per cent of the total US dollar stock (Porter and Judson, 1996; United States Treasury, 2000). Furthermore, several countries, namely Panama, El Salvador and Ecuador, have opted for full and formal dollarization, abandoning their national currencies, and a number of other countries are considering the idea (even if the enthusiasm for this has diminished somewhat with the dramatic end of the Argentinean currency board regime).

This paper, however, is centred on the argument that dollarization is not the only option of regional monetary integration to be considered in Latin America. For this, we will single out the two most striking, yet greatly contrasting cases of Mexico/NAFTA and of Mercosur. The Mexican case is particularly interesting because, as we argue, even if NAFTA fails to include any formal agreement for monetary coordination, the past ten-year experience has shown that there is good reason to interpret it as a case of implicit monetary coordination (pp. 127–32). In the case of Mercosur, the Southern Cone's free trade agreement covering Brazil, Argentina, Uruguay and Paraguay, the ambitious plans for monetary coordination have found their maximum expression in the project of a common regional currency (popularly labelled the 'merco', in obvious allusion to the euro). In analysing the prospects of a common Mercosur currency as a case of South–South monetary coordination (pp. 132–40), we will particularly focus on first, the lack of internal hierarchies in terms of currency quality which, in our view, severely limits the stabilization gains to be obtained by a regional common currency; and second, on the question as to how far the differing debt structures in the Mercosur economies constitute an obstacle to establishing common exchange-rate regimes; and third, on the importance of a common regional exchange-rate policy due to increased symmetries with regard to external shocks. In the Conclusions (pp. 140–1) we will draw a preliminary balance of the diverging prospects of monetary regimes within the informal dollar bloc of the western hemisphere.

NAFTA as North–South trade integration with no monetary coordination

NAFTA is a paradigmatic case of a North–South regional integration, bringing together economies with no or low 'original sin' – the United States and Canada (the 'North') – and a net foreign-currency debtor economy, Mexico (the 'South'). The North American Free Trade Area (NAFTA), established in 1994 between the United States, Canada and Mexico, had intensive effects in terms of regional integration of the participating economies. With 50 per cent of foreign trade staying within the free trade zone, the degree of integration is much higher than in the case of other Latin American free trade agreements (data for 2000; IDB, 2002, p. 26f.). However, the NAFTA agreement does not include any kind of macro-economic or monetary coordination. While, against the original intention, efforts are underway in some areas to move from the free-trade zone towards a common-market scheme (Gratius, 2002), there are as yet no such initiatives for institutionally coordinated monetary or exchange-rate policies. The only exception is the so-called swap line, an agreement between the central banks of the three countries to dedicate a quite limited sum of money to supporting transnational payments.[4] Since Mexico on its own – being a country afflicted by original sin – can manage exchange rate fluctuations only to limited degree, and at high economic cost, the lack of supra-national monetary coordination within NAFTA is problematic for the economy. The country has to undertake great efforts to achieve comparable levels of competitiveness if it wants to avoid major economic losses due to integration, while there is no coordinated support or effort to stabilize its currency from the US central bank. Effectively, there are no indications that the United States should be willing to actively promote an explicit integration of Latin American economies into its currency area, as would be achieved by admitting the Mexican central bank as the thirteenth member of the Federal Reserve. An explicit, institutionalized and rules-based extension of the Fed's lender-of-last-resort function to Mexico's financial system, which would enable a lowering of its interest rates due to substantially decreased devaluation expectations, does not seem to be in the offing in the foreseeable future (Cohen, 2004; FitzGerald, 2001). As a consequence, Mexico seems stuck between a rock and a hard place. While on the one hand the project of bilateral, coordinated dollarization seems unrealistic in the short and medium term, on the other, the Mexican government rules out – for good reason (see Chapter 1) – the option of unilaterally dollarizing the Mexican economy.[5]

Since the 1970s, with the breakdown of Bretton Woods and the turn towards an international currency regime based on flexible exchange rates, various types of informal or implicit forms of monetary cooperation have emerged. In the past decades, repeated short-term cooperation agreements have marked the relationship between the key currency blocs. However, in general current policies are essentially based on implicit monetary coordination, in which central banks, for the planning and definition of their policies, take into account the manifest or expected actions of other central banks (Muchlinski, 2002, p. 23f.).

Our hypothesis is that a form of monetary coordination has evolved between Mexico and the USA that is not rules-bound and formalized, but marked by a series of discretionary ad hoc policies. In a first step, we analyse the way the United States dealt with the Mexican currency crisis in 1994–5, arguing that economic actors could read the strong US commitment as a signal that the Mexican peso in fact could rely on backing from the US monetary and fiscal authorities – or, in other terms, that within the NAFTA framework, the United States and Mexico were moving towards an implicit monetary coordination arrangement. To support our argument, we will briefly recall the measures taken by the US authorities in response to the crisis as well as the major pros and cons of the debate over the US intervention in favour of the peso. In a further step, we analyse the course of Mexico's monetary policy after the crisis, which gave priority to bringing down inflation quickly, even at a potentially high macroeconomic cost.

The US reaction to the Mexican currency crisis of 1994–5: defending the US economy's southern flank

The series of currency crises in emerging markets in the 1990s in most cases led to sharp economic contractions with severe social consequences. In Mexico, too, the economy suffered a sharp decline, with GDP shrinking by 6.2 per cent in 1995. However, the following years (until the beginning recession of the US economy in 2001) were marked by an impressive growth of an average of 5.4 per cent annually in real terms.

The Mexican economy's 'soft landing' is partly explained by the privileged access to US markets, which permitted an increase in exports – on the basis of significantly reduced real wages[6] – by almost 50 per cent in only two years; this included both *maquila* and other industries (data from *Informe de Gobierno*, 2003). Beyond this, however, the quick and strong US response in favour of stabilizing the Mexican peso certainly was of fundamental significance, since it allowed the Mexican central bank to avoid an extremely restrictive monetary policy in the wake of the peso's collapse.

Within a few days after the spectacular collapse of the Mexican peso, the Clinton administration had achieved three things: it had provided an official US credit line of $20 billion,[7] it had convinced the IMF to extend a similarly large loan of $17.8 billion, and it had mustered additional support from the Bank for International Settlements (BIS) in Basle funded by European central banks. The explanation given for these highly unusual steps is instructive. President Clinton argued that Mexico's financial troubles were not only a problem for the United States' southern neighbour, but also a danger for the future prospects of the US economy (Weintraub, 2000, p. 139).

The critics, mainly from the conservative side of the US political establishment, rejected this intervention as a mere bail-out of investors who had underestimated the risks of their business dealings, and advocated leaving the resolution of the currency crisis to market forces. In fact, there is little doubt that the losses US investors would have had to face in the case of Mexico's insolvency was a driving force behind the government's action.[8] In contrast to most South American countries, US–Mexican trade and financial relations are intensive also from the US viewpoint, in whose currency the great majority of its debt is denominated. This is an advantageous situation to the extent that the US hence must have a genuine interest in maintaining the Mexican economy's fundamental functioning and solvency. In line with this, the USA conditioned its credit guarantees on, among other things, the mortgaging of Mexican oil revenues.

This rapid and large US credit line was essential for the consolidation and reactivation of the Mexican economy, since it reestablished the country's solvency thus enabling its return to the international capital market within a very short time. What it did not prevent, however, was a profound crisis of the Mexican banking sector that has had devastating consequences for Mexican growth during the following years. Even years after the crisis, non-export-oriented Mexican companies continue to suffer from a chronic lack of credit opportunities, which severely affects their international competitiveness. As the ratio of credit to GDP decreased from 49 per cent in 1994 to 17 per cent in 2002 (Martínez *et al.*, 2004, p. 295f.), the credit sector turned into a bottleneck for the productive sector oriented towards the domestic market, as most firms in this sector suffer from restricted access to international finance (Krueger and Tornell, 1999). The reasons for these shortcomings are to be sought partly in the financial crisis itself, that created strong balance-sheet effects for most banks and deteriorated the loan quality, as a large number of Mexican companies and consumers faced insolvency. But in addition to crisis effects, there are also structural reasons for the growth-limiting functioning of the Mexican banking sector. Bad privatization in the early 1990s laid the basis for the crisis, as the government failed to create adequate institutions to promote prudential rules and to adequately supervise the sector. Moreover, after the crisis, the problem was further aggravated as bad credits in the banks' books were recognized only gradually, leading to high fiscal costs and highly prudent behaviour by the banks; also, such institutional reforms as an effective insolvency law have remained incomplete to this today (Haber, 2004; Martínez *et al.*, 2004).

Mexico's monetary policy after the crisis: the dilemma of unilateral exchange-rate stabilization

Mexico is no longer seeking monetary convergence with the US through the pegging of its exchange rate, but rather through a policy of inflation-targeting. Nevertheless, the country still suffers from a problem typical of developing economies with no formal integration into regional monetary coordination schemes and with open capital accounts. As Flassbeck points out (Chapter 4), even a slightly diverging inflation trend between two open economies is sufficient for short-term interest-rate-differential-driven capital flows to force the central bank of the country with higher inflation to let its currency appreciate – or face severe fiscal costs of sterilization. However, such appreciation reduces the international competitiveness of the country's production, creating balance-of-payment problems in the medium term.

Mexico is a prime example of this dilemma. In 2001, the Mexican central bank established inflation targets of 6.5 per cent for 2001, 4.5 per cent for 2002, and 3.0 per cent for 2003 (Ortiz, 2001),[9] allowing a margin of deviation of one percentage point in each direction. So far, this highly ambitious policy can claim remarkable success, with actual inflation rates not far off the mark (see Table 7.1).

The flip side of this success in inflation control was a contractive monetary policy that accentuated the US recession and let Mexican growth rates decline from 2001 through 2003. In addition, and in part due to a historical low of inflation rates in the US, Mexican inflation remained above that of the US. The result was a strong real appreciation of the Mexican peso, due to interest rate-driven capital imports.[10]

According to official Mexican data, the real exchange rate, on the basis of 1990, in May 2002 was overvalued by 37.5 per cent (*Informe de*

Table 7.1 Mexico: selected data, 1995–2003

	1995	1996	1997	1998	1999	2000	2001	2002	2003
Real growth (annual change)	−6.1	5.4	6.8	5.1	3.6	6.7	−0.3	0.7	1.2
Annual inflation in %	52.0	27.7	15.7	18.6	12.3	9.0	4.4	5.7	4.0
Real exchange rate (1990 = 100)	117.3	103.1	86.0	84.8	77.8	69.0	63.0	59.0	n.a.
Current account	−0.6	−0.8	−1.9	−3.8	−2.9	−3.1	−2.9	−2.1	−1.4

Sources: *Informe de Gobierno* (2003); and CEPAL (2004)

Gobierno, 2002, p. 289). This was even higher than the real exchange rate value prior to the 1994–5 currency crisis – a crisis widely explained as a consequence of a non-sustainable overvaluation of the Mexican currency. In this context, the rigid pro-cyclical policy of the Mexican central bank met with harsh criticism. However, strict adherence to orthodox recipes as a signal to the US government and central bank would provide the best possible argument for renewed intervention in favour of the peso, in the case of the peso again being interpreted as an overvalued currency, since the causes for crisis could then hardly be seen in domestic policy errors, but rather in external shocks.

If in fact the United States accepts such a role, including the willingness to repeat a similarly comprehensive intervention as in the 1994–5 crisis, Mexico would be in a unique and privileged position among the uncoordinated dollar-bloc countries of the western hemisphere. Mexico would not be left alone in its attempt to stabilize its exchange rate, but could count on the lender-of-last-resort facilities of the US central bank in a more or less explicit manner. The consequence most probably would be increasing confidence in the stability of the peso, permitting lower interest rates and higher domestic investment, and resulting in higher growth rates.

At present however, US acceptance of such a role as the *de facto* lender of last resort for the Mexican peso is anything but certain. If it were to come about, such an implicit regime of monetary coordination could induce speculative attacks aimed at testing the interventionist commitment of the Federal Reserve. Therefore, to gain the full benefits of monetary coordination, the implicit coordination scheme should at some point give way to a formal monetary arrangement within NAFTA.

A common currency for the Mercosur: narrow limits – better than nothing

The proposal for a common currency in Mercosur has been launched on several occasions and by very different actors over the past ten years (see Chapter 6 of Carvalho in this book). The Argentinean and Brazilian presidents, Néstor Kirchner and Lula, have both repeatedly declared the deepening of the Mercosur integration process a high political priority, and they have underscored their political will to establish a common currency. Although these declarations have not yet materialized in practical policy, this fact should not be an argument against advancing the academic debate on the issue.[11] According to the World Bank's criteria for grouping debtor economies, Mercosur unites a group of economies which are not able to borrow abroad in domestic currency, but which instead are highly indebted in foreign currency. Therefore, all of them are rated as economies with a maximum index of original sin (Eichengreen, Hausmann and Panizza, 2003, p. 43). This means that any regional monetary coordination within Mercosur, ranging from ad hoc exchange-rate coordination all the way to a common regional currency, would suffer from the fundamental limitations of an SSC agreement. The introduction of a 'merco' would not be able to fundamentally change the rather low stabilization capacity which is the result of the member states' common status as net external debtors in foreign currency, and their consequent problems of currency mismatches and limited lender-of-last-resort facilities, except that the effects of an increased size of the currency area could provide international investors with an incentive to include the 'merco' in their portfolios, as Panizza argues in his chapter in this book.

Most existing literature ignores these limitations, both in the general treatment of currency unions (i.e. Alesina and Barro, 2000; Bayoumi and Eichengreen, 1994; De Grauwe, 1994) and in the cost-benefit evaluations for a common Mercosur currency. Comparing the project of a common Mercosur currency with that of the euro – by now the natural reference for all common currency projects – most of the literature mainly emphasizes the disciplining effects of a type of Maastricht Treaty for the Mercosur countries (e.g. Giambiagi, 1999; Zahler, 2001). Some authors point out specific problems of the EMU process which the Mercosur should avoid repeating (Eichengreen, 1998, p. 31; Arestis *et al.*, 2003). The only exceptions to be found are those of the IDB (2002, p. 194) and Levy Yeyati and Sturzenegger (1999, p. 86f.). These commentators do indeed point to the lack of credibility gains due to the absence of a regional key currency.

The following analysis of the Mercosur's common currency project will – along the lines of arguments drawn in Fritz/Metzger in this book – focus first on the problem of the lack of internal hierarchies within Mercosur, second on the additional problem of differing debt structures of the member states; and third on the question of symmetries with regard to external monetary and financial shocks.

Lack of internal hierarchies

Argentina and Brazil, Mercosur's two main economies, show certain differences in the level of external indebtedness (liability dollarization), the most striking one being that Argentina has been in default for part of its external debt since 2001, whereas Brazil is making major efforts to maintain its payment capacity (for external as much as for internal public debt), receiving continued IMF liquidity assistance. However, this certainly is not sufficient to enable the Brazilian real to serve as a regional anchor currency. Even if the Brazilian economy is considered to be in better shape than the Argentinian, at least since the Argentinian default, the Brazilian central bank cannot intervene to stabilize the Argentinian currency *vis-à-vis* the US dollar, if needed, as this would require large quantities of foreign currency. Brazil itself, however, suffers from a severe foreign currency shortage, making continued IMF assistance and an extremely tight monetary and fiscal policy necessary to preclude any doubts regarding its ability to service its debt.

Furthermore, in almost none of the macroeconomic indicators conventionally taken as references is Brazil's performance convincing enough to place it in the role of a regional leader. Since the beginning of the 1990s, Brazilian inflation rates have been constantly higher than those in Argentina (the only exception is 2002, due to the maxi-devaluation of the Argentinian peso). Based on the criterion of the nominal result of the public budget, both countries are currently running moderate fiscal deficits. Where Brazil in fact stands out with significantly better results is the stock of public debt in relation to GDP; while in Brazil this at present is approximately 60 per cent, the net public debt in Argentina has reached 140 per cent of GDP (Dec. 2003; all data from GMM).

Except for the fact that accepted supra-national rules for monetary and fiscal policy could contribute to minimizing the influence of political pressure groups at the national level pushing for inflation-financed public expenditure, and that the merco would represent an increased currency area that could in the long run possibly help to reduce original sin, the core problems of macroeconomic instability in the Mercosur countries stemming from original sin would remain, at least in the short run.

Implications of different debt structures

Even if there is no significant difference in the level of international original sin between Argentina and Brazil, the monetary regimes of the two economies have differed markedly. As Fernández-Arias *et al.* (2002, p. 24) state:

> Differences in the structure of liabilities may lead countries to respond to common shocks with different policies. A country where most financial liabilities are short-term and denominated in domestic currency is more likely to respond to a shock with a devaluation than a country where most liabilities are denominated in foreign

currency... Different debt structures may therefore generate important exchange-rate disagreements. Should countries take into account the potential divergence in exchange rates when choosing partners for regional integration agreements?

Debt structure in terms of currency, maturity and coupon (fixed or indexed rate) has been differing widely between Argentina and Brazil. Dollarization of the domestic financial system in Argentina until the mid-1990s was below 40 per cent, climbing to more than 70 per cent, in terms of deposits, in 2001 (Mecon, cited in Hujo, 2002, p. 263). In Brazil, however, dollarization during the 1990s has been below 20 per cent,[12] leaving much more room for financial contracts in domestic currency.[13]

The difference in the level of dollarization helps to explain the differences in the exchange-rate regime options followed by both countries during the 1990s (see Fritz, 2000). Both opted for a peg, seeking to fight inflation by stabilization import. After its traumatic hyperinflationary experience at the end of the 1980s, Argentina in 1991 opted for a very strict peg in the form of a currency board with an extreme fix on the exchange rate. The conventional explanation focused on the credibility import aspect, by tying the national politicians' hands. However, seen from the perspective of a highly dollarized economy, the Argentinian convertibility plan can also be understood as a strategy of market-driven de-dollarization, and of the re-establishment of the domestic currency, by subjecting both currencies to equal conditions on the domestic market.

On the other hand, the Brazilian *Plano Real*, implemented in 1994 with a quasi-fixed exchange rate, should not be understood as an 'easier version' of exchange-rate-based stabilization requiring less efforts in terms of fiscal adjustment and productivity gains, but as an attempt to combine the coordination advantages for the price level by a fixed exchange rate with the reduction of incentives for dollarization by loosening the exchange-rate peg (Fritz, 2002, p. 162ff.). Part of this strategy was the introduction of a fictitious unit of account, called URV (*unidade real do valor*), prior to the introduction of a new currency. This step served to reestablish the relative price equilibrium which had been severely distorted by the highly sophisticated system of indexation which operated until the beginning of the 1990s. Dollarizing the economy would have had a similar effect for relative prices, as Gustavo Franco, then president of the Brazilian Central Bank, pointed out (Franco, 1996, p. 8). It may be an exaggeration to say that the plan 'avoided the dollarization process following exactly the opposite path' (Franco, 1996, p. 11), but the Brazilian authorities certainly made it an important goal of their monetary policies to limit effective currency substitution.

While it is important to note these differing inclinations towards a specific exchange rate regime, their consequences for the question debated here should not be overestimated. Even if, during the 1990s, Brazil at first glance appeared more inclined towards a more flexible regime than Argentina, because its lower degree of dollarization reduced currency mismatch costs in case of exchange-rate devaluation (Fanelli and Gonzáles-Rosada, 2003, p. 10), this does not hold true in the broader sense. And even if, compared to Argentina, Brazil's economic crisis after the maxi-devaluation was less dramatic; a closer look shows that the devaluation still had severe consequences for the country's economy.

First, the proportion of financial contracts in domestic currency in Brazil has always been higher, but most internal credit relationships are short-term and often not fixed, but are rather indexed to the interest or the exchange rate; second, the Brazilian government stands out as the major debtor of the Brazilian economy in domestic currency. The composition of public bonds varies over time (see Figure 7.1): with increasing uncertainty, maturities shorten and the share of interest-rate or exchange-rate-indexed bonds increases. The latter especially gain weight in periods with high devaluation expectations. In the pre-devaluation

Figure 7.1 Currency and quasi-currency mismatch of Brazil's public sector debt

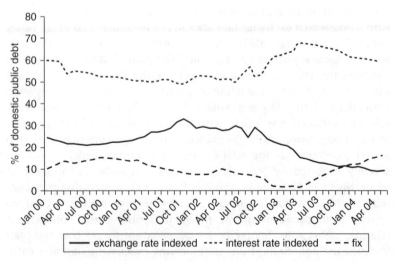

Source: Banco Central do Brasil, Séries temporais

period of 1997–8 for example, these increased from 9.4 per cent of public internal debt in December of 1996 to 21 per cent in December of
1998 (data from the Banco Central do Brasil), with demand coming primarily from private debtors in foreign currency in the form of hedging
against devaluation. This means that in the case of a currency devaluation, the Brazilian state is not only exposed to the negative wealth
effects due to its own foreign debt denominated in foreign currency, but
also to costs of quasi-currency mismatch, as exchange-rate-indexed
bonds are to be honoured not in foreign but in domestic currency – only
that their nominal value has significantly increased. To this must be
added the maturity mismatch, as expressed in the increase of real debt
stemming from interest-rate-indexed bonds, in consequence of tight-
ened monetary policy aimed at avoiding the spillover effects of devaluation upon the price level.

As a result, in the case of the Brazilian maxi-devaluation of 1999, real
income reduction was initially limited, because the costs of currency
mismatch mainly affected the state, whereas the private sector as a
whole was largely shielded from these costs, as the sum of exchange-
rate-indexed public bonds equalled more or less the value of recently
accumulated private foreign debt.[14] In consequence, due to the devaluation, the stock of public debt increased dramatically within a very short
time, from 41.7 per cent of GDP in December 1998 to 50.5 per cent in
January 1999. In spite of the government's continuous austerity policy
since then, public debt has never fallen significantly below 50 per cent,
due to very high real interest rates. Consequently, in 2001, and
especially in 2002, rising uncertainty about the Brazilian state's capacity
(or willingness) to fulfil its extremely high debt-service obligations led to
a new increase in the share of exchange-rate and interest-rate-indexed
bonds. As a result, in combination with a large nominal devaluation and
another tightening of monetary policy, public debt temporarily
increased to more than 60 per cent of GDP in September of 2002 (all
data from the Banco Central do Brasil, Annual Reports; see Figure 7.2).
As uncertainty about Brazil's public payment capacity persists to this
day, and prospects for a decrease in the stock of debt are rather long-
term, total costs stemming from devaluation must be considered very
significant.

This means that even when the timing and sectoral distribution of
devaluation-related effects has been markedly different in Brazil and
Argentina, with more weight given to maturity and quasi-currency mismatches in the case of Brazil,[15] in principle, both are economies marked
by fear of floating: taking into account all macroeconomic consequences,
their exchange-rate-regime preferences should not be significantly

Figure 7.2   Brazil: public debt as a percentage of GDP

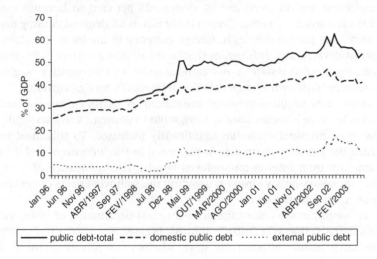

Source: Banco Central do Brasil, Séries temporais

different. Neither of the two economies will quickly return to fixed exchange rates, so that perspectives for regional monetary coordination will probably encounter fewer barriers than in the past. However, it seems to be a precondition for a common monetary and exchange-rate policy that both countries agree on a similar policy towards their creditors, especially the IMF.

Symmetric reactions to external shocks

Even if a 'merco' would not *per se* reduce the regional economies' exposure to international financial volatility, a system of bloc floating towards the rest of the world still could make sense as a tool for facing common external shocks. Of course, the advantage might not consist so much in the elimination or full absorption of these shocks; nonetheless, stabilization or even elimination of intra-regional exchange-rate variability could prevent beggar-thy-neighbour-policies with their potentially highly negative effects for the entire region. Furthermore, it could to a certain extent elevate the efficiency of regional monetary policy in response to external shocks, as it would minimize diverging and potentially conflicting macroeconomic responses.

There is broad agreement that the volatility of international capital flows has grown greatly over the past decades, due to increasing capital account liberalization; that the level of volatility has been constantly

much higher in southern than in northern economies; and that financial shocks have come to outweigh terms-of-trade shocks, and have
gained in significance. This holds true, too, for regional economic
arrangements (IDB, 2002, p. 153): volatility of capital flows towards
South–South free trade areas, including Mercosur, has always been significantly higher than capital flow-related volatility towards the
European Union, and it has been increasing constantly since the 1970s.
Empirical studies on the reaction to these volatile capital flows within
the Mercosur member economies confirm the symmetry hypothesis.
Carrera (1998) found that external shocks did hit the Mercosur
economies in a more symmetrical manner than did internal shocks.
Fanelli and Gonzáles-Rozada (2003), by calculating the trend growth
rate of the real GDP of three Mercosur economies (Argentina, Brazil and
Uruguay), found a very strong correlation between the Mercosur common cycle and the weighted average of country risk premium that signals the volume and direction of capital flows. By contrast, Carvalho
(see Chapter 6) argues that even if the Mercosur economies show a
rather symmetrical behaviour in relation to capital inflows (as both
Brazil and Argentina did receive large amounts of capital from the early
to mid-1990s), shocks related to capital outflows have been more idiosyncratic. Indeed, net capital flows to Brazil did turn negative from 1997
to 2000, and almost did so again in 2002 (data from Banco Central do
Brasil, Balanço de Pagamentos). The first period was marked by increasing devaluation expectations and, from January 1999 onward, by the
crisis in the wake of a maxi-devaluation; 2002 was marked by a high
level of uncertainty over the Brazilian public and international payment
abilities, while in Argentina, net capital flows turned negative only from
2000 onward (CEPAL, 2004). The divergence in capital outflows thus
can be understood as a result of diverging exchange-rate regimes during
the 1990s, due to diverging debt structures.

Between 1999 and 2001, Brazil's flexibilized and strongly devalued
real contrasted sharply with Argentina's currency board and its fixed
exchange-rate regime. This extreme divergence in exchange-rate regimes
caused a serious setback in the real integration of both countries, with
Argentina resorting to strong protectionist reactions against the Brazilian
maxi-devaluation.[16] Here, Mercosur became a paradigmatic case for the
importance of beggar-thy-neighbour problems related to exchange-rate
disagreements in regional free trade agreements (Fernández-Arias *et al.*,
2002; Bobik, 2002). As real integration within Mercosur has been rather
low, with intra-regional trade barely surpassing 20 per cent of the total
foreign trade of its members (data for 2000; IDB, 2002, p. 26f.), this

episode also contrasts with the widespread wisdom[17] that only an advanced degree of integration requires intra-regional exchange rate coordination. This argument may be valid for monetary coordination projects that involve a northern economy. But if we assume highly symmetrical external shocks, which in southern economies cause rather large macroeconomic volatility, the sum of external shock and intra-regional devaluation[18] within an SSC will probably damage regional integration, even if intra-regional trade is at a rather low level.[19] This leads to the conclusion that if members are able to reach an agreement on a common exchange-rate regime, symmetry with regard to reaction to external shocks will increase, facilitating coherence in regional monetary policy-making and endogenously increasing regional integration, fairly independently of the original level of intra-regional trade.

Conclusions

As we have seen, the US dollar's 'sphere of influence' in the Americas forms anything but a monolithic bloc. Taking a closer look at monetary strategies in Latin America, diversity is the game of the day. While some – mostly small Central American – countries are still considering the option of unilateral dollarization, the three major economies of the region, Argentina, Brazil and Mexico, are pursuing alternative options.

NAFTA failed to include any formalized agreement on monetary coordination, and as we have shown, Mexico still has little to expect from NAFTA in terms of *explicit* monetary coordination. However, on the basis of the analysis of the United States' dealing with the Mexican currency crisis in 1994–5 and of the Mexican central bank's monetary policy after that crisis, we argue that Mexico is seeking an implicit regional monetary coordination with the United States. After overcoming the turmoil of the maxi-devaluation, the Mexican central bank in the late 1990s sought monetary convergence with the US at the cost of significantly revaluing the exchange rate. Although this strategy indeed seems to be running some risk of a new currency crisis, it shows some plausibility: only strict adherence to such a rigid market-oriented policy course can hope to convince US authorities to intervene a second time in favour of the Mexican peso, thereby establishing an irregular and informal – but effective – implicit regional monetary coordination within NAFTA. If such coordination were to materialize, it probably would bring fewer gains for Mexico in terms of exchange-rate stabilization and interest reduction than an explicit, formal arrangement. Nevertheless, it would still put Mexico in a privileged position, compared to the rest of Latin

America, as no other economy can count, even if in a reduced and hidden form, on US lender-of-last-resort facilities.

After the traumatic outcome of the Argentinian currency-board experience, the Mercosur economies today are far from considering unilateral dollarization as a viable option; at the same time, however, they are also far from being able to benefit from the Federal Reserve, even as an occasional lender of last resort, in moments of crisis. In this context, and given the member countries' evident difficulties in unilaterally maintaining the domestic currencies' value at a given level and the weight (economic as much as political) given to sub-regional integration by the current governments, there is good reason to look into the prospects for regional monetary coordination. Our analysis shows that due to the lack of an internal hierarchy among currencies all marked by high original sin, only rather limited stability gains can be expected. The main benefits of increased regional monetary coordination will likely consist in a certain reduction in the degree of original sin by creating a common currency with an enlarged area, compared to the existing national currencies, and in eliminating beggar-thy-neighbour policies that can be highly damaging for the whole region. The latter argument, the experience of extremely divergent exchange rates between 1999 and 2001 and their serious negative consequences for regional trade and growth (as well as for the political commitment to the integration project) serves to argue that, against conventional wisdom, exchange-rate coordination in South–South regional integration is necessary, even in cases of a relatively low degree of regional economic integration.

In fact, regional monetary coordination requires rather substantial efforts to make it successful. But in a global financial environment that is expected to continue to be highly unstable at least in the medium term, a regional option will have some attraction, even if its stability gains may be limited.

Notes

1. See Frankel and Wei (1995); Mundell (1995, p. 27f.). The definition is valid independently from the causal nexus between increasing economic regionalization and intra-regional exchange-rate stabilization.
2. Canzeroni (1995, p. 156) estimates exchange-rate variability of the Western Hemisphere at twice the world average. Berg *et al.* (2002, p. 10ff.), evaluating the prospects of a common Latin American currency, do not find more symmetries in exchange-rate variations between Latin American economies than between emerging markets in general.
3. Berg *et al.* (2002), based on IMF data for 2000, distinguish three groups: the first, with dollarization under 20 per cent, includes Chile, El Salvador (prior to

its full dollarization) and Mexico; the middle group (dollarization between 20 and 70 per cent) is made up of Argentina, Costa Rica and Honduras; in the third group of highly dollarized economies (dollarization over 70 per cent) we find Bolivia, Nicaragua, Peru and Uruguay. Brazil and Guatemala are not listed, because foreign-currency deposits are not permitted. Colombia and Venezuela have negligible foreign-currency deposits. Of course, the participation of foreign-currency deposits is not the only – and for certain countries, probably not the most adequate – way of measuring de facto dollarization, but it has the advantage of relying on comparable data.

4. Since the 1940s, the United States and Mexico have a bilateral agreement on a limited central bank credit to support bilateral trade. In the context of the NAFTA agreement, this *swap-line* has been institutionalized while at the same time limited to a total sum of US$6 billion. The statute of this agreement explicitly rules out using this line of credit for the stabilization of the Mexican currency (United States Treasury, 1999). A similar *swap-line* was established between Canada and Mexico, limited to a maximum of US$1 billion.

5. The option of unilateral dollarization for Mexico is critically discussed in Ibarra and Moreno-Brid (2001a und 2001b); FitzGerald (2001). Berg et al. (2002), however, consider Mexico a candidate for unilateral dollarization.

6. As elsewhere, so also in Mexico, the crisis had a negative effect on income distribution. Due to the inflation surge as a result of the peso devaluation, real wages decreased by about 20 per cent between 1994 and 1996, and did not recover their 1994 level until 2001.

7. The government initially planned to ask the US Congress for a credit guarantee of $40 billion, but in the face of resistance there, it chose a different path not requiring congressional approval, and drew on the Exchange Stabilization Fund administered by the US Treasury.

8. An example are the numerous US pension funds that held large-scale investments in Mexican bonds, putting at risk the savings of many small depositors (Stern, 1995, p. 2).

9. The first years after the peso crisis of 1994–5 (with one of its consequences being the return of inflation) were marked by a new monetary regime officially labeled as 'free floating', but largely regarded as insufficient and non-transparent (Mishkin and Savastano, 2002). At the same time, inflation was gradually but steadily brought under control, falling from 52 per cent in 1995 to 9 per cent in 2000.

10. As Flassbeck shows in Chapter 4, Mexico is one of the economies that offers the highest rates of return to international investors; a fact that the author interprets as indicating an unsustainable exchange rate in the medium or long term.

11. Illustrative is the case of the 'Instituto de la Moneda del Mercosur'. Heralded as the embryo of a regional central bank, it has initially been designed as a centre for academic research on the topic. However, even as such it has not yet moved beyond the drawing board (*La Nación*, 15 January 2003). The most important practical advance to date is the formation of a 'Grupo de Monitoreo Macroeconómico' (GMM: Group for Macroeconomic Monitoring for the Mercosur).

12. Data from Freitas (1999, p. 46); since dollar accounts are not permitted in Brazil, we are here using the measure of dollar liabilities in relation to total liabilities of the domestic financial sector.

13. Hausmann and Panizza (2003) define a series of indices for domestic original sin that captures different types of domestically-traded public debt. Therefore, they look first only to the currency in which domestically-traded public bonds are issued (DSIN1), and in a second and third step expand the domestic original-sin index towards short-run and interest-rate-indexed public bonds (DSIN2) and bonds indexed to the price level (DSIN3). Consequently, for 2000, Brazil is computed with an index of DSIN1 of only 0.309, but with a DSIN2 and DSIN3 of respectively 0.915, whereas Argentina's DSIN1 is 0.644, and its DSIN2 and DSIN3 are both at 1 (0 indicates the lowest and 1 the highest index for original sin; Hausmann and Panizza, 2003).

14. Carvalho (1999). The only costs to be covered by the private sector were those of hedging, as exchange-rate-indexed bonds offered lower yields than non-indexed bonds.

15. See the first definition of original sin in Hausmann (1999) that – in addition to the currency mismatches resulting from foreign currency debt – includes maturity mismatches, because it assumes that finance in domestic currency will be exclusively for the short term. By quasi-currency mismatch we mean costs related to exchange-rate-indexed debt.

16. For a detailed description of trade-related disputes and protectionist measures, see Rozemberg and Svarzmann (2002).

17. Eichengreen (1998) has stated this explicitly for the case of Mercosur.

18. Of course the impact of intra-exchange-rate volatility depends on the relative economic weight of the devaluating country within the regional agreement, as Eichengreen also emphasizes (1998, p. 11).

19. This may help to explain why until the 1990s South–South regional integration efforts have not advanced significantly (Schelkle, 2000), and why South–South monetary coordination projects have surged mainly within the context of regionally expanding financial crises.

Bibliography

Alesina, A. and Barro, R. J., *Currency Unions*, NBER Working Paper 7927 (2000).

Arestis, P., Ferrari-Filho, F., Paula, L. F. de and Sawyer, M., 'The Euro and the EMU: Lessons for Mercosur', in Arestis, P. and Paula, L. F. de (eds), *Monetary Union in South America: Lessons from EMU* (Cheltenham: Edward Elgar, 2003).

Banco Central do Brasil, *Boletim do BC – Relatório anual*, various issues. http://www.bcb.gov.br/?BOLETIMANO

Banco Central do Brasil, *Séries temporais*: http://www.bcb.gov.br/?SERIETEMP

Bayoumi, T. and Eichengreen, B., 'One Money or Many? Analyzing the Prospects for Monetary Unification in Various Parts of the World', *Princeton Studies in International Finance*, No. 76 (Princeton, NJ, 1994).

Berg, A., Borensztein, E. and Mauro, P., *An Evaluation of Monetary Regime Options for Latin America*, IMF Working Paper 02/211 (2002). http://www.imf.org/external/pubs/ft/wp/2002/wp02211.pdf

Bobik, M. B., 'Volatilidade cambial, comércio e integração econômica', *Carta Internacional*, Vol. X, No. 122 (2002): 11.

Canzeroni, M., 'Comment on Frankel and Wei', in Genberg, H. (ed.), *The International Monetary System* (Berlin and Heidelberg: Springer, 1995), pp. 154–70.

Carrera, J. E., *Análisis integral de las fluctuaciones macroeconómicas en Argentina y Brasil*. Documento Técnico, No. 1 (Buenos Aires: Centro de Asistencia a las Ciencias Económicas y Sociales, Universidad de Buenos Aires, CACES-UBA, 1998).

Carvalho, C. E., *Surpresas da economia brasileira depois da desvalorização* (São Paulo, 1999), unpublished manuscript.

CEPAL, *Anuario estadístico de América Latina y el Caribe 2003* (Santiago de Chile, 2004).

Cohen, B. J., 'America's Interest in Dollarization', in Alexander, V., Melitz, J. and Furstenberg, G. M. von (eds), *Monetary Union: Why, How, and What Follows?* (London: Oxford University Press, 2004). http://www.polsci.ucsb.edu/faculty/cohen/inpress/#

De Grauwe, P., 'The Need for Real Convergence in a Monetary Union', in Johnson, Christopher and Collignon, Stefan (eds), *The Monetary Economics of Europe* (London: Pinter, 1994), pp. 269–79.

Eichengreen, B., *Does Mercosur Need A Single Currency?* NBER WP No. 6821 (1998).

Eichengreen, B. and Hausmann, R. and Panizza, U., *The Pain of Original Sin*, unpublished manuscript, August 2003.

Fanelli, J. M. and González-Rozada, M., *Business Cycles and Macroeconomic Policy Coordination in Mercosur*, unpublished manuscript, September 2003.

Fernández-Arias, E., Panizza, U. and Stein, E., *Trade Agreements, Exchange Rate Disagreements*, unpublished manuscript (2002).

FitzGerald, V., 'The Winner's Curse: Premature Monetary Integration in the NAFTA', in Bulmer-Thomas, V. (ed.), *Regional Integration in Latin America and the Caribbean: The Political Economy of Open Regionalism* (London: Elgar, 2001).

Franco, G., 'The *Real* Plan', *PUC/RJ*, Dep. Economia, Texto para Discussão, No. 354 (1996).

Frankel, J. A. and Wei, S.-J., 'Emerging Currency Blocs', in Genberg, Hans (ed.), *The International Monetary System* (Berlin and Heidelberg: Springer, 1995), pp. 111–53.

Freitas, C. P. de, 'A ampliação recente da participação estrangeira no sistema bancário', in Paula, L. F. R. de (ed.), *Anais do Seminário 'Perspectivas para o Sistema Financeiro Nacional'* (Rio de Janeiro: Universidade Candido Mendes, 1999).

Fritz, B., *Development or Growth-cum-Debt? Reflections on Latin America's Economic Strategy in a Time of International Financial Instability*, Diskussionsbeiträge des Fachbereichs Wirtschaftswissenschaft der Freien Universität Berlin No. 2000/10, Volkswirtschaftliche Reihe, April (2000).

Fritz, B., *Entwicklung durch wechselkursbasierte Stabilisierung? Der Fall Brasilien*, Studien zur monetären Ökonomie, vol. 28 (Marburg: Metropolis, 2002).

Giambiagi, F., *Mercosul – por que a unificação monetária faz sentido a longo prazo?* Ensaios BNDES (Rio de Janeiro), No. 12, December (1999).

GMM (Grupo de Monitoreo Macroeconómico), *Estadísticas fiscales armonizadas*. http://gmm.mecon.gov.ar/

Gratius, S., 'Acht Jahre NAFTA: vom Freihandelsabkommen zur Nordamerikanischen Gemeinschaft?', *Brennpunkt Lateinamerika*, No. 15 (2002): 153–60.

Haber, S., *Mexico's Experiments with Bank Privatization and Liberalization, 1991–2002* (2004), unpublished manuscript. http://www.worldbank.org/research/wdr/WDR2004/papers/haber_mx.pdf

Hausmann, R., 'Should There Be Five Currencies or One Hundred and Five?', *Foreign Affairs*, Fall: (1999): 66–79.

Hausmann, R. and Panizza, U., 'The Determinants of Original Sin: An Empirical Investigation', *Journal of International Money and Finance*, Vol. 22 (7) (2003): 957–90.

Hujo, K., *Soziale Sicherung im Kontext von Stabilisierung und Strukturanpassung: Die Reform der Rentenversicherung in Argentinien* (Freie Universität Berlin, 2002), unpublished manuscript.

Ibarra, D. and Moreno-Brid, J.-C., 'Currency Boards and Monetary Unions: The Road Ahead or a Cul de Sac for Mexico's Exchange Rate Policy?', in Martín, P. A. and Punzo, L. F. (eds), *Mexico beyond NAFTA: Perspectives for the European Debate* (London and New York: Routledge, 2001a), pp. 3–20.

Ibarra, D. and Moreno-Brid, J.-C., 'La dolarización: Antecedentes y perspectivas para la economía mexicana', *Nueva Sociedad*, No. 172, March–April (2001b): 138–49.

IDB, *Beyond Borders: The New Regionalism in Latin America. Economic and Social Progress in Latin America*, 2002 Report (2002).

Informe de Gobierno [Informe de Gobierno del C. Presidente Vicente Fox Quesada], various issues, Anexo Estadístico. http://cuarto.informe.presidencia.gob.mx/index.php

Jameson, K. P., 'Latin America and the Dollar Bloc in the Twenty-first Century – To Dollarize or Not?', *Latin American Politics and Societey*, Vol. 43, No. 4 (2001): 1–36.

Krueger, A. and Tornell, A., *The Role of Bank Restructuring in Recovering from Crises: Mexico 1995–98*, National Bureau of Economic Research, WP No. 7042 (1999).

Levy Yeyati, E. and Sturzenegger, F., 'The Euro and Latin America III: Is EMU a Blueprint for Mercosur?', Quadernos de Economía, Vol. 37, No. 110 (1999): 63–99.

Martínez, L., Tornell, A. and Westermann, F., 'Globalización, crecimiento y crisis financieras: Lecciones de México y del mundo en desarrollo', *El Trimestre Económico*, Vol. LXXI (2), No. 282 (2004): 251–351.

Mishkin, F. S. and Savastano, M. A., 'Monetary Policy Strategies for Emerging Market Countries. Lessons from Latin America', *Comparative Economic Studies*, Vol. 44, Nos 2–3 (2002): 45–82.

Muchlinski, E., *Explicit or Implicit Monetary Coordination? A Consideration of Historical Aspects*, Diskussionsbeiträge des Fachbereichs Wirtschaftswissenschaft der Freien Universität Berlin, No. 5 (2002).

Mundell, R., *Prospects for the International Monetary System*, Columbia University, Research Study No. 8 (1995).

Ortiz, G. M., *La Política Monetária en México: el esquema de objetivos de inflación y la reducción de la incertidumbre* (2001). www.banxico. org.mx/gPublicaciones/Discursos/ ConvencionBancariaGOM.PDF

Porter, R. D. and Judson, R. A., 'The Location of US Currency: How Much Is Abroad?', *Federal Reserve Bulletin*, Oct., No. 82 (1996): 883–903.

Rozemberg, R. and Svarzmann, G., *El proceso de integración Argentina-Brasil en perspectiva: conflictos, tensiones y acciones de los gobiernos*. Documento elaborado para la División de Integración, Comercio y Asuntos hemisféricos del Banco Interamericano de Desarrollo (2002).

Schelkle, W., 'Regional Integration among Less Developed Economies: Discordant Variations on an Evergreen', Metzger, M. and Reichenstein, B. (eds), *Challenges for International Organizations in the 21st Century* (Basingstoke: Macmillan, 2000), pp. 65–88.

Segundo Informe Presidencial, Anexo Estadístico (2002). http://nt.presidencia. gob.mx/Informes/2002Fox2/website/cfm/anexo.cfm?Id=Informe2-3& NoDiscos=14

Stern, P., *The Mexico Crisis – Doing the Right Thing*, Progressive Policy Institute, Backgrounder (27 January 1995). http://www.ppionline.org/ppi_ci. cfm?knlgAreaID=108& subsecID=900009&contentID=1769

United States Treasury, *Treasury Secretary Robert E. Rubin Statement on Mexico. Office of Public Affairs*, 15 June 1999), RR-3206. http://www.treasury.gov/press/ releases/ rr3206.htm

United States Treasury, *The Use and Counterfeiting of United States Currency Abroad* (Washington, DC, 2000).

Weintraub, S., *Financial Decision-Making in Mexico: To Bet a Nation* (Pittsburgh, 2000).

Zahler, R., 'Estrategias para una cooperación / Unión Monetaria', *CEMLA Boletín*, No. 4 (2001): 161–209.

8
The Common Monetary Area in Southern Africa: A Typical South–South Coordination Project?

Martina Metzger

Introductory remarks

Monetary coordination currently is *en vogue* in Africa. With the transformation of the OAU to the African Union and the launching of the initiative of the New Partnership for African Development (NEPAD; both in 2001) the old idea of a common African currency seems to be within reach. A common African currency and a common central bank for all AU member countries is set for 2021 (Masson and Milkewicz, 2003; Masson and Pattillo, 2004). According to NEPAD, the transition process to monetary union in Africa is to be marked by the establishment of regional monetary unions for already existing integration projects. One of the prime candidates among existing integration schemes is the Common Monetary Area (CMA) in Southern Africa, which is regarded as an unusually longstanding and successful monetary coordination project. It is based on a tripartite arrangement between South Africa, Lesotho and Swaziland that came into effect in 1974, at which time these countries were known as the Rand Monetary Area. From our point of view, to understand the functioning of the CMA and the outstanding role of the Republic of South Africa, we need to take into account the political and historical framework in which the Common Monetary Area has been set from the very beginning. Therefore, we will give a brief overview of what relations were like in the region of Southern Africa pre-1990. We will then discuss the functioning of the CMA, including issues of institutions, interdependence and convergence (pp. 149–56). Finally, we shall try to assess, on the basis of the typology of both North–South coordination (NSC) and South–South coordination (SSC) projects, whether the CMA can be regarded as a typical SSC.

Political and historic framework of the Common Monetary Area (CMA)

The Republic of South Africa was governed between 1948 and 1994 by the National Party, which not only implemented one of the most sophisticated and drastic racial segregation systems in its own territory, but carried out a harsh destabilization policy throughout Southern Africa and decisively influenced the region's economic and political destiny.[1] The UN Commission on Africa tried, for instance, to assess the direct costs in terms of GDP loss during the 1980s of the South African destabilization policy against neighbouring countries which were all members of the Southern African Development Coordination Conference. Estimated losses during the period 1980 through 1988, measured in relation to the 1988 GDP, ranged from 26 per cent for Tanzania to 550 per cent to 600 per cent for Angola and Mozambique (see also p. 160, Table A8.1: GDP loss in the SADCC region).[2]

Swaziland and Lesotho, as members of the CMA, were relatively little affected by direct costs. Lesotho is surrounded by South African territory and has depended heavily on South Africa for remittances by Lesotho workers in that country's mining industry. Furthermore, one of its major export products is water, the main customer for which is South Africa. Swaziland is also a landlocked country, surrounded by South Africa on all sides but the north-east, where it has a common border with Mozambique. Swaziland was in the position of a buffer zone between South Africa and Mozambique, thereby realizing some transient gains e.g. in subsidies to encourage use of South African transport infrastructure instead of Mozambican railways. Furthermore, Swaziland developed a processing industry, especially packaging and labelling, to camouflage South African exports and imports, which were targeted by a boycott and other measures.

Lesotho and Swaziland became independent from Great Britain in 1966 and 1968, respectively. After a *coup d'état*, Lesotho had its first internationally accepted democratic elections in 1993, while Swaziland is the last absolutist monarchy in Africa, where King Mswati III appoints the prime minister and the members of the cabinet. Although Namibia was not formally a member, it was integrated in the CMA from the very beginning. South African troops had invaded Namibia during World War I and this status of occupation was maintained until 1990, when Namibia saw its first democratic elections ever and thereafter issued its own currency, the Namibian dollar.[3]

The functioning of the Common Monetary Area

The South African pound was already legal tender in the so-called BLS-states (Botswana, Lesotho, Swaziland) in the 1920s, when the South African Reserve Bank was established. After World War II, South Africa dissociated itself from Great Britain and its policies in stages, culminating in the introduction of the South African rand (ZAR) and departure from the Commonwealth in 1961. After the independence of the BLS-states from Great Britain, negotiations between them and South Africa began which resulted in the first official agreement about the establishment of a Rand Monetary Area (RMA) in 1974.

Brief overview of CMA history	
• Before 1961	Informal monetary union: SA pound as common currency
• 1961–74	SA rand replaces the SA pound
• 1974	Rand Monetary Area Agreement
• 1986	CMA replaces RMA; additional provisons were made for seigniorage compensations and intrazone fund transfers Swaziland abolishes SA rand as legal tender
• 1992	Namibia formally becomes a member; officially the Multilateral Monetary Agreement replaces the trilateral CMA

Although Botswana participated in the negotiations, it opted out in favour of a managed floating of its currency, the pula. Since then however, Botswana has pegged the pula to a basket comprised of estimated 60 per cent to 70 per cent ZAR, which is the reason why it is often called a *de facto* member of the current CMA (e.g. Grandes, 2003). Swaziland and Lesotho began to issue their own currencies, the lilangi and the loti, in 1974 and 1980 respectively. The CMA today formally consists of four countries, to which we will mainly refer: Lesotho, Swaziland, Namibia and South Africa.

Concretely, the CMA arrangement covers the following features:[4]

- Each of the four members has its own central bank, which is formally responsible for monetary policy within the respective country, and issues its own currency.
- Both Lesotho and Namibia have to back their currency issues by South African Rand assets. In order to maintain financial stability within the CMA, the South African Reserve Bank acts as a lender of last resort.
- In both Lesotho and Namibia the ZAR serves as legal tender; Swaziland abolished the legal status of the ZAR in 1986, although *de facto* it is still widely used. By contrast, none of the other currencies is legal tender in South Africa, nor are they commonly used within South Africa. A clearing system repatriates ZAR coins and notes circulating in the other member countries.
- Already in 1986, South Africa committed itself to making compensatory payments to CMA members in return for circulating the ZAR within their currency areas; therefore Lesotho and Namibia partly share the seigniorage of the ZAR; this does not apply to Swaziland.
- The loti of Lesotho and the Namibian dollar are all pegged at par to the ZAR; Swaziland abolished this commitment in 1986, but it is still valid *de facto*.[5]
- Within the CMA, there are no restrictions on capital movements; *vis-à-vis* the rest of the world, CMA members apply a common exchange control system, determined by the South African Department of Finance and administered by the South African Reserve Bank in cooperation with central banks of the other members.
- Member countries share a common pool of foreign exchange reserves, managed by the South Africa Reserve Bank and increasingly also managed by South African authorized dealers (commercial banks); central banks and authorized dealers of other member countries have free access to the foreign exchange market in South Africa. On request, the South Africa Reserve Bank will make the foreign exchange of the common pool available to other member countries.
- Lesotho, Namibia and Swaziland may hold additional foreign exchange themselves for direct and immediate needs; up to 35 per cent of this foreign exchange may be held in currencies other than the ZAR.

Institutions

From the very beginning, the South African Reserve Bank (SARB) has enjoyed a close relationship with the central government, which can be characterized as relatively devoid of conflict. This refers not only to those policy areas, such as exchange and capital controls, which lie in the competence of the central government and for which the SARB is only the executive agency. It also applies to such core functions of the central bank as interest-rate policy and regulation of the domestic money and credit market. Although the SARB is autonomous with regard to the design of monetary policy,[6] it has always seen itself as only one of several domestic macroeconomic actors, which is therefore an integral part of the overall structure of domestic economic policy. Hence, the following characterization made almost forty years ago is still valid: 'the Bank enjoys "independence *within* the government rather than *of* the government" '.[7] The two governors of the SARB, which ruled the SARB after the abolition of the apartheid regime, declared their adherence to this political consensus. Chris Stals, governor of the SARB until 1999, stated that 'the central bank, vested with the right to create money, cannot be allowed to be a power supreme to the sovereign government of the country. Even monetary policy must in the end be subject to the overall macro-economic objectives of government'.[8] While stressing that the power to spend money needed to be separated from the power to create money, Tito Mboweni, the current governor of the SARB, stressed that 'central banks are powerful institutions. They are staffed and managed by a bunch of unelected officials and governors. The power of central banks permeates society as a whole – particularly as they determine the cost of money.'[9] Therefore, he rejects the position that central banks were not accountable to government, parliament and even the people.

However, the SARB has not followed a – for other countries so typical – 'stop-and-go' approach, but has rather adopted an official policy of inflation-targeting to which the other member countries of the CMA adhere.[10] Therefore, it can be said that the SARB *de facto* determines monetary policy for the CMA although every member has its own central bank with formal competence for the design of monetary policy. In addition to a technical committee, the Common Monetary Area Commission meets prior to the SARB's Monetary Policy Committee, which is responsible for designing interest rates. Each member country sends a representative and advisors to the Common Monetary Area Commission, in which the different interests of the member countries in the formulation and implementation of monetary and foreign exchange policies are to be reconciled via a consultation mechanism. If for instance, some member country other than South Africa intends to change its foreign exchange controls, it is first obliged to enter into consultations with the Common Monetary Area Commission. In Namibia, criticisms have increasingly been raised against the dominance of South Africa in designing monetary policy for the whole region. These voices charge that since independence Namibia has never had the opportunity to influence South African monetary policy, and they call for the democratization of the CMA via the establishment of a common central bank for the CMA (e.g. Sherbourne, 2003, p. 3).

Interdependence

In the table below, exports and imports of the CMA countries and Botswana are listed, which all belong to the South African Customs Union (SACU). Except for Swaziland, exports from SACU members are overwhelmingly directed to the rest of the world, e.g. the European Union and the US. By contrast, 70–90 per cent of all imports by Botswana, Lesotho, Namibia and Swaziland come from SACU, specifically from South Africa. Hence, the four countries earn export revenues in foreign exchange other than rand, while paying for their imports in rand, to which at least Lesotho and Namibia have unlimited access.

We cannot identify a balanced *inter*dependence between these four countries and South Africa; the former are clearly depended on South African imports. Accordingly, the relevance of intra-regional trade flows for these four countries is significantly higher than for member countries of other regional projects, e.g. in Latin America (see Chapter 6). From the point of view of South Africa, however, the market share of goods and services from Botswana, Lesotho, Namibia and Swaziland on its domestic market is marginal, since regional income is concentrated in South Africa, which accounts for 96 per cent of regional GDP. Besides the concentration of regional income, there are broad income divergences both within each country and between them. Average GDP per

Table 8.1   Directions of trade in CMA countries in 2000 (in percentages)

	Exports to SACU	Exports to RoW	Imports from SACU	Imports from RoW
Botswana	6.7	93.3	73.9	26.1
Lesotho	39.1	60.9	88.2	11.2
Namibia	n.a.	n.a.	n.a.	n.a.
South Africa	n.a.	n.a.	n.a.	n.a.

Note: There was no data available for Namibia in 2000; in 1996 24 per cent of all Namibian exports were directed to SACU and 76 per cent to the rest of world, while 88.5 per cent of Namibian improts had SACU as their origin. South Africa exports about 10 per cant of its goods and services to SACU, while imports from SACU amount to between 2 and 3 per cent

Source: Grandes (2003)

capita per year is $1,825 (in 1997 prices), ranging from $505 for Lesotho to $3,331 for South Africa (Sparks, 2002). With regard to average GDP per capita, Lesotho disposes of an income level of 28 per cent, Swaziland of 78 per cent, Namibia of 112 per cent and South Africa of 183 per cent respectively. Hence, the economic relations within CMA (and SACU) are characterized by a clear hierarchy, with South Africa at the top.

Furthermore, the banking sector within the CMA is also highly concentrated with regard to ownership, both in each respective country and within the CMA as a whole. The South African banking sector is dominated by four South African commercial banks which together have a market share of about 90 per cent; the market is relatively equally distributed between them. A similar concentration in the banking sector can also be seen in Lesotho, Namibia and Swaziland, with the only difference being that ownership of the banks which control a similar market share in these countries is foreign – i.e., South African.[11] Okeahalam (2002, p. 5) even states that 'given the size of South Africa relative to the other members, the nature of CMA membership regulations, the compliance of these regulations by the authorities of all members and the high level of ownership which South African banks have in the three other countries, it is not difficult to perceive the CMA as one banking market'.

Convergence

Although it is difficult to assess how Lesotho, Swaziland and Namibia would have developed had they not been part of the CMA, it is widely acknowledged that the process of inflation assimilation to the South African level is due to CMA membership. The central banks of the three countries vary their interest rates to defend the nominal peg and thereby 'import' price-level stability. Although the deepening of the financial sector in Lesotho, Namibia and Swaziland is fairly limited, it is interesting to note that they are said to have slightly *lower* short-term interest rates than South Africa, so as to more easily mobilize financial resources for developmental issues. 'Regulatory authorities in the three non-core countries continue to strive to *minimize* interest-rate differentials with those prevailing in South Africa, to prevent the outflow of capital to South Africa and thus reduce the likelihood of liquidity problems for the domestic economy' (Okeahalam, 2002, p. 5, emphasis not in the original).

For Namibia, the only country for which reliable medium-term data is available, the repo rate of the Namibian central bank is fixed at about 25 basis points *below* the South African repo rate, so that the Namibian prime lending rate is only slightly higher than the South African, due to a perception of higher risk and higher operational costs of commercial

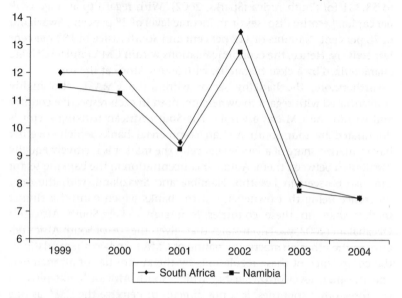

Figure 8.1 Repo rates in South Africa and Namibia at the end of year

Source: Bank of Namibia (2005)

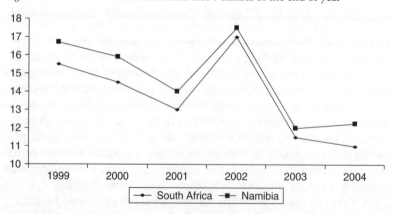

Figure 8.2 Prime rates in South Africa and Namibia at the end of year

Note: For the respective interest rates of all countries, see Table A8.2: Repo rates in the CMA and Table A8.3: Prime rates in the CMA, pp. 160 and 161

Source: Bank of Namibia (2005)

banks operating there. Hence, long-term interest rates in Namibia are only 25 to 50 basis points higher than in South Africa, to which Namibia pegs its currency (Kalenga, 2001, p. 4f).

One reason for the relatively low interest rate spreads between the non-core CMA member countries and South Africa is the almost complete absence of foreign capital other than South African in their countries. These countries do not face the risk of high capital outflows of foreign investors as typical emerging market economies do, for the simple reason that they are non-existent in these countries. Private domestic actors in the three countries are the only potential capital exporters – in their majority to South Africa. Thus these three countries can apply an interest-rate policy to steer their domestic money market under the restriction of maintaining the nominal peg to the South African rand. And as South Africa is a net debtor with regard to the other CMA member countries (see also p. 161, Table A8.4: South African assets and liabilities), interest rate policy of the three countries does not need to be very restrictive in itself.

There is also a business-cycle assimilation aspect in the downturn, and to some extent even in the upturn. The typical transmission belt of business-cycle assimilation in slowdowns or even recessions within a monetary coordination project are interest rates and intra-regional trade flows, whereas in the upturn, business cycle assimilation is not automatically ensured. With regard to the downturn this is also valid for the CMA, but there is one more and probably more relevant transmission

Figure 8.3 Lesotho: labour income from abroad to trade deficit (as a percentage)

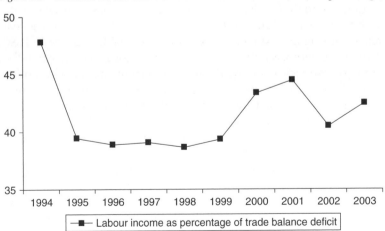

Sources: Central Bank of Lesotho (2003)

channel in the CMA, both in the downturn and the upturn. South Africa has many migrant workers from CMA countries, especially in the mining industries and agriculture (for details with regard to Lesotho workers in the South African mining industry see p. 161, Table A8.5: Lesotho: mineworkers employed in South Africa). Although there is no reliable comprehensive data on these issues (Brunk, 1996), it is said for example that imports to Lesotho from South Africa are overwhelmingly due to remittances of the migrant workers who either physically bring South African goods back to their homes when they take a break after months of work, or send money back via South African banks. Merely the *recorded* labour income from abroad in the official balance of payments statistics of Lesotho amounted to some 38 to 48 per cent of its trade deficit during the past ten years (see Figure 8.3).

Hence, in an upturn of the South African economy, the demand for migrant workers will increase quite rapidly; whereas in a downturn, migrant workers will be dismissed relatively easily with a time lag, as they have only fixed-term labour contracts and temporary resident's permits which will not be prolonged in a recessive economic environment. Thus, migrant workers and their remittances may explain the high synchronicity of GDP movements of all non-core CMA countries with regard to South African GDP movements, rather than intra-regional trade or financial flows.[12]

Is the Common Monetary Area a typical South–South coordination arrangement?

With regard to the disadvantages developing countries are plagued with, such as 'original sin' and the lack of a lender of last resort in foreign currency, the Common Monetary Area cannot be qualified as a typical SSC. Although Lesotho, Namibia and Swaziland are not able to issue bonds in domestic currency, either on the international financial markets or the South African market, they have free access to the South African money and capital market, on which they are able to raise debt denominated in South African rand (Van der Merwe, 1996, p. 19). Furthermore, the South African Reserve Bank acts as a lender of last resort, at least for Lesotho and Namibia. These two countries also participate in the seignorage of the rand circulating in their own territories. All this results in relatively low interest-rate differentials, both in nominal and real terms. The South African Exchange Control Regulations even state that 'Namibia, Lesotho and Swaziland should be treated as part of the domestic territory and not as foreign'.[13] While Lesotho and Namibia *de jure* and

Swaziland *de facto* are obliged to defend their peg to the rand, the South African Reserve Bank is responsible for defending the external value of the rand *vis-à-vis* the rest of the world, which results in a common bloc floating of the CMA against the key currencies, the euro and the US dollar. This 'division of labour' is based on a strong hierarchy in economic relations within the CMA with South Africa at the top. Hence, from the point of view of Lesotho, Namibia and Swaziland, the Common Monetary Area is rather a North–South coordination project than a South–South coordination arrangement.

There are two further specific features in economic relations within CMA which deserve mention. Like many other developing countries, Lesotho, Namibia and Swaziland show current-account deficits. But they realize export revenues overwhelmingly in either euros or US dollars, while their import liabilities are denominated in rand. Taking into account that the access to the South African rand is not restricted, this *favourable currency mismatch* rules out balance-of-payments crises in Lesotho and Namibia, and to some extent, too, in Swaziland. The second specific characteristic consists in the high relevance of remittances transferred from migrants working in South Africa to their home countries. Hence, Lesotho, Namibia and Swaziland have different

Figure 8.4 Exchange rates of the South African rand (annual change in percentages)[14]

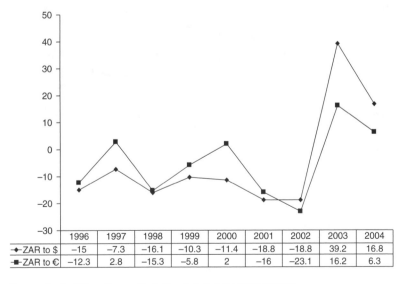

	1996	1997	1998	1999	2000	2001	2002	2003	2004
ZAR to $	−15	−7.3	−16.1	−10.3	−11.4	−18.8	−18.8	39.2	16.8
ZAR to €	−12.3	2.8	−15.3	−5.8	2	−16	−23.1	16.2	6.3

Sources: South African Reserve Bank, *Quarterly Bulletin*, various issues

opportunities to satisfy their demand for rand: the seignorage, their own foreign exchange in key currencies which they can use to buy rand, the foreign exchange in the common foreign exchange pool of the CMA, which they can also use in case of emergency to buy rand, the conclusion of debt denominated in rand on the South African financial market, and, last but not least, the remittances.

From the point of view of South Africa, the CMA is more an SSC project than an NSC arrangement, due to its own position in international markets. South Africa is an emerging market economy, which was hit three times over the past ten years by high net capital outflows resulting in double-digit depreciation rates of the rand in some years (see Figure 8.4). Due to the relatively low level of South African foreign debt, in other words the low foreign original sin (see Chapter 2, Eichengreen *et al.*, 2003; Hausmann and Panizza, 2003) compared to other emerging market economies in Asia or Latin America, these instances did not result in balance-of-payments crises, or put the banking sector at a risk of bankruptcy.

However, South Africa is highly vulnerable, and has become even more vulnerable over the past fifteen years, as capital controls have been

Figure 8.5   Total foreign debt of South Africa (in percentages, at end of year)

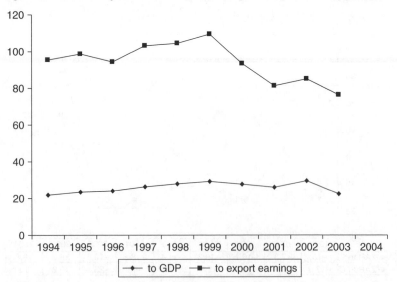

Source: South African Reserve Bank, *Quarterly Bulletin*, various issues

continually dismantled (Kahn, 1996). Whenever there is a crisis which is assumed to be a general 'emerging market crisis', South Africa is negatively affected, even if it has not been directly involved. This was the case in the aftermath of the East Asian crisis, when South Africa was confronted with high outflows. Whenever there is a crisis which is assumed to be restricted to some identifiable emerging market economies, such as Argentina and Brazil, South Africa serves as a 'save heaven' for institutional investors and is confronted with high inflows, as was the case in 2003. Hence, the rand exchange rate is highly volatile, although the South African Reserve Bank tries to stabilize it through interest-rate policy and interventions in the foreign exchange market.

With regard to the integration in world financial markets, it can be said that CMA member countries are *not* in a similar market constellation, which once more emphasizes that the CMA is more a NSC for the weaker countries. Lesotho, Namibia and Swaziland do not dispose of a high level of capital inflows, be it in the form of portfolio investment – which is almost non-existent – or in the form of foreign direct investment, of which the major share is owned by South African companies or banks. Nor do these three countries have access to financial markets other than the South African market. We interpret this phenomenon that these countries are involuntarily marginalized. Hence, the monetary coordination with South Africa is here understood as a way to open one door which otherwise would have also been shut. However, exchange-rate fluctuations of the rand are transferred via the nominal peg to the loti, Namibian dollar and the lilangeni which have to follow the depreciations and appreciations of the rand. Furthermore, all non-core CMA countries have to follow the South African Reserve Bank if it increases its interest rates. Depending on the extent to which public finance and production in the non-core member countries is based on credit financing, the interest-rate increase in the CMA in case of depreciation has either a severely or only slightly negative effect. The depreciation of the rand indisputably has one directly negative effect on the GDPs of the non-core CMA countries. When the income-generating process in South Africa is depressed by high interest rates, unemployment will increase and migrant workers are among the first to be dismissed. This then results in a loss of substantial income for those households and countries affected.

Relatively low interest-rate spreads and the absence of both intra-regional financial instability and competitive devaluations between the member countries might be an explanation of slow but continuous convergence in GDP per capita. The structural deficiencies of some or even all CMA member countries, such as – to name a few – high dependence on raw material exports, lack of diversification in exports and production, high income inequality, a low level of infrastructure, a lack of financial deepening and – worst of all for human development – the paralysis of all governments in the fight against HIV – will not under any circumstances be overcome by a monetary coordination arrangement. Thus, monetary integration might successfully create structural conditions which allow low inflation, stable exchange rates and stability in the financial sector – which is all true for the CMA – but it is no panacea for all development problems.

Annex

Table A8.1   GDP loss in the SADCC region, 1988 and 1980–8

Country	1988 in % of actual GDP	1980–8 in % of 1988 GDP
Angola	90	600
Mozambique	110	550
Zimbabwe	25	145
Malawi	30	133
Zambia	20	200
Tanzania	10	26
Botswana	10	40
Lesotho	7	42
Swaziland	5	33
All SADCC	43	210

Source: UN Economic Commission for Africa (1989)

Table A8.2   Repo rates in the CMA (at end of year)

	1999	2000	2001	2002	2003	2004
South Africa	12.0	12.0	9.5	13.5	8.0	7.5
Namibia	11.5	11.25	9.25	12.75	7.75	7.5
Swaziland	12.0	11.0	n.a.	n.a.	n.a.	n.a.
Lesotho	n.a.	n.a.	n.a.	n.a.	n.a.	n.a.

Sources: Data from Bank of Namibia (2005), Central Bank of Lesotho (2003), Central Bank of Swaziland http://www.centralbank.org.sz/interate.html

Table A8.3 Prime rates in the CMA (at end of year)

	1999	2000	2001	2002	2003	2004
South Africa	15.5	14.5	13.0	17.0	11.5	11.0
Namibia	16.7	15.9	14.0	17.5	12.0	12.25
Lesotho	18.0	17.0	16.33	17.67	17.67	n.a.
Swaziland	15.0	14.0	n.a.	n.a.	n.a.	n.a.

Sources: Data from Bank of Namibia (2005), Central Bank of Lesotho (2003), Central Bank of Swaziland http://www.centralbank.org.sz/interate.htm

Table A8.4 South African assets and liabilities against CMA member countries (in R millions, end of 2003)

	Botswana	Lesotho	Namibia	Swaziland
Assets (+)	1497	1155	4895	1372
Liabilities (−)	1383	1792	17573	1481
Total	114	−637	−12678	−109

Source: South African Reserve Bank, *Quarterly Bulletin*, March 2005

Table A8.5 Lesotho: mineworkers employed in South Africa and earnings

	Average numbers employed	Average earnings in loti (per person)	Total earnings (millions of loti)	Trade and services deficit (millions of loti)
1994	112722	14562	1641.48	−2523.08
1995	103744	16801	1743.00	−3076.10
1996	101262	19186	1942.81	−3577.73
1997	95913	21193	2032.68	−3771.45
1998	80445	24678	1985.22	−3647.72
1999	68604	27657	1897.38	−3745.86
2000	64907	30131	1955.71	−3583.42
2001	61412	32030	1967.02	−3497.90
2002	62158	35326	2195.79	−4231.57
2003	61415	38333	2354.22	−4398.84

Sources: Central Bank of Lesotho (2003), own calculations (for 2002 and 2003 preliminary figures)

Notes

1. For a comprehensive and impressive overview of South Africa during these years see O'Meara (1996).
2. There are three different methods to estimate losses. In one way or the other, these methods are based on estimates of costs with regard to direct war damage, extra defence spending, higher transport costs, higher energy costs, assistance for domestic displaced persons and refugees etc., trying to assess non-war growth; although such estimates are concretely very approximate, they all indicate losses of a comparable extent. For further information see the UN Commission for Africa (1989, p. 11ff).
3. Namibia, or Southwest Africa as it was formerly named, shares a colonial past with other African countries; it was a German colony until World War I. South Africa, at that time still part of the British Empire, wished to incorporate Namibia into its own territory, but this was rejected both by the League of Nations (1920) and the United Nations (1946). For Namibia's history during the occupation, see also United Nations (1982), Moorsom (1984) or Kössler (2002).
4. See Grandes (2003), Sherbourne (2003), Van Zyl (2003), Okeahalam (2002), Sparks (2002), Van der Merwe (1996).
5. On 10 April 2005, 1 euro was valued at 7.99060 rand and 5.94485 pula; 1 rand was equivalent to 1 loti of Lesotho, 1.00652 Namibian dollar, and 1.01358 lilangeni of Swaziland respectively.
6. The legal independence of the SARB is even provided for in the South African constitution, where its primary goal, the protection of the internal and external value of the rand 'in the interest of balanced and sustainable economic growth in the Republic', is established. See Republic of South Africa (1996), Article 224.
7. Crick (1965, p. 43 (emphasis in the original)).
8. Stals (1994, p. 7). See also Kiblböck and Williams (1996).
9. Quoted from Sherbourne (2003, p. 2).
10. See Appendix to the *Statement of the Monetary Policy Committee* (2000) and van der Merwe (2004). In the 1990s, monetary stability was defined by the SARB not only as a stable internal and external value of the rand, but more comprehensively, as the stability of financial institutions and markets. However, interest rate policy by the SARB consists of reactive measures to changes in the rand exchange rate, rather than constituting true inflation-targeting. For a critique of the SARB's interest rate policy see also Botha (1997).
11. Therefore, the banking sector in all CMA countries is known to comply with international banking standards and regulations, such as Basel I.
12. An econometrical estimate for the synchronicity of business cycles can be found in Grandes (2003), while Jenkins and Thomas (1997) prove a long-term convergence in GDP per capita over a thirty-year period. However, migration and remittance flows are not taken into account.
13. 'Orders and Rules under the Exchange Control Regulations' (1998), Section Instructions.
14. A positive sign indicates an appreciation of the South African rand.

Bibliography

Appendix to the Statement of the Monetary Policy Committee, *A New Monetary Policy Framework*, Statement issued by Mr T. T. Mboweni, Governor of the South African Reserve Bank, 6 April 2000.

Bank of Namibia, *Quarterly Bulletin*, March (2005).

Botha, D. J. J., 'The South African Reserve Bank and the Rate of Interest', *South African Journal of Economics*, Vol. 65 (4) (1997): 532–67.

Brunk, M., *Undocumented Migration to South Africa: More Questions than Answers*, IDASA Public Information Series No. 4 (Cape Town, 1996).

Central Bank of Lesotho, *Annual Report Statistical Tables* (2003). www.centralbank.org.ls.

Central Bank of Swaziland, www.centralbank.org.sz

Crick, W. F., 'The Framework of Inter-Relations', in Crick, W. F. (ed.), *Commonwealth Banking Systems* (Oxford: Clarendon Press, 1965), pp. 1–54.

Eichengreen, B., Hausmann, R. and Panizza, U., *The Pain of Original Sin*, unpublished manuscript (2003).

Grandes, M., *Macroeconomic Convergence in Southern Africa: The Rand Zone Experience*, OECD Development Centre Working Paper No. 231 (2003).

Hausmann, R. and Panizza, U., 'The Determinants of Original Sin: An Empirical Investigation', *Journal of International Money and Finance*, Vol. 22 (7) (2003): 967–90.

Jenkins, C. and Thomas, L., *Is Southern Africa Ready for Regional Monetary Integration?* LSE CREFSA Research Paper No. 10 (London: Centre for Research into Economics and Finance in Southern Africa, 1997).

Kahn, B., *Exchange Control Liberalisation in South Africa*, IDASA Public Information Series No. 3 (Cape Town, 1996).

Kalenga, P., *Monetary Policy Framework in Namibia*, Conference on Monetary Policy Frameworks in Africa, 17–19 September 2001 (Pretoria, South Africa, 2001).

Kiblböck, I. and J. Williams, J., 'South African Banking Culture Changes to Accommodate the Demands and Aspirations of the "Unbanked" Community', in Schuster, L. (ed.), *Banking Cultures of the World* (Frankfurt: Fritz Knapp, 1996), pp. 59–69.

Kössler, R., *Struggling for Survival and Dignity: Two Traditional Communities in Southern Namibia under South African Rule* (Windhoek and Frankfurt am Main: Macmillan and Gamsberg, 2002).

Masson, P. and Milkiewicz, H., *Africa's Economic Morass: Will a Common Currency Help?*, Policy Brief No. 121 (The Brookings Institution, 2003).

Masson, P. and Pattillo, C., 'A Single Currency for Africa?', *Finance and Development*, December (2004): 9–15.

Moorsom, R., *Walvis Bay: Namibia's Port* (London: International Defence and Aid Fund for Southern Africa in cooperation with the United Nations Council for Namibia, 1984).

Okeahalam, C. C., *Concentration in the Banking Sector of the Common Monetary Area of Southern Africa*, Paper presented at the Development Issues in the New Economy Conference, University of Cape Town, South Africa, 24–26 March (2002).

O'Meara, D., *Forty Lost Years: The Apartheid State and the Politics of the National Party, 1948–1994* (Randburg: Ravan Press, 1996).

'Orders and Rules under the Exchange Control Regulations', as published in Government Notice R1112 of 1 December 1961 and amended up to Government Notice R. 791, *Government Gazette* No. 18970 of 5 June 1998, mimeo (1998).

Republic of South Africa, Constitutional Assembly, *Constitution of the Republic of South Africa Bill*, as amended by the Constitutional Committee, no year, no location (1996).

Sherbourne, R., 'Tito Mboweni, Governor of the South African Reserve Bank, "On Monetary Policy" ', *IPPR Interview*, No. 7, October 2003.

South African Reserve Bank, *Quarterly Bulletin*, various issues.

Sparks, D. L., *The Future of Monetary Integration in Southern Africa: Will SADC Join the Rand Monetary Area?* Paper presented at the Conference 'Exchange Rates, Economic Integration and the International Economy', Ryerson University, Toronto, Canada (2002).

Stals, C. L., 'Monetary Policy and Financial Stability in the Developing Economies', address at a Conference on Money, Foreign Exchange and Capital Markets, Valletta, 2–4 November 1994, printed in *Deutsche Bundesbank, Auszüge aus Presseartikeln*, No. 89, 2 December 1994: 6–8.

UN Commission for Africa, *South African Destabilization: The Economic Cost of Frontline Resistance to Apartheid* (Addis Ababa: United Nations, 1989).

United Nations, *Plunder of Namibian Uranium*, Major Findings of the Hearings on Namibian Uranium Held by the United Nations Council for Namibia in July 1980 (New York: United Nations, 1982).

Van der Merwe, E. J., 'Exchange Rate Policies in South Africa: Recent Experience and Prospects', *Occasional Paper of the South African Reserve Bank*, No. 9 (Pretoria: South African Reserve Bank, 1996).

Van der Merwe, E. J., 'Inflation Targeting in South Africa', *Occasional Paper of the South African Reserve Bank*, No. 19 (Pretoria: South African Reserve Bank, 2004).

Van Zyl, L., 'South Africa's Experience of Regional Currency Areas and the Use of Foreign Currencies', *BIS Papers*, No. 17 (2003): 134–9.

9
The CFA Zone: A Positive Example of Monetary Coordination?

Jan Suchanek

Introduction

In the Asian crisis of 1998–9, many East Asian currencies came under pressure and had to devalue. By what was later called the effect of contagion, even countries with weak trade links to Asia were affected. The aftermath of the Asian crisis saw the awakening of new interest in monetary coordination. Remarkably, the Franc CFA Zone in Africa, which may well be the oldest arrangement of this type, was left untouched by the East Asian eruptions. The following article looks into the question of whether this makes the Franc CFA Zone a positive model. It begins with a short statement of the need for monetary cooperation, briefly outlines the origin and function of the Franc CFA system, then recalls selected features and failures of the arrangement and briefly discusses their impacts. The next section (pp. 171–2) outlines the current discussion on this monetary arrangement and its future, with attention being drawn (pp. 172–4) to the role of the Zone for Europe, and vice versa. Finally, there is a review of the lessons to be learned from a study of the Franc CFA Zone for monetary coordination arrangements in general. The focus is on economic arguments, while the interesting field of political economy is only touched on briefly; Kohnert, in his commentary on Chapters 8 and 9, addresses the political aspects more directly.

Monetary cooperation to stabilize exchange rates

Large unpredictable shifts in exchange rates can have devastating effects on economies. Countries that are less diverse, small, open, and indebted in foreign currency – typically poor countries – have to face permanent devaluation pressure originating from their market constellation, that eventually erupts in speculative attacks followed by harsh, capital-flight-induced devaluations. With debt denominated in foreign currency, devaluations increase the burden of this debt, thus leading to increased pressure to further devaluate. While the debt burden increases, import prices rise. If import and export elasticity are low, an increase in the debt burden quota per current-account deficit will be a direct result. In short, unpredictable devaluations can bring major distortion to local price vectors, leading economies into unsustainable indebtedness, and economic turbulences or crisis, and thus hampering their stable growth.

Unilateral pegging of the exchange rate does not seem to be a sustainable alternative for small and open economies, as international capital flows can exceed the central bank's capability to stabilize the exchange rate. The ever-increasing volume of international portfolio investment flows demands that ever-increasing reserves to be held by central banks. Monetary cooperation offers the advantage of pooling reserves and thereby diminishing dependence on international donors in case of speculative attacks, and has in itself a discouraging effect on capital markets speculating against the cooperating currencies.

Looking at existing arrangements of monetary cooperation, the Franc CFA Zone deserves special interest. Not only did this arrangement survive the currency turbulences of the late 1990s, but since it has a very long history, it also suggests itself as a perfect object of study. It includes fourteen member states in Africa, and France. Following the terminology proposed by Fritz and Metzger (Chapter 1), it therefore comprises both South–South coordination (SSC) between its member states, and North–South coordination (NSC) with France, i.e. Europe.

Origin and function of the Franc CFA system

The Franc CFA monetary coordination arrangement dates back to colonial times. Until 1962, the abbreviation 'Franc CFA' meant *Franc des colonies françaises de l'Afrique*. Today, this label stands for *Franc de la Communauté Financière Africaine* in West Africa and as *Franc de la Coopération Financière en Afrique Centrale* in Central Africa. Both currencies follow almost identical monetary arrangements, involving a fixed peg to the French franc – i.e. the euro – and full convertibility backed by France; hence, in the following, we will not differentiate between them. The West African Franc CFA is legal tender in Benin, Burkina Faso, Ivory Coast, Guinea-Bissau, Mali, Niger, Senegal, and Togo, while the Central

African Franc CFA is the currency of Cameroon, Central African Republic, Chad, Republic of the Congo (Brazzaville), Equatorial Guinea and Gabon.

The balances of the two 'central banks' that issue the two Franc CFA in Dakar and in Yaoundé respectively are simply operations accounts of the French treasury at Quai de Bercy in Paris. While the debit side of these accounts is denominated in CFA, the credit side is denominated in euros. On all major decisions of these 'central banks', France has a *de facto* veto stemming from its presence in all major bodies, where decisions can only be made if all members are present (cf. König, 2001). The Franc CFA arrangement obliges its African members to the following:

(i) to deposit 65 per cent of their foreign reserves on the operations account at the French treasury,

(ii) to provide for an exchange cover of at least 20 per cent of their sight liabilities, and

(iii) to impose a cap on credit extended to each member country equivalent to 20 per cent of that country's public revenue in the preceding year (cf. Mazzaferrro *et al.*, 2002; Semedo and Villieu, 1997).

In return, the French treasury originally guaranteed an exchange rate of 50 FCFA = 1 FF by providing unlimited liquidity in French francs. It continued to do so until the operations accounts became persistently negative. By 1994 it had become apparent that it would be impossibly expensive for France to further support the existing exchange rate, and the CFA was devaluated by 50 per cent. The switch from the franc to the euro left the monetary arrangement of the Zone Franc untouched. France, when becoming part of the Euro area, did so with the understanding that decisions regarding new members or changes in the exchange rate of the CFA system would be communicated in advance to European institutions. The agreement between the French treasury and its African partners is of a budgetary nature for France. The contracts that constitute the Zone do not involve any obligation for the ECB to support the peg (EU Council decision of 23 November 1998). Since then, France has guaranteed the rate of 655.957 FCFA = 1FF = €0.154490. Along with the euro, the CFA franc has primarily undergone an appreciation against the US dollar, and most observers today consider the CFA overvalued *vis-à-vis* the dollar area.

Selected features and failures of the CFA arrangement

Since the political independence of its African members, the CFA system has not been much more than a group of independent countries sharing a colonial past and a common currency. The year of crisis and devaluation, 1994, saw the founding of the regional economic communities, the *Union Economique et Monétaire Ouest-Africaine, UEMOA* (West African Economic and Monetary Union, WAEMU) and the *Communauté Economique et Monétaire de l'Afrique Centrale, CEMAC* (Economic and Monetary Community of Central Africa, EMCCA). This was driven by the insight that the advantages of a monetary union could only emerge through interdependence, but interdependence has up to now been virtually non-existent. Trade flow between member countries is still very limited, accounting for only 11 per cent of foreign trade. This is due to poor infrastructure, the countries' heavy dependence on tariff revenues, and a lack of diversification within local economies. The member countries of the Zone are extremely diverse, from desert to jungle, and comprising states dependent of the export of various goods, from gold to fish. Some, if not all of its members, can be characterized as *rentier* states in the sense of Mahdavy and Yates (cf. Mahdavy, 1970; Yates, 1996): the main source of government revenue stems from the export of non-manufactured goods. Accordingly, all surveys resting on the 'classical' criteria of an optimum currency area concluded that the Zone would not be optimal (cf. Gehle, 1998; Gurtner, 1999; Fielding and Shields, 2001). The literature, however, agrees that the common pooling of reserves and the saving of administrative costs is advantageous (e.g. Michelsen, 1995).

Until the 1980s, the countries in the Zone nevertheless seemed to have profited from the arrangement: inflation rates were lower, while growth rates were on average higher than in neighbouring countries. This situation changed in the 1980s, as both prices of both primary goods and exchange rates became more and more volatile. The Zone was at a disadvantage as it lacked the flexibility to adjust to external shocks (cf. Devarajan and Rovik, 1991). Thanks to the peg, the CFA became overvalued, and the Zone lost competitiveness due to the competitive devaluations of its neighbours and competitors on the world market. Since then, the output of the Zone has generally been low, and economic growth in some years lower than population growth.

The Zone's growth was particularly slower than in comparable areas (cf. Michelsen, 1995), and in most years since 1996 economic performance generally lagged behind that of comparable neighbouring countries, e.g. Ghana. The current crisis of Ivory Coast and at least partly contradictory French policy in response, is placing additional tension on the functioning of the Zone.

Since the breakdown of the Bretton Woods system, the franc CFA and its anchor the franc – i.e. now the euro – have floated. The appreciation of the euro has had a negative impact on local economic stability, as all participating countries are heavily dependent on exports of primary goods, which are still mainly quoted and invoiced in US dollars. The rising euro, falling export prices and high oil prices have supported further deterioration in the current accounts of member countries. The austerity policies imposed by the Bretton Woods institutions and by France, along with the need to follow the ECB's monetary policy, have put deflationary pressure on the Franc CFA Zone, while it remained impossible to reduce inflation rates to zero. The rising euro has made imports from Europe more expensive in real terms. The devastating effect has only been moderated by the fact that fuel import prices measured in euros have remained more or less stable, a situation very likely to change in the near future.

The peg made it impossible to adjust the exchange rate to changes in the prices of raw materials (*Prebisch-shocks*). According to the much quoted study by Devarajan and Rovik (1991), this disadvantage rules out the stability advantage if the volatility of prices is high. They tested their model on the Franc CFA Zone in particular, and found it to be proof that the arrangement has been disadvantageous since the mid-1980s, when raw material prices became more volatile.

The Zone survived the Asian crisis, when many emerging countries came under pressure (e.g. South Africa). A larger monetary area comprising diverse economies can cushion external shocks from assets markets (*Calvo-shocks*). However, for the Zone as a whole, foreign investment plays an almost insignificant role. The investment activities are mainly those of companies exploiting natural resources. For the most part, foreign direct investment in the Zone does not seem to follow the patterns known as contagion. The Zone has never attracted much foreign investment, so there was not much to withdraw. Inasmuch as the Zone's design might be responsible for the low level of investment, it also cushioned it against withdrawal as well.

The fact that the current-account balances of the member countries are pooled in the operations accounts in the French treasury has led to free-rider behaviour in fiscal politics, while it is worth noting that the richer countries, notably Ivory Coast and, to a lesser extent, Senegal, have expanded their expenditures at the cost of the poorer Sahel states. Solving the problem of the incentive to free-ride will be among the most

Figure 9.1   Interest rates of the BCEAO and of Banque de France, 1993–2002

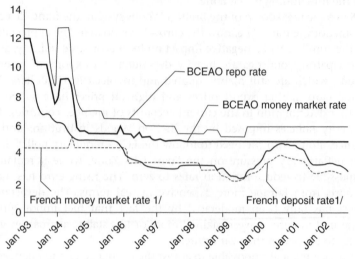

Source: IMF, 2003, p. 33

urgent tasks for any reform of the Zone's constitution, a task that would seem crucial for any monetary coordination.

Interest rates in the Franc CFA Zone have always followed the rates of the Banque de France and thus now follow those set by the European Central Bank. Nonetheless, they are always significantly higher (IMF, 2003) (Figure 9.1).

This margin can partly be explained by the reasonable fear of further devaluations and other risk premiums, mirroring a lower liquidity premium in respect to the euro (cf. Lüken genannt Klaßen, 1993). This is a direct consequence of the fact that money supply is delivered from the outside. The region does not have its own lender of last resort.

For sustainable development, real interest rates have proved to be too high. There is a severe lack of reasonable investments in current rates (cf. Khane Camara, 1998). Market imperfections are common, and in rural areas there is a vast need for credit that is not being fulfilled, mostly due to problems in infrastructure and the dissemination of information (cf. Stiglitz, 1989; Khane Camara, 1998). Local banks in the area tend to serve only a small formal urban sector of the economy, while the European (mainly French) banks with the facilities to refinance directly through the ECB system tend to restrict their activities to European customers active in the region. Table 9.1 shows indicators of financial development.

Table 9.1 Indicators of financial development, Sub-Saharan Africa and euro area (unweighted averages 2000)

	Sub-Saharan Africa	Euro area
M2 / GDP	30.7	66.7
Domestic Credit / GDP	26.0	134.5
Currency / M1	42.2	18.8

Source: Mazzaferro *et al.*, 2002, p. 47f.

The CFA in the current discussion

With very few exceptions, dissatisfaction with the present arrangement is found throughout the literature, and the discussion on the future of the Zone is lively (cf. Ben Hammouda and Kassé, 2001; Ouedraogo, 2003; Masson and Pattillo, 2004; Kohnert in this volume).

At first sight, multiple currencies seem a good option for African countries, due to their reliance on exports of various primary goods. Individual currencies allow exchange rates to be adjusted to external (*Prebisch-*) shocks more easily. However, achieving monetary unity could also be conducive to stronger regional trade links, and thus a single West African or even pan-African currency could be *ex post* optimal (cf. Frankel, 1999).

The dissolution of the south–south-cooperation component of the arrangement is rarely proposed. Plans for rearrangement usually originate from more visionary concepts anxious to redraw the monetary map of the whole continent. The most ambiguous and at the same time the most predominant concept has a single African currency as its final objective. An African central bank, an African investment bank and an African monetary fund are foreseen in Article 19 of the Constitutive Act of the African Union. Monetary and political union are to both be achieved at the end of an integration process, which is to begin by strengthening existing regional economic cooperative communities (RECs). There are many such RECs (Figure 9.2).

In West Africa, the non-CFA countries are planning to set up a single currency uniting the Nigerian naira with the currencies of Ghana, Liberia, Sierra Leone, Guinea and Gambia; then, in a second step, this currency is to be united with the West African Franc CFA, which will give all of ECOWAS a single currency; the convergence criteria have already been established. Both the European Union and Bretton Woods institutions support these plans, and it is interesting to note that the

Figure 9.2   Overview, regional economic communities in Africa

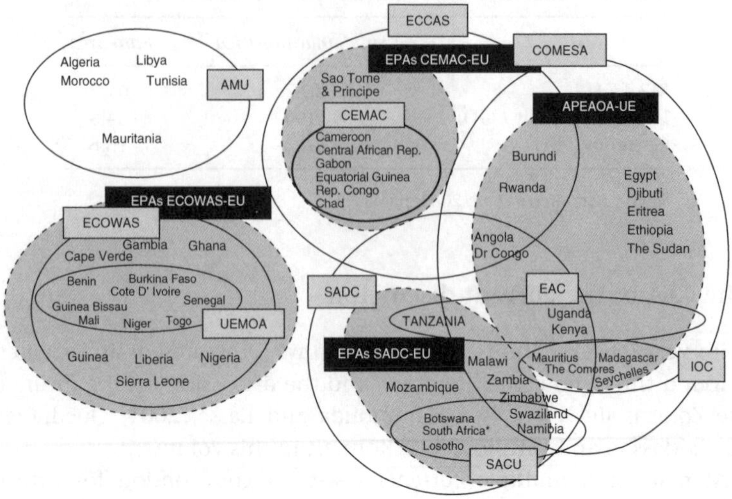

Source: African Union, 2004, p. 8

convergence criteria are the same as the obligations stemming from the HIPC initiative. At present, however, military conflicts, such as those in the Manu river region and in Ivory Coast, as well as rising tensions in other areas, such as eastern Chad, are impeding progress. Moreover, at present, not even the WAEMU members can meet the convergence criteria.

There is an astonishing lack of literature and discussion about which exchange rate regime the new currency should follow. There is also an obvious conflict of interest between enlarging the WAEMU by means of the CFA system, and strengthening the ECOWAS by switching to block floating. All this will depend on the relationship between the French-speaking region and its giant anglophone partner, Nigeria.

The CFA Zone and Europe

'*Meine Karte Afrikas liegt in Europa*', 'my map of Africa is located in Europe', Otto von Bismarck once said (1888). He presided over the 1884–5 Berlin Conference, also known as the Congo Conference, during which Africa was divided between the colonial powers. The negotiating countries were Great Britain, Austria-Hungary, France, Germany, Russia, USA, Portugal, Denmark, Spain, Italy, the Netherlands, Sweden, Belgium and Turkey. It was considered dangerous to ship gold-equivalent hard currency of the 'mother country' into the colonies. Thus, currency-board-like systems were created, precursors to the CFA franc. It was in the logic of colonial rule to have a currency that could eventually be dropped without danger for the 'mother country', while at the same time guaranteeing price stability in a foreseeable horizon, and thus the income of colonialists who received their profits mainly from exporting raw materials to the 'mother country'. This resulted in a market constellation of rentier states as defined by Mahdavy (1970) and Yates (1996). While *rentier*-class rulers, be they black or white, enjoy the advantages of a hard currency, the local economy is permitted to access it only by paying much higher interest rates than these entrepreneur-colonizers would have to pay their home banks in the colonies. Thus, the basic economic relationship between these southern countries and their colonizers (Europeans) has not changed since independence, even though the means for upholding that relationship may have. Of course, in such a system, the dependent country does not have its own lender of last resort. It is not only an indebted currency, but also a currency which is in and of itself already debt, the 'original sin' of underdeveloped countries.

Today, European unification sheds a new light on the map of Africa. Now that there is only one European currency, it is hard to see any reason for maintaining multiple African currencies within borders stemming from colonial times, and even harder to see why a currency called the 'franc' should continue to exist in Africa, when there is no such currency even in France anymore.

The whole Zone is of little economic importance to Europe, its aggregated GDP adding up to no more than 0.5 per cent of the Euro Zone's GDP. If there is any advantage of the CFA system for Europe, it is rather limited, given the Zone's relative insignificance in international trade both with Europe and abroad. By contrast, Europe is very important for the Zone. The European Union, France in particular, is the most important 'partner' of these countries in terms of commerce, financial flows, and political influence in general. This is a typical case of small open economies pegging their currencies to those of larger partners. The North–South arrangement thereby fulfils the classical OCA criteria. The small partner concentrates on stabilization of the current account, while the larger partner focuses on internal stabilization. French Africa policy, however, have not always been helpful in achieving stability: in many cases, corrupt, brutal, undemocratic and sometimes outright racist regimes have been scandalously supported by French elites (cf. Péan, 1988, 1990; Verschave, 1998, 2000, 2004; Yates, 1996, 2000).

The heavy indebtedness of most sub-Saharan countries results in their inability to cover even the costs of negotiating individually with multinational institutions. Given the importance of Europe to the Zone, and the huge administrative costs involved in dealing with so many independent states and currencies, there are obvious reasons for promoting further African unification. Almost all African frontiers were drawn by the colonial powers.

Conclusions

The Franc CFA Zone system of monetary cooperation comprises a group of extremely poor, heavily indebted countries with almost non-existent infrastructures and major market shortcomings. These economies are dependent on the export of a wide variety of primary goods, and foreign investment does not play a significant role. The reasons for the existence of the monetary cooperation structure are mostly of a political nature: to save administrative costs and to tie the region to France, i.e. Europe. Since the 1980s, it does not seem to have favoured the development of its African members. The mechanism of a true peg to the euro leads to considerable costs for the European side – be they France financing the current-account deficits via its budget and the *compte d'operations* mechanism, or Europe, providing development aid.

There is a great need to find a method of monetary cooperation that would offer more flexibility than under the current system, and allow the Zone to have its own lender of last resort and better achieve financial deepening. This question, though, is naturally linked to the question how to find a strategy to end the heavy indebtedness of these countries (cf. Chapter 2). The idea of reshaping the composition and constitution of the Zone with the broader perspective of the establishment of a single pan-African currency floating free seems appealing, though global conflict lines still crossing on the continent make this less realistic.

In terms of theory, the Franc CFA Zone demonstrates the dilemma that countries in this market constellation are facing: there is no way to avoid devaluation. In this constellation, any announced peg, such as the 'true' peg of the CFA, is intrinsically suspect. It might well serve to avoid turbulences in the short run, but always bears the danger of only postponing devaluation. Its advantage lies in the better short-run predictability, but this security is achieved by certain sacrifices, including, due to high interest rates, financial deepening. The result is a low-growth steady state, constantly under the Damocles' sword of threatening devaluation.

Bibliography

African Union, *Strategic Plan of the Commission of the African Union*, Volume 2: 'Strategic Framework of the Commission of the African Union' (2004).

Ben Hammouda, H. and Kassé, M. (eds), *L'Avenir de la zone franc. Perspectives africaines* (Paris/Dakar, 2001).

Devarajan, S. and Rovik, D., *Do the Benefits of Fixed Exchange Rates Outweigh their Costs? The Franc Zone in Africa*, NBER Working Paper No. 3727 (Cambridge, MA, 1991).

Fielding, D. and Shields, K., *Currency Unions and International Integration: Evidence from the CFA and the ECCU* (Leicester, 2001). http://www.le.ac.uk/economics/research/RePEc/lec/leecon/econ02–8.pdf

Frankel, J. A., *No Single Currency is Right for all Countries or at all Times*, NBER Working Paper No. 7338 (Cambrigde, MA, 1999).

Gehle, S., *Die Franc-Zone als inhomogener Währungsraum: Zur Optimalität der Währungskooperation der Franc Zone für ihre afrikanischen Mitgliedsländer* (Baden-Baden, 1998).

Gurtner, F. J., 'The CFA Franc Zones and the Theory of Optimum Currency Area', *africa spectrum*, 34 (1999): 33–58.

IMF, *West African Economic and Monetary Union: Recent Economic Developments and Regional Policy Issues*; and Public Information Notice on the Executive Board Discussion (Washington, DC, 1999). http://www.imf.org/external/pubs/ft/scr/2003/cr0370.pdf

Khane Camara, M., *Die Finanzsektorreform in Afrika: Das Beispiel der Franc-Zone* (Frankfurt, 1998).

König, T., *Das regelgebundene Währungssystem der Franc-Zone im Wandel der Zeit* (Marburg, 2001).

Lüken gennant Klaßen, M., *Währungskonkurrenz und Protektion. Peripherisierung und ihre Überwindung aus geldwirtschaftlicher Sicht* (Marburg, 1993).

Mahdavy, H., 'Patterns and Problems of Economic Development in Rentier States: The Case of Iran', *Studies in the Economic History of the Middle East* (Oxford, 1970).

Masson, P. and Pattillo, C., 'A Single Currency for Africa?', *Finance and Development*, 12 (2004): 8–15.

Michelsen, H., *Auswirkungen der Währungsunion auf den Strukturanpassungsprozess der Länder der afrikanischen Franc-Zone* (Frankfurt, 1995).

Mazzaferro, F., Mehl, A. and Sturm, M. *et al.*, *Economic Relations with Regions Neighbouring the Euro Area in the 'Euro Time Zone'*, ECB Occasional Paper Series No. 7, December (2002).

Ouedraogo, O., *Une monnaie unique pour tout l'Afrique de l'Ouest?* (Paris, 2003).

Péan, P., *L'Argent Noir: Corruption et sous-développement* (Paris, 1988).

Péan, P., *L'homme de l'ombre: Eléments d'enquête autour de Jacques Foccart, l'homme le plus mysterieux et le plus puissant de la République* (Paris, 1990).

Rat der Europäischen Union, 'Entscheidung des Rates vom 23. November 1998 über Wechselkursfragen in Zusammenhang mit dem CFA-Franc und dem Komoren-Franc', *Amtsblatt der Europäischen Gemeinschaften* (Luxemburg, 1998).

Semedo, G. and Villieu, P., *La zone franc: mécanismes et perspectives macroéconomiques* (Paris, 1997).

Stiglitz, J. E., 'Markets, Market Failures, and Development', *American Economic Review*, May (1989): 197–203.

Verschave, F.-X., *La Françafrique: Le plus long scandale de la République* (Paris, 2000).

Verschave, F.-X., *Noir Silence. Qui arrêtra la Françafrique?* (Paris, 2000).

Verschave, F.-X., *De la Françafrique à la Mafiafrique* (Paris, 2004).

Yates, D. A., *The Rentier State in Africa: Oil Rent Dependency and Neocolonialism in the Republic of Gabon* (Asmara, 1996).

Yates, D. A., 'Die Elf-Skandale: Eine Fallstudie von Elementen französischer Afrikapolitik unter dem Ancien Regime', *Afrika-Jahrbuch* (Hamburg, 1999): 73–84.

Comment on Chapters 8 and 9

Dirk Kohnert

On the relevance of rational economic reasoning under African conditions

Monetary coordination is high on the agenda of different regional organizations such as the African Union (AU), the Economic Community of West African States (ECOWAS), the West African Monetary Zone (WAMZ), or between the East African Countries of Kenya, Tanzania and Uganda. Economic benefits of a common currency, like lower transaction cost, increased macroeconomic stability, or the shielding of central banks against political pressure from nationalist elites and their inclination for excessive spending are undoubtedly expected. But the most important underlying aim of monetary integration in Africa is derived from its history, particularly the legacy of the slave trade and colonialism, and the subsequent striving for pan-African ideals, which has become manifest in the promotion of African unity in a crisis-prone continent. However, whether it is feasible to achieve this ambitious political aim through the economic means of regional economic and monetary cooperation is open to question. Experts and the international donor community periodically caution about diverting attention from the most pressing needs of African countries by pursuing over-ambitious monetary policies. African governments should get the priorities right, i.e. they ought to first implement sustainable solutions to the problems of crisis resolution and prevention, the fight against corruption and rent-seeking elites, in order to promote good governance, transparency and accountability. The realities of African economies suggest that the grand new projects of monetary unions are unlikely to succeed (cf. Masson and Pattillo, 2004).

In view of these prerequisites it is difficult to find a common denominator in the different views presented in Chapters 8 and 9 and to match it with the author's own convictions. In addition, it is questionable whether economic, result-orientated reasoning and the discussion of monetary concepts (e.g. that of the Optimum Currency Area or of the Original Sin), which might be duly applied to Western or Latin American societies, have the same relevance in the African context. The underlying vision of rational economic reasoning as a remedy for the major ills of development planning is a fallacy, at least under the prevailing African cultural and political conditions, insofar as it covers only part of the truth. Some three centuries ago, Francisco Goya chastised a similar form of hubris in his famous Capricho 'The dream [sleep] of reason produces monsters.'[1] On the one hand, the Cartesian ideal of rationalism is valid: if reason sleeps (is not vigilant), monsters like corruption, misappropriation of funds, politically instrumentalized xenophobia (witch-hunts against foreigners, as in the Côte d'Ivoire under the pretext of Ivorité), and other violent conflicts may arise. On the other hand, the dream of social, economic and political structures, based on the hubris of rational behaviour, may result in grand development projects and other 'white elephants', growing inequality and ensuing social and political conflicts. One only needs to point to the evils caused by the terrible excesses of ill-advised structural adjustment programmes of multinational donors in the 1980s (cf. Barré, Shearer and Uvin, 1999; Storey, 1999, p. 15; Uvin, 1998), and to the double talk of propagated unlimited rule of free markets over developing economies without due regard to major industrialized countries (cf. OXFAM, 2002; Cadot, Melo and Olarreaga, 1999). The dangers incorporated in the hubris of rationalism in development planning go far beyond the age-old controversy about the validity of the concept of the *homo oeconomicus* or of culture-specific rationalities. The ongoing debate on brain research shows that rational behaviour is influenced by deep-seated emotions at least as much as by empirical knowledge and rational reasoning. In fact, human beings cannot act rationally without the motivation of emotions.[2] But even more importantly in this context, the neuro-biological linkage of reason and emotions, born out of and developed within specific socio-cultural settings, is of immediate relevance for the resolution of pressing social needs and conflicts typically addressed by development cooperation (cf. Damasio, 1994, pp. 326–9, 344–52). And finally, if particular manners of reduction of complexity, based on culture-specific emotional structures, and not different rationalities are a major distinction between African and Western rational reasoning (cf. Kohnert, 2004a), then generations of social anthropologists since Evans-Pritchard are right in stressing (apparently without much effect) that Western-educated development experts and politicians should be particularly careful not to cultivate the hubris of rationality in their dialogue with stakeholders deeply rooted in foreign cultures.

Despite several, often competing projects of monetary cooperation in Africa there are only two functioning regional monetary zones: the Francophone CFA Zone, and the Anglophone CMA Zone.[3] However, even in these zones the monetary arrangements are of questionable viability. In addition, the CFA and CMA Zones are vivid examples of the limited practical value of abstract economic models, like that of Optimum Currency Areas (OCAs), in the African context.

The major structural deficiencies within and between member states of each zone cannot be solved by monetary coordination. They require sustainable political and economic solutions, adapted to the specific needs of each of its members, and aimed at the ownership of the measures and instruments by each country and/or sub-zone concerned. Concentrating efforts and scarce means on over-ambitious plans for monetary integration, like that of the West African Monetary Zone (WAMZ), pushed by the Anglophone West African governments of Nigeria, Ghana, Sierra Leone, Gambia, Guinea, Liberia, in order to establish the *eco* as a common virtual currency until July 2005, would divert attention from more important bottlenecks of development in the region and would lead to a sub-optimal allocation of resources and the temptation for fiscal wastefulness through prospects of a bail-out, or costs that are diluted through the membership (cf. Debrun, Masson and Pattillo, 2002; Doré and Masson, 2002; Masson and Pattillo, 2001, 2002; IMF, 2003; Page and Bilal, 2001). The same holds for rival efforts of Francophone circles to establish the Franc CFA as anchor currency of the future WAMZ.

Working hypotheses: on the primacy of external politics and informal economics

Monetary stability is not sufficient: three decisive elements impacted on the zones performance. All three had little to do with endogenous economic requirements of member states, but very much with external politics and informal economics; i.e.:

- The colonial heritage and 'Northern' interest in up-keeping its dominance as well as political stability in the region (cf. Monga, 1997; Chapter 9).
- Hierarchical structures of dependency maintained by the major economic and political powers, France and South Africa (cf. Kohnert, 2005; Chapter 8).

- Rent-seeking elitist informal transnational social networks, such as the *messieurs Afrique* (cf. Glaser and Smith, 1992; Joly, 2000; Verschave, 1998, 2000; Yates, 2000).

The CFA Zone: ambiguous perspectives of monetary integration

The CFA Zone is basically composed of two sub-zones, characterized by significant structural economic and political differences within and between its member countries: the West African Economic and Monetary Union (WAEMU/UEMOA) and the Economic and Monetary Community of Central Africa (EMCCA/CEMAC).[4] Neither of these sub-zones meets the classical criteria of the Optimum Currency Area (OCA). In contrast, they show a low degree of diversification of production and exports, low factor mobility (except of labour in some countries) and price and wage flexibility, different levels of infrastructure and of inflation, low intra-regional trade and a strong exposure to asymmetrical external shocks (e.g. different terms of trade development for oil and agricultural exports). The growing structural divergences between UEMOA and CEMAC have been intensified by the recent development of world oil markets, booming production in Equatorial Guinea and the arrival of Chad in the club of oil producers. Nevertheless the CFA Zone in general, and the UEMOA in particular, have been considered as model case for economic and monetary integration in Africa.

The crucial common denominators of the CFA Zone are:

- Common roots in African cultures;
- A shared colonial heritage, including a social and economic infra-structure, orientated at the *mise en valeur* of African resources for the former colonial power, which entailed considerable loss of economic and political sovereignty on the part of African member states.
- An informal transnational network of French and African political elites (*les messieurs Afrique*) with a vested interest in maintaining its inherited privileges (Yates, 2000). Certainly, this transnational lobby has lost much of its influence due to generational change. The several times postponed and belated decision on the CFA-devaluation, just four weeks after the death of Houphouët-Boigny (7 December 2003), may serve as just one example. However, the Balladur–doctrine of La Baule (1990), meant to initiate a radical shift in France's African policy, away from dependence of its African partners on aid, towards

increasing self-reliance, private sector investment and closer regional integration, still does not apply, if vital interests of Paris are put into question (cf. the French *Operation Turquoise* in Rwanda, or the handling of the Congo crisis or the present unrest in Ivory Coast). And even the current pressure of the French government within the EU to recognize the Eyadéma-Regime of Togo despite of its human rights violations in order to revitalize economic cooperation, shows that the old links are still very much alive.

• The rules of the informal sector (e.g. neo-patrimonialism, prebend-economy, rent-seeking etc.), which are more important in structuring the CFA Zone than the institutions and policies of the formal economic sector, including its monetary institutions. For decades, prices of French imports were overpriced (by 35 per cent on average, compared with the world market, due to protection by tied aid and other political and cultural non-tariff barriers: Yeats, 1989). The cost of this rent-seeking was carried not only by the French Treasury, who guarantees the peg, but by the French and EU-taxpayers, who financed budgetary bail-outs and development aid, and finally by the poorer member countries and social strata (cf. also the free-rider thesis, cf. Fielding, 2002, pp. 64–71; Suchanek in Chapter 9).

Economies of both zones are heavily dependent (for different reasons) on exports of primary commodities quoted and invoiced in US dollars. The high volatility to asymmetrical external shocks results, last but not least, from the peg to the French franc/euro, which does not allow adjustment of the exchange rate to the divergent commodity terms of trade development over time. The majority of African countries, including the members of the CFA zone, have been forced, among others by misguided structural adjustment programmes (SAPs) of the international donor community, into a trading structure that subjects them to secular terms-of-trade losses and volatile foreign exchange earnings, the 'African commodity trap' (cf. UNCTAD, 2004). A typical result is the overvaluation of the real exchange rate of the Franc CFA *vis-à-vis* the US dollar and deflationary pressure.[5] An opportune devaluation of the Franc CFA has been prevented by prevailing fears concerning political destabilization and its considerable social cost, notably for the poor, and probably not so much by the 'original sin' which could have made the devaluation undesirable (cf. Chapter 9; Kohnert, 2005).

The Franc CFA viability has been hurt by its dependency on the monetary policy of the Euro zone, which does not necessarily correspond to the needs of African member countries. Ambitious convergence criteria had been introduced with the 1994 devaluation and the founding of the UEMOA and CEMAC respectively. However, its implementation had been hampered by the lack of political will and the aftermath of the Ivorian crisis since September 2002 (cf. Kohnert, 2005).

In summary, the inherited Franc CFA Zone arrangement is suboptimal for both sides, the EU and francophone African countries (cf. Chapter 9). To overcome the significant structural differences within and between these zones, specific monetary regimes would be helpful. This is even more so since the potential flexibility of the CFA Zone monetary arrangements has not been fully exploited in order to cope better with the wide discrepancies of economies. Thus, the regrouping of member countries either along economic lines, or according to size has been proposed. The first option would unite all those likely to experience similar external shocks; the second would prevent large countries from hijacking the Operations Account and thus making smaller land-locked Sahel countries of the UEMOA finance the debt of their larger partners Senegal and Côte d'Ivoire (cf. Fielding, 2002, pp. 71, 190; for more detailed alternative proposals cf. Monga, 1997; Hugon, 1998).

If the CFA Zone wants to perform efficiently in the future, it should no longer be based on its inherited colonial culture, but on the economic needs of the population in the respective member countries. Unfortunately, overriding concerns on the political stability of the region, and dependency on its traditional allies concerning crisis resolution, prevented any meaningful transformation of CFA Zone structures. Violent conflicts in both regions (e.g. Ivory Coast since September 2002, and civil war in Congo Brazzaville 1997/98) made a mockery of several regional convergence criteria and put the gains of the 50 per cent CFA-devaluation in 1994 at risk. Nevertheless, international concern for political stability and the preservation of the status quo were mainly responsible for maintaining the CFA Zone in its present form. These shared political interests will continue to supersede national economic aims in the foreseeable future, as, under the prevailing political conditions, neither sub-zone could defend its own currency without the link to the euro and a sustainable solution to crisis–prevention, backed by the international community.

Ambiguous perspectives of the CMA

The CMA (Lesotho, Namibia and Swaziland; including Botswana as a de facto member) is, as the CFA Zone, characterized by severe structural divergences. These stem from its colonial past and the power politics of the apartheid regime, and from hierarchical monetary structures, with South Africa dominating both economically and politically (cf. O'Meara, 1996). This holds notably for Swaziland and Lesotho, both land-locked countries, surrounded by South African territory (with the exception of the north-eastern parts of Swaziland which border with Mozambique). Similar to the former South African 'homelands', Lesotho heavily depends on remittances by migrant workers in South Africa's mining industry, as well as on exporting water to its main South African customers (cf. Chapter 8). All countries are highly dependent on imports from South Africa, but the latter's major trading partners are outside the CMA, notably the EU, UK and USA. Monetary integration has not boosted intra-zone trade. Nor has the countries' adherence to the region's leading economic integration organization, the Southern African Development Community (SADC), as well as to the South African Customs Unions (SACU), with common external tariffs, which provide a common revenue pool tending to make up for imbalances in tax revenues that arise from asymmetric trade patterns (cf. Grandes, 2004, p. 4).

The SADC is opposed to joining the CMA not just for economic reasons, i.e. because SADC economies do not form an OCA, and because there are only minor chances of SADC as a whole to meet the necessary convergence criteria for a viable monetary union (cf. Jenkins and Thomas, 1998, pp. 153–68). Decisive for the reluctance to join the CMA is the lack of political will to implement a common currency arrangement in view of its political and economic cost, notably the loss of sovereignty (cf. Sparks, 2002). The threat of selfish South African dominance is pretty much alive, last but not least, in view of the painful past experience with the harsh destabilization policy of the Apartheid regime *vis-à-vis* its neighbours (cf. O'Meara, 1996). The *coup d'état* in Lesotho, provoked in 1986 by South Africa, was just one example, although not CMA countries, but Mozambique and Angola were the major targets of the destabilization policy.

CMA members may form an Optimal Currency Area (OCA), given the existence of common long-run trends in their bilateral real exchange rates (cf. Grandes, 2004). But this has never been a serious criterion for influencing the aims or actions concerning the monetary or financial policies of the CMA, all the more so since an OCA does not provide for the autonomous sustainable development of its member states, and macroeconomic policies have been dominated by vested South African political and economic interests. Additional microeconomic efficiency gains might still be accrued if the CMA countries developed to a fully-fledged monetary union (cf. Grandes, 2004, p. 22). But reliance on monetary integration will probably lead to consolidating and deepening the dependency of the junior partners of the CMA, thereby endangering not only its economic, but also its political independence. Although formally a South–South coordination arrangement, the CMA is de facto – like the CFA Zone – a North–South coordination project.

Although regional economic integration and monetary cooperation is fashionable, it is not necessarily the appropriate strategy to pursue (cf. Jenkins and Thomas, 1998, p. 145). The grave structural deficiencies of the junior partners of the CMA cannot be solved by monetary coordination arrangements, neither within the CMA, nor within the wider framework of the SADC. First and foremost, the member countries would have to get the priorities right.

Certainly, it is debatable whether it is against the interest of the populations concerned for at least Swaziland and Lesotho to be incorporated long-term into the economic and political structures of South Africa. In fact, it sounds revealing that even the South African Exchange Control Regulations of 1998 state that 'Namibia, Lesotho and Swaziland should be treated as part of the domestic territory and not as foreign' (cf. Chapter 8). But if the junior partners of South Africa want to preserve their political independence or to prevent an intolerable loss of sovereignty, and at least Namibia does demand more democratic monetary rules (cf. Chapter 8), they have to go for political solutions that answer their most pressing problems. That is, they would have to create initially an enabling cultural and political framework for sustainable growth and development, including good governance, transparency, accountability, and elimination of corruption.

Notes

1. Francisco Goya, Capricho 43, 1797–8: *El sueño de la razón produce monstruos*, in English, 'The dream [sleep] of reason produces monsters', which derives its ambiguity from two antagonistic interpretations, arising from the fact that the Spanish word *sueño* means 'sleep' as well as 'dream'. For the image cf. website: www.museum.cornell.edu/HFJ/handbook/hb128.html, 01.06.04. For the risks involved in results-based management, demonstrated by the example of the new poverty agenda of multinational donors cf. Maxwell, 2003, pp. 12–20.
2. In contrast to the Cartesian postulate on the fundamental separation of body and soul (*cogito, ergo sum*), human decision-making, by its very biological structure, is never determined by reasoning alone, but guided by emotions grown on, and deeply embedded, in the respective culture of the actor (Damasio, 1994, pp. 325–8). One may go even one step further in discussing the relevance of Gerald Edelman's (1992, pp. 232–6) hypothesis that the biological self, at

least vital parts of the human brain, have been conditioned and structured in the course of human genesis by basic values needed for survival; thus, the evolution of mankind provided for the acceptance of basic human value-systems guiding its actions. Possibly Edelman's thesis even sheds new light on the controversy concerning the existence of universal human rights. According to recent neuro-physiological theories on cognition, the perception of the world in the human brain is directed through the filter of positive and negative sentiments from birth. There is a close neuro-biological link between feeling and thinking, which means that the existence of emotions (based on the respective socio-cultural setting) is a precondition for any rational action. This applies to all human beings, and hence to Africans and Europeans alike.

3. For an overview on the Communauté Financière Africaine or CFA Franc Zone cf. Fielding, 2002; Kohnert, 2005; Monga, 1997; Suchanek in Chapter 9; for the Common Monetary Area, or the former Rand Zone, cf. Grandes, 2004; Metzger in Chapter 8.

4. A third sub-zone of the Comoros will not be examined in this paper because of its minor importance.

5. Cf. Devarajan, 1997. The real exchange rate (RER) is an index of relative prices of two goods: RER = price of tradeable goods / price of non-tradeable goods; it is an indicator of competitivity of domestic economy *vs* foreign economy, relative to the base year. A currency is under devaluation pressure when the RER increases. Determinants of RER are factors that affect the supply of foreign exchange, i.e. export earnings (price of exported goods or volume), foreign capital inflow (aid, debt, interest rate), and factors that affect the demand for foreign exchange, such as import expenditures (import price or volume), capital flight and foreign capital outflow (debt service), trade policy (import tariff); Demand for imports is itself influenced by domestic inflation (government deficit, increase in wages, increase in money supply (credit)). Since 2000/01 the overvaluation of the US dollar *vis-à-vis* the Franc CFA has been more than +35 per cent.

Bibliography

CFA Zone

Debrun, X., Masson, P. and Pattilo, C., *Monetary Union in West Africa: Who Might Gain, Who Might Lose, and Why?*, IMF Working Paper, WP/02/226 (Washington, DC: IMF, 2002).

Dembélé, D. M., 'Abwertungsängste in Afrika' (Anxieties about Devaluation in Africa; in German), *Le Monde Diplomatique* (German edition, in *die tageszeitung* (taz)), June (2004): 17.

Devarajan, S., 'Real Exchange Rate Misalignment in the CFA Zone', *Journal of African Economics*, 6 (1997): 35–53.

Doré, O. and Masson, P., *Experience with Budgetary Convergence in the WAEMU*, IMF Working Paper, WP/02/108 (Washington, DC: IMF, 2002).

Fielding, D., *The Macroeconomics of Monetary Union: An Analysis of the CFA Franc Zone* (London: Routledge, 2002).

Glaser, A. and Smith, S., *Ces messieurs Afrique. Le Paris-village du continent noir*, 2 Vols (Paris: Calmann-Levy, 1992 and 1997).

Hugon, P., 'Les avatars de la Zone Franc face à l'Euro', *Cahier GEMDEV* (Groupement d'Intérêt Scientifique pour l'Étude de la Mondialisation et du Développement), No. 25 (1998): 363–94.

Joly, E., *Notre affaire à tous* (Paris: Editions les Arènes, 2000).

IMF, *West African Economic and Monetary Union: Recent Economic Developments and Regional Policy Issues; and Public Information Notice on the Executive Board Discussion*, IMF Country Report No. 03/70 (Washington, DC, 2003) www.imf.org/external/pubs/ft/scr/2003/cr0370.pdf; 06.07.04

Kohnert, D., 'Kooperation auf französisch: was die frankophone westafrikanische Wirtschaft (noch) zusammenhält', *Der Überblick*, 40: 1 (2004): 50–4.

Kohnert, D., 'Die UEMOA und die CFA Zone. Eine neue Kooperations-Kultur im frankophonen Afrika?', in Nabers, Dirk *et al.* (eds), *Perspektiven regionaler Zusammenarbeit in den Entwicklungsländern* (Hamburg: Deutsches Übersee Institut, 2005): 115–36.

Masson, P. and Pattillo, C., *Monetary Union in West Africa (ECOWAS): Is it Desirable and How Could it be Achieved?*, Occasional Paper, no. 204 (Washington, DC: IMF, 2001).

Masson, P. and Pattillo, C., 'Monetary Union in West Africa: An Agency of Restraint for Fiscal Policies?', *Journal of African Economics*, 11 (2002): 387–412.

Monga, C., 'A Currency Reform Index for Western and Central Africa', *World Economy*, January (1997): 103–25.

Page, S. and Bilal, S., *Regional Integration in Western Africa*, Report prepared for and financed by the Ministry of Foreign Affairs, the Netherlands, September (London: ODI, 2001).

Verschave, F.-X., *Françafrique* (Paris: L'Harmattan, 1998).

Verschave, F.-X., *Noire Silence* (Paris: Les Arènes, 2000).

Yates, D., 'Die Elf-Skandale: Eine Fallstudie von Elementen französischer Afrikapolitik unter dem Ancien Regime', in Hofmeier, Rolf (ed.), *Afrika-Jahrbuch 1999* (Opladen: IAK/Leske & Budrich, 2000), pp. 73–84.

Yeats, A. J., *Do African Countries Pay More for Imports? Yes*, World Bank, Working Paper No. 265 (Washington, DC: World Bank, 1989).

CMA Rand Zone, Southern Africa

Grandes, M., *Macroeconomic Convergence in Southern Africa: The Rand Zone Experience*, OECD, Development Centre, Working Paper No. 231, DEV/DOC 29, (2004).

Jenkins, C. and Thomas, L., 'Is Southern Africa Ready for Regional Monetary Integration?' in L. Petersson (ed.), *Post-Apartheid Southern Africa: Economic Challenges and Policies for the Future*, Proceedings of the 16th Arne Ryde Symposium (London, New York: Routledge, 1998), pp. 145–70.

O'Meara, D., *Forty Lost Years: The National Party and the Politics of the South African State, 1948–1994* (Randburg and Athens, OH: Ravan Press and Ohio University Press, 1996).

Sparks, D. L., *The Future of Monetary Integration in Southern Africa: Will the SADAC Join the Rand Monetary Area?* Paper presented at the conference 'Exchange Rates, Economic Integration and the International Economy', Ryerson University, Toronto (2002).

General and Africa

Barré, A., Shearer, D. and Uvin, P., *The Limits and Scope for the Use of Development Assistance Incentives and Disincentives for Influencing Conflict Situations: Case-Study: Rwanda*, OECD Development Assistance Committee Informal Task Force on Conflict Peace and Development Co-operation (Paris: OECD, 1999).

Cadot, O., Melo, J. de and Olarreaga, M., *Asymmetric Regionalism in Sub-Saharan Africa: Where Do We Stand?* CEPR Discussion Paper, No. 2299, 8 November 1999.

Damasio, A. R., *Descartes' Error: Emotion, Reason and the Human Brain* (New York, 1994) (Quoted according to the German translation: *Descartes' Irrtum*. dtv, München, 1997).

Edelman, G. M., *Bright Air, Brilliant Fire: On the Matter of the Mind* (New York, 1992).

Kohnert, D., 'Local Manifestations of Transnational Troubles: Different Strategies of Curbing Witchcraft Violence in Times of Transition in South Africa', in Ossenbrügge, Jürgen and Reh, Mechthild (eds), *Social Spaces of African Societies. Applications and Critique of Concepts of 'Transnational Social Spaces'* (Münster: Lit, 2004a), pp. 151–4.

Masson, P. R. and Pattillo, C., *The Monetary Geography of Africa* (Brookings Institute Press, 2004).

Maxwell, S., 'Heaven or Hubris: Reflections on the 'New Poverty Agenda', *Development Policy Review*, 21 (1) (2003): 5–25.

OXFAM, *Rigged Rules and Double Standards: Trade, Globalisation, and the Fight Against Poverty. Make Trade Fair Campaign* (London: OXFAM, 2002).

Storey, A., *The World Bank's Discursive Construction of Rwanda: Poverty, Inequality and the Role of the State* (1999). http://www.cddc.vt.edu/host/lnc/papers/storey_rowanda.htm (17.07.04)

UNCTAD, *Economic Development in Africa: Trade Performance and Commodity Dependence*, UNCTAD/GDS/AFRICA/2003/1, released 26 February 2004. http://www.unctad.org/en/docs/gdsafrica20031_en.pdf (07.07.04).

Uvin, P., *Aiding Violence: The Development Enterprise in Rwanda* (West Hartford, CT: Kumarain, 1998).

10
The Advancement of Monetary Regionalism in East Asia[1]

Heribert Dieter[2]

Introduction

Since the Asian financial crisis of 1997, East Asia has been exploring the possibilities for enhanced monetary cooperation. The experience of the weaknesses of existing regional institutional economic arrangements encouraged scholars and policy-makers alike to examine the potential for regional – as opposed to national or global – mechanisms for the stabilization of financial markets. In 2005 both progress and stumbling blocs can be identified. Whereas cooperation progresses on the level of central banks, the prospects for comprehensive integration in East Asia appear to be not very bright. The conflict between Japan on the one side and China as well as South Korea on the other seems to have hollowed out the modest progress of the recent past. Nevertheless, monetary regionalism continues to be plausible, but probably not in the medium term. One of the questions to be considered today is whether integration in East Asia without the participation of Japan could be developing.

The crises of late 1990s have contributed to the evolution of a new type of regionalism in Asia. The existing regional integration projects, in particular the ASEAN and APEC since then have had a diminishing role. Both illustrate the inability of conventional, trade-based integration systems to avoid or mitigate financial crises. Although ASEAN (at 30+) is one of the oldest regional integration projects it had nothing to offer in 1997. Neither liquidity, nor even good advice, was provided.[3] ASEAN emerged damaged from the crisis (Higgott, 1998; Rüland, 2000) and its vision – the establishment of a free trade area and the continuation of an institutionally low-key approach to regional integration – appears to be problematic. Although un-stated by regional policy-makers, the benefits from this type of supranational regionalism are now deemed in many quarters too limited to warrant other than minimum effort. Successful exporters to *world* markets can expect few advantages from the creation of a *regional* free trade area.

APEC's failure to provide any meaningful response to the biggest economic crisis in the Asia-Pacific region since 1945 made it, if not irrelevant, then less important, for many Asian members. As with ASEAN, not even good advice was provided. The Vancouver Leaders' Declaration (APEC, 25 November 1997) did discuss the crisis, but the suggested responses were limited to surveillance and, above all, the endorsement of the central role of the IMF as the key agent for any improved global regulatory capacity. With hindsight, this appeared to drive the region deeper than necessary into crisis and contributed little to its solution (Dieter, 1998; Stiglitz, 2002).

True, control of financial volatility was never part of APEC's remit, and, more positively, Harris argues that the Asian crisis did not result in a regional protectionist backlash and this could be credited to APEC (Harris, 2000, p. 13). But Harris offers a correlation rather than a proof and it is not clear why a protectionist backlash should have been expected in the first place. The countries in crisis were confronted with a sudden shortage of capital, not with an inflow of goods from other countries.

Increasingly, Asian observers evaluate APEC as a tool of American foreign economic policy. And the resistance of Asian policy-makers to a strengthened APEC was caused by their fear of US dominance (Kahler, 2000, p. 568). APEC has not been successful in creating a joint identity as the basis for further pan-Pacific cooperation and the lack of tangible benefits has been progressively criticized (Ravenhill, 2000). APEC's concentration on facilitating contacts in the corporate and private sector, accompanied by an almost total neglect of developing an intra-regional network at the wider civil society level, has resulted in a weak or nonexistent sense of community. As a consequence, APEC has failed to provide much needed political legitimacy for the wider regional liberal economic project.

Although rivalry between an Asian integration project and APEC is not new, policy elites in Asia do seem to be reconsidering the benefits of regionalism without the Anglo-Saxons. In particular, American opposition to an 'Asian Monetary Fund' sowed the seeds for a further polarization and bolstered the development of a dialogue between Southeast and Northeast Asia. The initial Japanese proposal of an Asian Monetary Fund (AMF) in September 1997 was opposed by the USA and the IMF (Wang, 2000, p. 207). In all probability, an AMF would not have stopped the initial crisis. But what contribution to limiting the magnitude of downturn it might have made, must remain conjecture. However, it is not unreasonable to suggest that the crisis in Korea, which started *after* the AMF proposal was rejected by the US and the IMF, could have been avoided as it was primarily a liquidity crisis, not a solvency crisis.

The Asian crises of 1997–8 also underlined the weaknesses of the *informal personalized* 'ASEAN way' approach to regional integration, in which both ASEAN and APEC had previously taken pride (Rüland, 2000, p. 445). Before the crises, protagonists of APEC were happy to declare it as a new type of regionalism – economic integration without bureaucratic institutions, with the European Union being the model to avoid (Higgott, 1995). The crises demonstrated the limits of non-formalized institutional commitment. The challenge for the Asian policy community since then remains to develop new forms of regionalism that address these deficiencies.

Due to the continuing political obstacles in the region, this paper does not argue the inevitability of monetary regionalism in East Asia so much as its *theoretical plausibility*. The next section outlines the traditional understanding of regional economic integration and poses an alternative model of 'monetary regionalism'. An improvement of the existing multilateral institutions would be an alternative to monetary regionalism. But the IMF continues to suffer from too much influence of the US Treasury and Wall Street, whose policies frequently result in doubtful results, in particular in East Asia and Russia. Joseph Stiglitz (2002) accused the IMF of implementing the wrong policies and asked if US and the IMF pushed policies because they 'believed the policies would help East Asia or because ... [they] ... would benefit financial interests in the United States and the advanced industrial world?' The question is pertinent but, for this paper, the answer is less significant than the perception it receives in East Asia, where many in the regional policy community have developed a very critical outlook on US economic policy.

The third section discusses the impact of this perception on policy. It identifies the decreasing importance of traditional forms of economic cooperation in East Asia and the emergence of a new trend: monetary regionalism. It also shows the piecemeal progress that is apparent in cooperation in East Asia: here the deepening of central bank cooperation in an East Asian context is a significant break with the policies of the past. In this context, the joint efforts for the creation of a regional bond market are important.

The final section addresses some elements of the politics of the new regionalism in Asia. First, it identifies a Japanese desire for greater regional leadership towards questions of monetary cooperation, albeit constrained by the realities of Japanese economic life in the late twentieth and early twenty-first centuries. Second, China's participation in the Chiang Mai initiative is argued to reflect its aspirations to greater regional leadership. The negotiations of China and ASEAN for a bilateral FTA, commenced in November 2001, underscore the growing acceptance of China as a leading regional power. Third, it is argued that successful regional policy coordination will be as much dependent on Sino-Japanese relations and leadership as on US relations with these two states, either singularly or collectively.

Finally, the main findings will be summed up in a conclusion.

Monetary regionalism: beyond conventional integration theory

Since the early 1960s, theorizing about regional integration has been under the influence of Bela Balassa's (1961, 1987) five-step approach: from free trade area over customs union to common market to economic and monetary union and finally political union. But this typology was first articulated well over forty years ago in a different historical context. In the 1960s tariffs, as the principal barriers to trade, were much more important than today. Financial flows across the borders of national economies were much less important. Most countries, including the United States, used controls to ensure that fixed exchange rates were not undermined by high inflows or outflows of capital. Trade integration offered an answer to the economic goals of many countries. They could protect their economies against the flaws of the world market or, in a more radical but popular version, they could dissociate their economies from the global economy, which was obviously easier for a group than for individual countries.

But that was then. Today, the most problematic aspect of Balassa's approach is that it provides no link between the monetary policies and the financial sectors of the participating economies on the first three levels of integration. In an era of globalization and liberalization, reflected in growing capital flows, this missing link constitutes major theoretical and policy deficiencies. Furthermore, the introduction of an economic and monetary union is a change of tune from the first three steps, which put the emphasis on trade.

A theory of monetary regionalism

In contrast to conventional regionalism, monetary regionalism aims to contribute to the stability of currencies and financial markets in a region without the need for formalizing trade links. Eric Giradin has emphasized that regions have a motive for cooperating in monetary and financial affairs. Although domestic financial stability cannot be ensured, for instance due to the increase of capital flows, a region can collectively provide the means to avoid systemic risk, i.e. the breakdown of the (regional) financial system. The gains from regional financial cooperation essentially stem from reducing regional systemic risk. Regional financial stability has the nature of a public good, in that no country would have an incentive to work toward it if others do not do it, while all benefit from it. Disruptions caused by financial crises, at a regional level, are a major incentive for cooperation. The public good nature of regional financial coordination is due to the fact that financial instability is a potential public bad that spreads across countries (Giradin, 2004, p. 334).

Like conventional regionalism, it requires participating states to enter a process which, if successfully implemented, will lead at least to the creation of a common currency. This requires a willingness to give up a traditionally central element of a nation's sovereignty and independence; the ability to issue one's own currency. This is central to monetary regionalism. Such an integration process could be organized in four stages (see Table 10.1).

Level 1: Regional liquidity fund

The central measure to be implemented at level 1 is the creation of a public regional liquidity fund. This is an attempt to provide a regional safety net if a financial crisis, primarily a credit crisis, emerges. Countries participating would earmark part of their foreign reserves for a liquidity pool. A participating central bank, in such a system, would not only be able to use its own reserves, but also those of the other central banks. Technically, such a liquidity fund could either be a system of credit lines or swap agreements.[4] Whereas a credit is possible, a swap appears to be superior. A participating central bank would have the right to swap domestic currency for foreign currency. If liquidity is provided by swap agreements, the central bank providing the foreign currency has some collateral, which is more difficult to provide with conventional credit lines.[5] At the same time, swaps have to be accompanied by penalties that discourage their use. Without financial sanctions the participating central banks could be using the regional liquidity fund outside emergency times. Finally, the regional liquidity fund would only be available for

Table 10.1   Key components of monetary regionalism

	Level 1 Regional liquidity fund	Level 2 Regional monetary system	Level 3 Economic and monetary union	Level 4 Political union
Main component	Creation of a public regional liquidity fund	Introduction of a regional monetary system with exchange rate bands	Permanent fixing of exchange rates and creation of a single currency	Creation of a political union; national political systems continue to exist and cover most issues
Political measures	Creation of a forum for the central banks of the region, i.e. a regional monetary committee	Regular meetings of the regional monetary committee	Creation of common political institutions, establishment of a regional central bank	Creation of supranational institutions in defined areas
Additional components (crisis management)	Creation of a private liquidity fund	Expansion of coverage of existing regional liquidity funds		
Additional components (crisis prevention)	Implementation of universal debt-rollover options with a Penalty (UDROP) Capital controls of the individual countries, in particular on inflows, may continue to exist		Phasing out of capital controls	
Trade components		Facilitation of regional trade by harmonizing norms and standards	Establishment of a customs union	Free movement of labour
Macroeconomic policy	Joint monitoring of monetary and fiscal policy; regional surveillance of financial markets	Coordination and harmonization of both monetary policy (in particular interest rate policy) and fiscal policy (in particular on debt levels)		

short periods (three to six months). The advantages of a public regional liquidity fund are substantial:

- A central bank using other central banks' reserves has a much higher chance to act as a lender of last resort for the domestic financial sector, thus limiting the consequences of a credit crisis. Given that loans denominated in foreign currency limit the ability of central banks to act as lender of last resort, a central bank gains leverage when it is using regional reserves; this is particularly relevant for economies that have partly or completely abandoned capital controls.
- Countries that experienced a severe foreign-exchange crisis often accumulate high foreign reserves. The drawback of foreign reserves is that they require a country to swap high-yielding domestic assets into low-yielding foreign ones.[6] Use of the region's foreign reserves reduces the need for individual central banks to maintain costly foreign reserves, typically held in highly liquid instruments that earn very small returns often of not more than two percent per year.
- The provision of liquidity in a region would put the participating countries in a position in which they can avoid to go immediately to the IMF when a financial crisis emerges. This is the biggest political advantage of a regional fund. In the past, writing a letter of intend to the IMF has been seen by many people in crisis-struck countries as a disgrace.[7]
- Although a liquidity fund would only be activated in the event of a crisis, it would encourage participating central banks to engage in permanent monitoring of regional economic developments. Joint regional surveillance of financial markets could begin.

The creation of a regional liquidity fund would, of course, require substantial political will and mutual trust on the part of the participating countries and, in addition, participants would have to possess significant foreign reserves. Even if not more than 10 or 20 per cent of any reserves were available for a regional liquidity fund, this would constitute a major obstacle for monetary regionalism in many parts of the world, *but not in East Asia*, as Table 10.2 (see p. 203) indicates.

The creation of a regional liquidity fund is not primarily targeted towards stabilizing exchange rates. At least initially, the main purpose of a fund is limited to the provision sufficient liquidity for banks and corporations that, due to sudden swings in market sentiment, may be confronted with an inability to rollover existing debt denominated in foreign currency. The reason for limiting the use of regional liquidity for credit crises is simple. Stabilizing exchange rates is difficult and may easily be unsuccessful. The risk of failure is more limited in credit crises. The central bank only has to deal with domestic borrowers that are confronted with a liquidity crunch. Although this type of credit crisis usually has implications for the (floating) exchange rate of an economy, at the first level of monetary regionalism the use of regional liquidity should be limited to the defined situation of a credit crisis.

Starting with an attempt to stabilize exchange rates is too risky a strategy. But the establishment of a regional monetary committee could contribute to the creation of 'intra-regional policy networks', which would enable policy-makers to deepen their knowledge of one another prior the evolution of a strategy for the exchange rate stabilization. Such a regional liquidity fund could also challenge the IMF monopoly on crisis management.

Moreover, a *public* regional liquidity fund could be accompanied by *private* regional liquidity funds in which private banks and other financial intermediaries create a system that also provides liquidity in the event of a banking crisis. When a bank gets into trouble, the other banks supply fresh money to the initially agreed limit. This is not as revolutionary as it sounds. Such a system has been in place in Germany since a major banking crisis in 1974. The creation of this system of two liquidity funds would be a significant step forward for a regional integration project. It would both provide powerful instruments to limit financial crises and generate the functional basis for further integration. This becomes particularly evident when the monitoring of financial markets and banking supervision are included in the integration process via the creation of bodies such as a regional monetary committee and a regional banking supervision system. Supplying foreign reserves of a country's central bank, even if it is limited, is not just an accounting exercise, but a genuine expression of confidence building.

The surveillance of financial markets plays an important role both in the discussion of a new global financial architecture and in our proposed regionalism scheme. However, one should not overestimate the role of surveillance. It is not a substitute for a liquidity fund and other hard measures to stop a crisis from spreading. As the recent financial history of the US, and albeit to a less extent Europe, demonstrates, even theoretically well-regulated markets can be subject to dramatic bankruptcies. From LTCM to Enron, WorldCom, Vivendi and others, the ability to hide liabilities reinforces how difficult surveillance is, especially when cronyism and corruption cannot be ruled out. Surveillance and supervision are no substitutes for other safety nets. And the installation of a regional body for banking supervision will not end the need for national banking supervision.

In addition to the creation of a regional liquidity fund, measures to reduce the likeliness of financial crises are a vital element of monetary regionalism. A major aim here is to force the private sector to consider the risks associated with lending and borrowing. Without strict accompanying measures, a large regional liquidity fund could cause moral hazard. Borrowers and lenders could assume that they would be bailed out and thus they would not properly evaluate risk in the first place. Kim, Ryou and Wang (2000, p. 41) have argued that the regional liquidity fund ought to be implemented with high interest rates in order to avoid moral hazard. However, high interest rates are not useful in the attempt to reduce moral hazard. Private borrowers and lenders would not be affected by high interest rates. The high rates would be charged for swap arrangements between central banks. A solution for this problem has to address the risk of moral hazard directly, i.e. at the level of borrower and lender.

Rollover options on loans from abroad could be one solution to this problem. Universal debt-rollover options with a Penalty (UDROP) (Sibert and Buiter, 1999) are an instrument which can be exercised upon maturity of a loan. The use of the option results in a short-term extension of the credit. The option has a price, which will have to be set before the deal is done. The cost of the option induces a market behaviour like a tax on borrowing abroad. Consequently, borrowing domestically becomes cheaper. As both parties would have to agree on the price they must consider the risk associated with the loan. Since financial crises tend to be characterized by panic and by a lack of sober evaluation, the implementation of UDROPs have several advantages (Dieter, 2000). The main ones are:

- Debtors gain valuable time. Liquidity problems caused by panic will be less likely.
- The necessity to find a price for the option increases the evaluation of the credit risk.
- Pressure on the exchange rate of a country affected by a credit crisis can be reduced significantly.
- The implementation of a UDROP requires neither a global consensus nor the approval from the IMF. Thus the regional collective introduction of a UDROP will strengthen the bargaining position of participating countries and reduce the isolation from international financial markets.

The disadvantages of UDROP, in particular when implemented by a group of economies, are limited. The UDROP can only provide help in the event of a liquidity crisis, not in a solvency crisis, thus a bank or company facing bankruptcy will eventually not be saved.

On the first level of monetary regionalism, as in conventional forms of regionalism, the economies of the participating countries are likely to be heterogeneous. Measures for the protection of weaker countries will be required. A main element of such protection would be the permission to continue the use of capital controls. In particular, countries should be allowed to limit the inflow of capital and to tie the inflow to certain conditions, especially favouring long-term over short-term loans. Also, taxes on short-term inflows, a policy successfully implemented by Chile in the 1990s, ought to be possible on the first level. But capital controls might also play a useful role in fighting financial crises. The experience of Malaysia in 1998 and 1999 shows how capital controls empower a government to follow a strategy of low domestic interest rates, a fixed exchange rate and the restoration of economic growth (Kaplan and Rodrik, 2000). The establishment of a formal scheme to facilitate trade is not necessarily a measure at level 1. The creation of a free trade area or customs union can be misinterpreted as the formation of a trade bloc and consequently can be used by policy-makers in other countries to justify retaliatory import restrictions. These notions are particularly relevant for economies producing high surpluses in their trade accounts over longer periods of time as in East Asia. Similarly, macroeconomic policy does not have to be coordinated and harmonized at level 1, but institutions should be created that permit the joint monitoring of macroeconomic developments. Such a step is not only an important precondition for the introduction of a monetary union, but also contributes to the creation of intra-regional policy networks.

Level 2: Regional monetary system

The second step should be characterized by further preparation for monetary union. The introduction of a regional monetary system, with exchange rate bands, enables the participating economies to gain macroeconomic stability. The advantage of this system over a system with permanently fixed rates is obvious; it permits adjustments of exchange rates. But there is no room for a currency system built around one individual currency, i.e. the Japanese Yen. The monetary policy of the Japanese central bank lacks the transparency and cohesion necessary to achieve the status of a widely accepted reserve currency (Wang, 2000).

Nor would China or other countries in East Asia agree to an effectively hegemonic role for the Japanese central bank.[8]

Moreover, finding the appropriate exchange rate bands is no easy task. If the bands are too broad, the benefits from such a scheme are limited. Exporters and importers in such an arrangement with wide bands would still have to hedge their receipts from transactions in foreign currency. Thus exchange rate bands wider than 10 per cent might be more symbolic than functional. On the other hand, the risk of markets testing narrow bands (±2 per cent say) with ensuing destabilizing effects seems to be quite high.

After the experience with the European Monetary System, which operated successfully for more than a decade until 1992, a regional monetary system may have lost some of its appeal. However, such a system in Asia has to be evaluated in comparison with other plausible alternatives and in the different regional context. Countries may either opt for completely flexible exchange rates or hard pegs in the form of currency boards. In the aftermath of the Asian crisis and the Brazilian crisis many influential economists were stressing that only two viable exchange rate regimes existed. This so-called bipolar view gained prominence in international policy circles (Fischer, 2001). But for regional players neither option is particularly attractive. Enhanced regional cooperation as a route to the stabilization of exchange rates may turn out to be a more plausible, albeit not perfect, strategy.

Although separate currencies will continue to exist, the establishment of a regional monetary system will require an intensification of cooperation between monetary authorities. The media coverage of regional meetings of central bankers could raise the awareness of the integration process among citizens of the region. When monetary cooperation is intensified and the coverage of the existing regional liquidity fund has been expanded, the additional measures taken for crisis prevention can gradually be phased out.

While the establishment of a free trade area is not suggested, trade facilitation could start to play a greater role at level 2. Given the undesired administrative costs and the potential political vulnerability caused by formal trade regimes, the creation of a free trade area could be interpreted as a protectionist measure. Despite these reservations, trade facilitation via the harmonization of norms and standards could make an added longer term contribution to the integration process.

In preparation for level 3, the economic and monetary union, monetary and fiscal policy will have to be harmonized. The experience of the Eurozone offers no blueprint for application elsewhere. But the criteria used in the process leading to the creation of the Eurozone have been useful, and the convergence criteria (below) provide a start for a more harmonized economic and fiscal policy:

- the level of existing public debt shall not exceed 60 per cent of GDP;
- new public debt has to be lower than 3 per cent of GDP;
- the inflation rate should not be higher than 1.5 per cent above the average inflation rate of the three countries with the lowest inflation;
- the economies must have participated successfully, i.e. without adjustments, in the European Monetary System for at least two years;
- long-term interest rates should not be higher than 2.0 per cent above the average respective rate of the three economies with the lowest long-term interest rates.

The combination of these measures to evaluate public debt and inflation is simple enough to be workable. It includes criteria primarily determined by markets (exchange rate, long-term interest rate) as well as criteria that directly reflect fiscal policy. Needless to say that the European experience has also demonstrated the pro-cyclical nature of the restrictions on fiscal policy. However, in the absence of a regional body for fiscal policy, there is a need for some form of regional surveillance of national fiscal policy.[9]

Level 3: Economic and monetary union

In the creation of an economic and monetary union, major conditions have to be met and an economic and monetary union has some disadvantages that participating countries may not wish to accept. The inability to react to differing economic developments within the union with exchange rate adjustments is a major disadvantage of this level of regional integration. However, an economic and monetary *union* clearly has advantages over a mere regional monetary system. Transaction costs are permanently reduced and competition within the union is strengthened. Above all, exchange rate adjustments within the union cease to be a threat. Companies no longer have to pay for hedging against exchange rate volatility. Once the third level of integration is reached, at least a customs union is required. Although, theoretically, trade within a project of monetary regionalism could still be subject to tariffs and other forms of trade restrictions, one of the aims of a common currency, i.e. the strengthening of competition, could not be fully achieved. A free trade area, however, should not be implemented, because of the need to administer certificates of origin: Trade would not be facilitated as much as in a customs union. At the same time, restrictions on migration could remain in place. In particular in areas with strongly differing levels of development, the introduction of the freedom of employees to move within the union ought to be limited to the last and final level of integration. This is particularly so in East Asia where it is clearly a very sensitive political issue.

Level 4: Political union

The completion of the integration process, the creation of a political union, will not require many additional measures with regard to economic policy, but rather demands political action. In particular, supranational political decision making bodies have to be founded. In most areas, economic policy integration will have been implemented already on lower levels of integration. A deepening of the integration process could show the reduction of national tax systems in favour of a uniform union-wide tax system. But measures of that nature do not seem to be vital for the success of the political union. A certain variation of tax rates would not undermine the integration project. The main benefits of the integration project continue to exist during the implementation phase of level 4. The region would gain independence and would be more immune to financial crises. The economic preconditions for such a scheme are high; hence, probably monetary regionalism can be successfully implemented only in East Asia.

The evidence from Asia?

The preceding discussion has been an exercise in speculative, but plausible, economic theorizing. But no economic integration system emerges in a political vacuum. Indeed, it is the political constraints and opportunities that are very often the most salient variables. Boldly stated, we believe that evidence of an emergence of monetary regionalism is indeed to be found in East Asia. The region – policy elite and wider community alike – perceived IMF policy throughout the late 1990s as humiliating and wrong. In the summer of 1997 the IMF and the US government impeded the Japanese initiative to create an Asian liquidity fund. The Asian Monetary Fund – AMF as it would have been called – was explicitly to apply softer conditions than those of the IMF. The AMF's concept corresponded more to that of a 'lender of last resort' than the IMF. Essentially, the AMF idea was about providing unconditional loans to overcome liquidity crises.

By the end of 1999, the worst impact of the Asian crisis was over and East Asian policy circles once again addressed the topic of more intensive regional cooperation. The regular ASEAN summits were expanded by the participation of Japan, China and South Korea, the new body being called ASEAN+3 (or APT). Since then, steps in the search for a new monetary regionalism have been numerous. Several are worth noting:

- The first East Asian Summit (EAS) took place in Kuala Lumpur in December 1997. Not surprisingly, monetary issues were discussed.
- During the ASEAN+3 meeting in Manila in November 1999, the scope for regionalism in Southeast and East Asia was discussed. The summit chair, then Philippine President Joseph Estrada, told the news media the goals were a common market, monetary union and an East Asian Community (*Financial Times*, 29 November 1999, p. 4).
- Increasing numbers of Japanese observers have begun to advocate monetary cooperation. Eisuke Sakakibara, former state secretary of the Japanese finance ministry, spoke out for a cooperative monetary regime in East Asia (World Bank, *Development News*, 12 January 2000).
- During the fourth ASEAN finance ministers' conference in March 2000 plans for a regional liquidity system were discussed (Conference declaration at www.asean.or.id).
- In May 2000, Japan suggested a network of currency swaps, in effect a regional liquidity fund, at the annual meeting of Asian Development Bank member finance ministers. The idea was that Asian countries should be able to borrow from each other via short-term swaps of currency reserves. As Il Sakong, chairman of the Korean Institute for Global Economics, noted at the now famous Chiang Mai Meeting: 'We need some kind of defence mechanism. Since not much is expected to be done at the global level, something should be done at the regional level' (*Financial Times*, 6/7 May 2000, p. 9). The finance ministers of the ASEAN countries, China, Japan and South Korea reached an agreement, although major elements of the proposal still have to be finalized.[10]
- In September 2000 Thailand's then deputy prime minister and now WTO-secretary general, Supachai Panichpakdi, underlined the need for an Asian liquidity Fund. Even taking US views on the future of the IMF into consideration (Williamson, 2000), he argued that IMF resources would be insufficient to cope with future crises.
- During the 2000 ASEAN+3-Meeting in Singapore, the Chiang Mai-initiative was reaffirmed. At the same time, the Chinese prime minister, Zhu Rongji, made a proposal for a free trade area between China and ASEAN (*Financial Times*, 27 November 2000, p. 3).

- In January 2001 France and Japan tabled a joint paper during the ASEM finance ministers meeting in Kobe. The paper suggested that stable exchange rates and financial flows are reachable at a regional level. The paper implicitly advocates monetary regionalism (www. mof. go.jp/english/asem/aseme03e.htm).
- In May 2001, the Chiang Mai-initiative was clarified during the annual meeting of the Asian Development Bank in Honolulu. The network of bilateral swap agreements was more precisely defined. Japan pledged up to $3 billion to South Korea, up to $2 billion to Thailand and up to $1 billion to Malaysia. However, only 10 per cent of these sums should be available automatically. For sums above the 10 per cent level the approval of the IMF will be required.[11]
- In December 2001 Thailand and China agree on a swap-agreement for 2 billion dollars (*China News Digest*, 26 June 2002).
- In March 2002 China and Japan agree on a swap-agreement for 3 billion dollars (*China News Digest*, 26 June 2002).
- China and South Korea agree in June 2002 on a swap-agreement for 2 billion dollars (*China News Digest*, 26 June 2002).
- In 2004 the number of bilateral swaps rose to 16; the volumes agreed upon rose to 44 billion dollars. Compared to the reserves of East Asians countries this continues to be a modest sum.
- In April 2004, the president of the Asian Development Bank, Tadao Chino, stressed in his opening remarks for the ASEAN+3 finance ministers' conference in Korea that monetary regionalism in East Asia already rests on three pillars: first the improved exchange of data and information; second, the pooling of currency reserves and, third, the development of an Asian bond market. Chino suggested replacing the bilateral swaps with a regional pool of currency reserves within three to five years.[12]

Apart from the emergence of cooperation with regard to exchange rates and capital flows, there is nascent cooperation in the field of financial market development at the same time. In the past, the lack of depth of national financial markets often forced borrowers to raise money at international markets, which inevitably attracted currency risk: borrowing in domestic currency has been impossible for most emerging market borrowers. The development of a regional bond market is supposed to solve this problem.

The ASEAN+3 finance ministers endorsed the creation of an Asian Bond Market Initiative (ABMI) in Manila in August 2003. The aim is to develop efficient primary and secondary bond markets. The ministers agreed not only on the principle, but established six working groups, e.g. on standardized debt instruments, the creation of credit rating agencies and the setting-up of guarantee mechanisms (De Brouwer, 2005, p. 7). The Asian Development Bank supports this process by issuing bonds denominated in Thai baht and Philippine pesos (*Financial Times*, 15 April 2005, p. 9). The aim of these processes is to develop a regional bond market which permits borrowing in domestic currency, thereby avoiding the currency risk that is normally associated with foreign borrowing. Apart from ASEAN+3, a similar, though not identical, group has also tried to promote a regional bond market. The Executive Meeting of East Asia-Pacific Central Banks (EMEAP) comprises the important East Asian central banks as well as Australia and New Zealand.[13] This group has flourished without making headlines, but it should not be underestimated. It has managed to deepen intra-regional policy networks as well as – a more tangible result – the creation of two initiatives for an Asian bond market. The theory of monetary regionalism only makes sense *in practice* if appropriate funding is available. It could not be countenanced in the absence of a sufficient level of foreign reserves; these funds are available in East Asia where reserves are not only high, but well distributed (see Table 10.2 below). The two largest economies, Japan and China, have also the largest reserves. In the event of a crisis, those two economies would have to make the highest contribution. Also, considering the high level of reserves, a regional liquidity fund is plausible even without using too

Table 10.2 Foreign reserves of East Asian economies

Country	Reserves in March 2000 (in US$ billion)	Reserves in July/August 2004 (in US$ billion)
China	156.8	483.0
Hong Kong	96.3	118.5
Indonesia	26.3	33.6
Malaysia	30.6	54.5
Philippines	12.9	12.7
Singapore	74.3	101.3
South Korea	74.0	170.4
Thailand	34.1	42.4
Japan	305.5	808.0
Total	810.8	1,824.4
Taiwan	103.5	231.6
Total (incl. Taiwan)	914.3	2,056.0

Sources: The Economist, 4.3.2000; *The Economist*, 25.9.2004; Japanese Ministry of Finance, http://www.mof.go.jp/english/e1c006.htm

high a percentage of the reserves of participating central banks. Asia has more foreign reserves than any other region. Between 2000 and 2004, reserves in the APT countries have risen by a staggering $1000 billion. Even without Taiwan, which alone enjoys reserves of more than US$ 230 billion, the central banks of East Asia together have more than US$ 1,800 billion at their disposal. The inclusive character of the project is underlined by China's participation. Today, China has no need for additional liquidity from the region. Together with Hong Kong's monetary authority, China's central bank has reserves of over US$ 600 billion, more than enough for an economy that enjoys the additional safety net of comprehensive capital controls.

East Asia is eschewing regionalism in favour of neither globalism nor bilateralism. No states pursue purely one-dimensional trade policies, or indeed foreign policies in general. Instead, the emergence of a new regionalism in Asia can be observed. This development exhibits three overlapping and complex trends:

(1) An interest in monetary regionalism arising from the desire to combat financial volatility that has emerged since the financial crises of the late 1990s.
(2) An interest in bilateral trade initiatives within the context of the wider multilateral system, largely at the expense of the APEC style open regionalism of the 1990s.
(3) The emergence of a *voice* of region beyond that of the sub-regions – Southeast and Northeast Asia – but more restricted than that of the Pacific as a mega region. Taking into account earlier analysis (Higgott and Stubbs, 1995) and in accordance with the analysis of others (Bergsten, 2000; Rapkin, 2001; Webber, 2001), the voice of region in the emerging global political economy is a new one, an 'East Asian' one. The most significant expression of this development is the first East Asian Summit, which is scheduled for December 2005 in Malaysia. It will include all important Asian and East Asian states, but will exclude the US.[14]

The politics of the 'new' Asian regionalism

Irrespective of the explanations of the Asian financial crises of the late 1990s[15] the closing years of the twentieth century have convinced Asian regional policy elites that, 'they no longer want to be in thrall to Washington or the West when trouble hits in' (Bergsten, 2000, p. 20). Bergsten, with Stiglitz, is rare amongst US observers in recognizing the degree to which East Asian states felt that they were 'both let down and put upon by the West' in the crisis. For others, triumphalism and *schadenfreude* was rampant (cf. Zuckerman, 1998). The Asian financial crisis was more an opportunity to displace the 'Asian developmental state' with the Anglo-American model. Since 1997 it is in this context that regional initiatives especially the dialogue about monetary regionalism and the process of East Asia wide summitry via the APT need to be located. The APT reflects a grouping of Asian states mirroring Malaysia's proposal for an EAEG that was strongly opposed by the Anglo-Saxon members of APEC, especially the US in the early 1990s.

It is becoming increasingly obvious that East Asian elites resent the dominance of Washington in regional and global affairs. Eisuke Sakakibara, an important Japanese government official and former deputy finance minister, sees a parallel between the decline of Britain after 1918 and the US decline today. Whereas World War I symbolized the end of the British Empire, today's so-called War on Terror indicates the end of Pax Americana. The watershed was the Asian crisis, a position that Sakakibara (2003, p. 232f.) spells out clearly:

> After the Asian crisis of 1997–98, Asian countries strongly perceived the vulnerability of their region, which does not have any viable regional cooperative scheme. They recognized that there is no global lender of last resort, that international organizations like the IMF and the World Bank were not of much use in preventing or addressing the crisis, and that the United States did not infuse much in the way of resources into Asian countries when the crisis broke out.

The Asian crisis therefore was not simply an unexpected and badly managed financial affair, it altered the relationship of East Asia with the US. Governments and elites were reminded that the US had a domestic agenda to deal with, and the interests of the US financial sector prevailed over the interests of US allies in the region.

It is hoped in the region, that APT and an AMF would give Asia added voice in determining the shape of the new international institutional architecture – a point not forgotten by the US in its opposition to the AMF proposal in 1997. The US clearly understood that, despite stated best intentions, an AMF would not long be likely to adhere IMF policy prescriptions if they appeared at odds with an Asian view of how the world economy should be organized. Thus a successful AMF would, *ipso facto*, contest the 'Anglo-American' view of global economic organization (Higgott and Rhodes, 2000). The factors that contribute to

East Asian monetary regionalism are both of a more technical nature as well as political. Regarding the former, there are a number of reasons why Asian governments are looking for regional solutions:

- Existing international institutions for the governance of the global economy are driven by neoclassical market fundamentalism, and the results with regard to capital flows and financial crises are mixed at best.
- These institutions, the IMF in particular, are staffed with economists who regularly demonstrate the desire to 'westernize' economies in crisis, which is a disguise for the take-over of the Anglo-Saxon model of capitalism.
- The lack of effective global governance, including the development of a lender of last resort and the regulation of capital flows, will not disappear quickly. National regulation can no longer provide sufficient regulation, but the region – from a theoretical perspective – is much more apt in providing these structures (Sakakibara, 2003, p. 234).

The perceived interest of the region in developing monetary regionalism does not indicate that all the countries have the same agenda. When state interests are disaggregated, different members of the APT have different goals. For the key ASEAN states, prospects of stronger relations with two of the world's major economic powers (Japan and China) – for all their current economic limitations – is self-evident. Moreover, it is not only the Malaysian government that recognized, a long time ago, that influence over the international institutional architecture depends on being part of a much larger group reflecting a collective position. ASEAN leaders like Lee Kuan Yew, and major opinion-formers in the region, such as Tommy Koh and Noordin Sopiee (see Koh, 1999, p. 8), have regularly expressed similar views.

But more important than the views of individual ASEAN partners to the longer-term evolution of the APT is the position of the major powers, notably Japan and China from within the APT, and the US from outside of it. For example, Japan has come under increasing pressure, both for internal and external reasons over the past decade, to sort itself out. Its economy is in a *cul-de-sac*, saddled with public debt, deflation, bad loans and a lack of consumer confidence that will, sooner or later, have to be addressed (Dieter, 2005). This economic reality according to Peter Katzenstein (2000, p. 360) has changed East Asia's perception of Japan. Today, the fear of too much influence of Japan has been replaced by the fear of too little power to deal with its own economic problems.

However, the tensions between Japan and its Asian neighbours in 2005 demonstrate that the region is in a state of flux not only *vis-à-vis* the rest of the world, but also within. It is becoming increasingly evident that the Japanese unwillingness to identify itself as a country that puts priority on its ties with Asia creates opportunities for other countries. The US government is using Japan as a tool to undermine the process of regional integration which would be – if successful – to the disadvantage of the US. Japan is encouraged to take sides with the US, whether it is in Iraq or with regard to issues debated by the UN Security Council. The US State Department courts Tokyo because a rift between Japan and its Asian neighbours weakens the entire region. The Japanese government has stated that it would defend Taiwan in case of an intervention from China, a deliberate provocation of Beijing. Even in seemingly secondary issues, such as China's wish to participate in the Inter-American Development Bank, Japan blocs the attempts of China to become a global player. The row over Japanese whitewashing of history is the expression, not the cause of the tensions.

However, such problems notwithstanding, there is considerable evidence of a Japanese agenda for greater regional monetary cooperation, although an AMF is an institution that presently dare not speak its name. Since the time of the abortive attempt in 1997, Japan has consistently developed initiatives of its own and backed the activities of others in the region wishing to advance policies that might lead to greater AMF-style monetary regionalism.

Indeed, on close inspection, Japan has played a greater leadership role on these issues over the last few years than most of its critics will concede.[16] Yet still to be tested is the Japanese will to resist a full assault by the US on Asia's attempts to smuggle in an AMF-style organization through the back door. The major problems in the organization of the region in the years to come reside in the relationship between the US and Japan on the one hand and between Japan and China on the other. As David Rapkin has argued, both the US and Japan are in a situation where neither can push its own vision of the policy future for the region in the absence of acquiescence from the other. By the US veto of the first AMF initiative and the Japanese veto of US desires for early sectoral trade liberalization within APEC, the two allies are shown to have 'blocking power' over each other (Rapkin, 2001).

A leading role for Japan in Asian integration might be accepted by smaller countries, but China is likely to be less acquiescent. The management of the Sino-Japanese relationship represents as big a challenge for Asian regionalism as does the relationship between the US and

Japan. According to Webber (2001) the past, the present and the future continue to strain the relationship. The past, because Japan has neither apologized in an accepted manner for the atrocities committed during World War II and the occupation of China and other countries in the region nor has Japanese society come to terms with its role in the region. At present there is an element of systemic competition between Japan and China. But most importantly the future casts a shadow over the relationship. If current economic trends continue it is not difficult to see the day when, in terms of the material and intellectual capacity for leadership, China might eclipse Japan.

Understandably, this makes Japanese leaders more nervous than their counterparts in China. China may worry about contemporary Japanese economic power, but the Chinese can imagine a day when this gap will be smaller than it is now. Japan conversely, can only speculate on what the decreasing asymmetry in the economic capabilities of the two countries implies for China's longer-term regional intentions in a range of policy areas, especially the security domain. This view will only be partially assuaged by China's increasingly responsible regional role in its strong support of the idea of an AMF style organization.

The fact that the year 2005 marks the outbreak of tensions is no coincidence. The second Bush administration – with Condoleezza Rice in charge of the State Department – is actively trying to limit the power of China and is, as already mentioned, finding willing support in the Japanese government, which continues to cling to its former role as the leading economy and leading country in East Asia. However, China's continuing political and economic rise enables Beijing to oppose attempts to reinstall Japanese leadership. Other, smaller, countries like South Korea and the ASEAN countries, are increasingly willing to take sides with Beijing, rather than with Tokyo. But it would be premature to assume that China has already achieved its goals.

We are thus faced with a paradox. The absence of acceptable or credible hegemonic power in East Asia remains a major obstacle to the successful implementation of the monetary regionalism project at the same time as it adds force to the very idea of, and need for, collective action problem-solving via a body like the APT. It is this paradox that gives ASEAN its strategic role (at least in the short run) in nurturing the APT dialogue. In so doing, playing the intermediary role between the two major regional powers provides ASEAN with a *raison d'être* at a time when its institutional viability has been under pressure from the financial crisis. This role, however, can be only a stop-gap measure. ASEAN has none of the material power of the larger players. Moreover, if something like an

AMF were to develop, it would need conditions attached to the financial support it offered. This means *rules*. But 'ASEAN way' diplomacy, built on consensus decision-making, remains inimical to the development of strong rule-driven conditionality. It would thus be necessary to move beyond ASEAN way decision-making. While not easy, such a movement may not prove impossible. Indeed, there are signs that this 'ASEAN way' approach may have outlived its usefulness.

Asian policy-makers are looking to create regional agreements that allow them to eschew hard line IMF medicine of the kind metered out in the late twentieth century. Small states in particular, for it is they that will rely on the support of the richer states, may be more willing to accept conditionality. They may be willing to accept it, if it emanates from a regional institution in which they feel like stakeholders in the process. In their relationship with the major international institutions most Asian states have seen themselves to-date largely as 'rule-takers' rather than 'rule-makers'. Thus seemingly cosmetic differences are more significant, albeit more intangible, than can ever be caught in any narrowly rational economic model of financial reform.

Conclusion

This article has proposed a theoretical approach to how regionalism in East Asia might develop over the near to mid-term future. But the article acknowledges the manner in which politics can derail theory. Thus it has located this exercise in theory-building within a realistic empirical context. Events on the ground in Asia, particularly the wishes of the regional policy elites for mechanisms to cope with financial volatility, are driving this process. In the wake of the financial crises of the late 1990s, and in the absence of cast-iron guarantees emanating from the international financial architecture, policy-makers aspire more to collective problem-solving at the regional level than in the past. It is this changing context that makes the kind of theoretical exercise developed in this paper germane.

It is also an *evolutionary* model, which takes account of the changing dynamics of economic interdependence under conditions of globalization – especially the increased importance of financial markets at the expense of markets in manufactures that prevailed at the time when the Balassian model or regional integration was developed. It is underwritten by assumptions of regional 'policy learning' that assumes that the mistakes of the past are not necessarily due to be repeated. Of course, in any specific historical circumstance, if diplomacy fails and a stable or balanced security environment breaks down, all other areas of policy are, inevitably, adversely affected.

But the 'learning' assumption of this paper is that Asian policy-makers do not automatically assume that conflict over contested issues in the politico-security domain is at some stage inevitable. For all its limitations, the multilateral security dialogue in the region has developed positively in the last decade of the twentieth century. There is no reason why this trend should not continue. Rather than ignore the security issues, or suggest that there is no linkage between them and economic questions, this paper argues that it is quite plausible to see regional policy communities pursuing different cooperative initiatives in the domains of security, finance and trade. In short, they are quite capable of playing a multi-dimensional diplomatic game.

Consider, for example, the relationship between Beijing and Tokyo – a central relationship in any discussion of the future of the region. Beijing has benefited from the developments of the late twentieth and early twenty-first century. But still the key question to be resolved in coming years is the degree to which increased economic ties between Japan and China might alleviate the climate of mutual distrust in other domains and allow them to cooperate in the enhancement of regional economic policy coordination. This is not an easy question to answer. However, Chinese diplomacy towards the region has been a tremendous success in recent years. Also, and notwithstanding that the 1994 Chinese devaluation of the renminbi was a significant factor in the Asian financial crisis, the general view in the region is that China has behaved responsibly and cooperatively in efforts to mitigate the prospects of further financial volatility (Wang, 2000, p. 210). The still-remaining distrust of China's motives amongst other sections of the East Asian regional policy elite is not at issue. The real question is to what degree this mistrust can be mitigated as a problematic factor in the development of (monetary) regionalism and the consolidation of the APT. Such issues will determine the prospects for East Asian cooperation via the APT in general, and the development of monetary regionalism specifically (by the creation of an AMF or some such like institution).

The financial crises of the 1990s may have been a sufficiently traumatic learning experience, especially for some of the weaker state policy-making elites, to recognize a need to shed a little sovereignty, in order to preserve wider state-building capacity and regional stability. Vulnerability to financial market volatility is now the major challenge to policy autonomy. It may be this sense of vulnerability that is the key to the further development of regional collective action in the monetary sphere.

Notes

1. A previous version of this article was published as 'Exploring Alternative Theories of Economic Regionalism: From Trade to Finance in Asian Co-operation' (together with Richard Higgott) in *Review of International Political Economy*, Vol. 10, No. 3 (2003): 434–54; see the journals website http://www.tandf.co.uk.journals.
2. The article was prepared during a visiting fellowship at Sydney University in 2005. The support from the German Research Council is greatly acknowledged.
3. Before March 1997, ASEAN finance ministers had never met officially. When they came together for the first time in Phuket, controversial issues were not debated (Rüland, 2000, p. 428).
4. A swap is an agreement to exchange one currency for another currency and to reverse this transaction at a fixed date in the future. A swap therefore always consists of two transactions: (1) A spot transaction of, say, Thai baht into US dollars; (2) A forward transaction, exchanging in this case US dollars for Baht at a fixed time. The rate for the forward transaction can be the current exchange rate, the market exchange rate at the time of the forward transaction or any other mutually agreed exchange rate. If the current exchange rate is chosen, there is no exchange rate risk for the party that provides the foreign currency. The same amount of, in our example, US dollars will have to be paid back.
5. Needless to say that domestic currency of a country that is faced with a financial crisis does not qualify as good collateral. But in a swap there is no exchange rate risk for the lending bank. However, if the borrowing bank has trouble to meet its obligations, the lending bank at least will have some, if devalued, collateral.
6. Conversely, countries that provide the reserves, i.e. in most cases the US, have a direct economic benefit from the provision of reserves, as they get access to large amounts of foreign capital at very low interest rates (Rajan and Siregar, 2004, p. 293).
7. For instance, in South Korea the 1997 crisis is referred to as the second national disgrace, the first being the invasion by Japan in 1910. The crisis was considered to be externally induced, and Korean citizens reacted by donating gold and jewellery (Milner, 2003, p. 290).
8. One may argue that Japan could have achieved this position in the past, when its own economy was growing fast and the economies of China and South Korea were so much smaller. This opportunity, however, passed by and is very unlikely to return.
9. It should be noted that there is a difference between the preparation phase of a currency union and the implementation. One could argue that it is more important to ensure convergence in the former. Before the currency union is implemented, the political will to reach the convergence criteria is probably as important as the actual numbers. However, this issue has been hotly debated in the EU in 2004 and 2005.
10. In the Chiang Mai meeting, the envisaged volume of the swap agreements was very limited. Thailand, Malaysia, Singapore, Indonesia and the Philippines discussed an expansion of their existing swap arrangements from $200 million to $2 billion (*Financial Times*, 8 May 2000, p. 10). Such a step is

clearly too limited for an effective regional liquidity fund, which needs both Japan and China as contributing partners. On a point of historical note, this plan is similar to the one drawn up in the early 1960s by the G10 industrial nations as a way of addressing similar global monetary questions.

11. Why create a separate credit facility if it cannot be used independently? Does the need to get IMF approval put the entire project of a regional liquidity fund into question? Maybe. But there are good historical-cum-practical reasons not to view it this way. Past crises have usually had a strong regional flavor. Support packages, although organized by the international institutions, have been primarily underwritten by regional funds. A regional body to coordinate such packages in the future thus makes sense and merely reflects reality on the ground. It could also focus greater attention on crisis *prevention*, as opposed to crisis management, which has been the principle *modus operandi* in the past (Rajan, 2000).

12. Speech of the president of the ADB on 15 April 2004. http://www.adb.org/ AnnualMeeting/2004/ Speeches/chino_asean+3_statement.html

13. The members are Australia, China, Hong Kong, Indonesia, Japan, Malaysia, New Zealand, Philippines, Singapore, South Korea and Thailand. Although the Federal Reserve is said to have liked to join the group, EMEAP-members have not endorsed US participation.

14. New Zealand, which was willing to sign ASEAN's treaty of amity and non-aggression, will participate in the summit. Australia's participation continued to be uncertain at the time of writing, mainly because the Howard government was not willing to guarantee non-aggression. The background for this decision is the so-called war on terror and Australia's inclination for pre-emptive strikes against terrorists in neighbouring countries, i.e. Indonesia, Malaysia or the Philippines.

15. But see *inter alia*, Dieter, 1998; Higgott, 1998; Jomo, 1998; Pempel, 1999.

16. Initiatives such as the Miyazawa agreement cannot be discussed here. But see Hayashi, 2002.

Bibliography

Balassa, B., *The Theory of Economic Integration* (Homewood, IL: Richard Irwin, 1961).

Balassa, B., 'Economic Integration', in Eatwell, John, Milgate, Murray and Newman, Peter (eds), *The New Palgrave. A Dictionary of Economics*, Vol. 2 (E to J) (London and Basingstoke: Macmillan, 1987), pp. 43–7.

Bergsten, C. F., 'East Asian Regionalism: Towards a Tripartite World', *The Economist* (15 July 2000): 19–21.

Buiter, W. H. and Sibert, A. C., *UDROP – A Small Contribution to the New International Financial Architecture* (London: Centre for Economic Performance, London School of Economics and Political Science), Discussion paper series, No. 2138 (1999).

De Brouwer, G., *Monetary and Financial Integration in Asia: Empirical Evidence and Issues*, mimeo (March 2005).

Dieter, H., *Die Asienkrise: Ursachen, Konsequenzen und die Politik des Internationalen Währungsfonds* (Marburg: Metropolis, 1998).

Dieter, H., *Monetary Regionalism: Regional Integration without Financial Crises*, Centre for the Study of Globalisation and Regionalisation (CSGR), Working Paper 52/00 (2000).

Dieter, H., *Die Zukunft der Globalisierung: Zwischen Krise und Neugestaltung* (Baden-Baden: Nomos, 2005).

Fischer, S., *Exchange Rate Regimes: Is the Bipolar View Correct?* (January 2001) www.imf.org/external/np/speeches/2001/010601a.htm

Giradin, E., 'Methods of Information Exchange and Surveillance for Regional Financial Cooperation', in Asian Development Bank (ed.), *Monetary and Financial Integration in East Asia*, Vol. 2: *The Way Ahead* (Basingstoke: Macmillan, 2004), pp. 331–63.

Harris, S., 'Asian Multilateral Institutions and their Response to the Asian Economic Crisis: The Regional and Global Implications', *The Pacific Review*, 13 (3) (2000): 495–516.

Hayashi, S., *Japanese Foreign Economic Policy and the Idea of an Asian Monetary Fund* (Warwick University, Department of Politics and International Studies, 2002).

Higgott, R., 'Economic Cooperation in Europe and Asia: A Preliminary Comparison', *Journal of European Public Policy*, 2 (3) (1995): 361–83.

Higgott, R., 'The Asian Financial Crisis: A Study in the International Politics of Resentment', *New Political Economy*, 3 (3) (1998): 333–56.

Higgott, R. and Stubbs, R., 'Competing Conceptions of Economic Regionalism: APEC versus EAEC in the Asia Pacific', *Review of International Political Economy*, 2 (3) (1995): 549–68.

Higgott, R. and Rhodes, M., 'After the Crisis: Beyond Liberalization in the Asia Pacific?', *The Pacific Review*, 13 (1) (2000): 1–19.

Jomo, K. Sundaram (ed.), *Tigers in Trouble. Financial Governance, Liberalisation and Crises in East Asia* (London: Zed Books, 1998).

Kahler, M., 'Legalization as Strategy: The Asia-Pacific Case', *International Organization*, 54 (3) (2000): 549–71.

Kaplan, E. and Rodrik, D., *Did the Malaysian Capital Controls Work?* NBER Conference on Currency Crises, mimeo (December 2000).

Katzenstein, P., 'Regionalism and Asia', *New Political Economy*, 5 (3) (2000): 353–68.

Kim, T.-J., Ryou, J.-W. and Wang, Y., *Regional Arrangements to Borrow: A Scheme for Preventing Future Asian Liquidity Crises*, Korea Institute for International Economic Policy, Policy Analysis 00–01 (2000).

Koh, T., 'Progress Toward an East Asian Free Trade Area', *International Herald Tribune* (14 December 1999): 6.

Milner, A., 'Asia-Pacific Perceptions of the Financial Crisis: Lessons and Affirmations', *Contemporary Southeast Asia*, Vol. 25, No. 2 (August 2003): 284–305.

Pempel, T. J. (ed.), *The Politics of the Asian Economic Crisis* (Ithaca: Cornell University Press, 1999).

Rajan, R. and Bird, G., 'Is There a Case for an Asian Monetary Fund?', *World Economics* 1 (2) (2000): 135–43.

Rajan, R. and Siregar, R., 'Centralised reserve pooling for ASEAN+3 countries', in Asian Development Bank (ed.), *Monetary and Financial Integration in East Asia*, Vol. 2: *The Way Ahead* (Basingstoke: Macmillan, 2004), pp. 285–329.

Rapkin, D. P., 'The United States, Japan, and the Power to Bloc: The APEC and AMF Cases', *The Pacific Review*, 14 (3) (2001): 373–410.

Ravenhill, J., 'APEC Adrift: Implications for Economic Regionalism in Asia and the Pacific', *The Pacific Review*, 13 (2) (2000): 319–33.

Rüland, J., 'ASEAN and the Asian Crisis: Theoretical Implications and Practical Consequences for Southeast Asian Regionalism', *The Pacific Review*, 13 (3) (2000): 421–51.

Sakakibara, E., 'Asian Cooperation and the End of Pax Americana', in Teunissen, Jan Jost and Teunissen, Mark (eds), *Financial Stability and Growth in Emerging Economies: The Role of the Financial Sector* (The Hague: Fondad, 2003), pp. 227–44.

Stiglitz, J., *Globalisation and Its Discontents* (London: Penguin, 2002).

Wang, Y., 'The Asian Financial Crisis and Its Aftermath. Do We Need a Regional Financial Arrangement?' *ASEAN Economic Bulletin*, 17 (2) (2000): 205–17.

Webber, D., 'Two Funerals and a Wedding? The Ups and Downs of Regionalism in East Asia and the Asia Pacific after the Asian Crisis', *The Pacific Review*, 14 (3) (2001): 339–72.

Williamson, J., 'The Role of the IMF: A Guide to the Reports', *Policy Briefs* (Washington, DC: Institute for International Economics, May 2000).

Zuckerman, M., 'A Second American Century', *Foreign Affairs*, 73 (3) (1998): 18–31.

Comment

Beate Reszat

The Asian financial crises of the late 1990s left deep scars – not only in the countries involved but also among economists who regarded the events as a sort of Lackmus test of prevailing theories of international economics. Among the vast array of proposals to cope with Asian-style financial crises the approach of Heribert Dieter is probably one of the most ambitious. He proposes a regional solution, a stepwise development of a framework of regional monetary cooperation proceeding in four stages: (i) the establishment of a regional liquidity fund, followed by (ii) a regional monetary system with exchange-rate bands which will create favourable conditions for establishing (iii) a regional common currency, and still later (iv) a political union.

Debates about this and other proposals often focus on practicality. However, the question to be asked in this context is about effectiveness rather than feasibility, which turns the attention to the aims of the proposal. For instance, the establishment of a liquidity fund cannot be intended to help individual banks getting out of a temporary liquidity crisis. This would mean risk supporting unsound management and phenomena such as 'crony capitalism'. Nor can it be thought to help individual countries' banking systems overcome a temporary liquidity crisis. Here, two scenarios must be distinguished. In cases where the banks are in need of domestic money it is clearly in the responsibility of the home authorities to find a solution. The situation looks different if the banking sector is in need of foreign money, as in the case of Korean financial institutions during the Asian crises, who found it difficult if not impossible to roll over short-term international debt. In such cases it is necessary to rethink the rules of the game in international financial markets, rules which were clearly violated in the Korean example. Lending in these markets is not as short-sighted as it looks at first view.

215

Participants rely on the principle that conditions are renegotiated at frequent intervals in order to limit the risks for international borrowers, which are much higher than in a national environment.

One target of establishing a regional liquidity fund is to avoid or limit a currency crisis. Very often, mounting pressures on a currency, which sooner or later may end up in a free fall of the exchange rate, mark the beginning of a financial crisis and fuel investors' panic in its further course. The higher the pressures on the currency, the stronger the vicious circle of successive rounds of depreciation, domestic failures, economic worsening and investors panicking, the longer will the financial crisis last, the deeper will it be and the greater is the danger of contagion. The sooner exchange-rate expectations turn again, the higher is the chance that the crisis will stay a local phenomenon. Thus, influencing exchange-rate expectations and/or curbing excessive trading in a currency becomes a matter of utmost urgency once crisis strikes. The question is: whose expectations and whose trades?

Table C10.1 indicates the role leading international banks played during the Asian crisis, showing bank exposure to Indonesia in 1998. This is hardly the group of actors that comes to mind debating about

Table C10.1   Bank exposure to Indonesia*

Bank	Exposure
HSBC	1,837
Standard Chartered	1,683
Citicorp	800
Chase Manhattan	2,500
Crédit Lyonnais	1,411
Deutsche Bank	564
DBS	729
Bank of Tokyo Mitsubishi	3,683
Fuji Bank	1,771
Bank of America	684
Daiwa	780
Sumitomo Trust	689
OCBC	758
JP Morgan	813
BNP	1,010
Société Générale	795

* Based on exchange rates as of 29 April 1998, in millions of US$

Source: *Financial Times*

'panicking investors' fleeing a currency. Observers often stress how much financial markets have changed. There are new regions and countries opening up their markets, new global players such as financial institutions from emerging markets, transnational corporations and institutional investors, new technologies and ever more sophisticated financial instruments. But, they tend to overlook how much, at least in currency trading, market mechanics have stayed the same since the early days. The bulk of trades in the foreign exchange market is still between banks in traditional foreign exchange instruments, that is spot transactions, outright forwards and swaps.

In many situations, the divide between 'normal' and 'excessive' trading is hard to tell. In principle, 'excessive' refers to some form of currency speculation. There is widespread agreement that speculation has a useful function in adding liquidity to a market in normal times. But, there is equal unanimity that, in the fragile environment on the brink of a financial crisis, its effects can become disastrous.

Liquidity and cost considerations require a direct market access for most expectation-driven foreign exchange transactions – in particular, those extending over a short time horizon. This explains why the foreign exchange market is still largely an interbank market. Whose trades are driving the market? In foreign exchange interbank trading, concentration is high and the circle of protagonists is limited. There are an estimated thirty to forty banks in the world which are internationally active in a narrow sense, making two-way prices in multiple currency

Table C10.2   Third-quarter 1997 foreign exchange trading revenues (in millions of US$)

	Year to date 1997	*Year to date 1996*	*% change*
Citibank[1]	1,043.0	640.0	63
Chase[1]	572.0	341.0	68
Bank of America[1]	312.0	269.0	16
JP Morgan[1]	302.0	206.0	47
State Street	170.0	91.0	87
Bank of New York[2]	87.0	43.0	102
Republic National	86.3	73.9	17
Northern Trust	77.8	42.7	82
Bank Boston	57.0	37.0	54

[1] Includes net interest income
[2] Includes other trading income

Source: *Financial Times*

pairs in usually more than one trading centre. Concentration is even higher in trading in emerging-markets currencies, the main targets of speculative attacks in recent years. In the US market, in April 1998, there were fifteen dealers reporting trades of US$ 250 and more in Thai baht, fourteen in Brazil real, five in Korean won, and only two in Chilean peso and Russian ruble respectively.[1]

Although information is a scarce good in this area, taking risks seems to pay for the banks, in particular in times of turbulence. For example, most of the world's leading institutions could be seen making large profits on the currency front out of the Asian crisis. The increases in foreign exchange trading revenues of American banks in the third quarter 1997, which in some cases ranged between 60 and 100 per cent (Table C.10.2), demonstrate this.

There is a long-standing debate about the nature of these revenues. The banks hint at the increase of customer trading in times of crisis. Rising volatility encourages speculators among their customers to bet on exchange rate moves, and companies and fund managers to stronger rely on hedging. On the other hand, the comparably small share of customer trading in the market, and the sheer volume of market turnover compared to flows of trade and investment worldwide, indicate that this cannot be the whole story.

Table C10.3 lists the top ten in trading in emerging-market currencies at the time of the Asian crisis. Except for Tokyo, there is a small circle of western banks dominating the overall scene. Those, as well as a few

Table C10.3   Top ten in emerging-market currencies trading

	Asian currencies		East European currencies		Latin American currencies
1	Citibank	1	Citibank	1	Citibank
2	HSBC	2	Deutsche Bank	2	Chase Manhattan
3	Standard Chartered Bank	3	Chase Manhattan	3	Bank of America
4 =	Chase Manhattan	4	JP Morgan	4 =	Deutsche Bank
4 =	Deutsche Bank	5	ABN Amro	4 =	JP Morgan
6	ABN Amro	6	ING Barings	6	ABN Amro
7 =	Crédit Agricole Indosuez	7	Merrill Lynch	7	Bank of Boston
7 =	Bank of America	8	Société Générale	8	HSBC
9	Barclays Capital	9	HSBC	9	ING Barings
10	SBC Warburg Dillon Read	10	Bayerische Vereinsbank	10	Merrill Lynch

Source: Euromoney

others, are the obvious target group of international policy efforts to cope with financial instability. It is the banks in this group which need to be integrated into a broader concept of international cooperation to contain financial crises. The question is what such a concept should look like. However, proposals for a regional solution such as the one presented by Heribert Dieter are no effective shield against currency instability.

Note

1. Federal Reserve Bank of New York, *Foreign Exchange and Interest Rate Derivatives Markets Survey Turnover in the United States* (New York, 29 September 1998), Table A5.

Index